Abbas J. Ali

Globalization of Business
Practice and Theory

Pre-publication
REVIEWS,
COMMENTARIES,
EVALUATIONS . . .

"Full of insights on the shape of globalization trends and what makes a corporation global, Abbas Ali offers a clear, convincing view of what is driving the changes already underway. The analysis of the top ten myths about global managers is compelling and instructive."

Margaret M. Carson, MSci
Director of Strategy,
Enron Corporation,
Houston, Texas

"This landmark work brings a new and most important dimension to the current crucial issue of the globalization of business. Dr. Abbas Ali clearly expresses the virtues of competition into innovation, and the risk and opportunities involved in a corporate or governmental global strategy. Dr. Ali's book offers insights into the competitive structure of global business, global strategies, the current global business environment, and the correlation between globalization and regionalism. I found the chapters that addressed global leadership, the structure of an effective global corporation, and globalization and competitiveness to be of the utmost importance; although, from a content standpoint, the entire work is a must-read. Those in leadership positions in business or government, or those with the responsibility for formulating strategy and/or providing strategic advice to leaders, must also read this book."

Robert L. Lattimer
Chairman and Managing Partner,
The Lattimer Group, Inc.;
Atlanta, Georgia

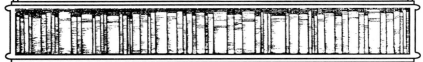

More pre-publication
REVIEWS, COMMENTARIES, EVALUATIONS . . .

"This is a must-read for all students and managers in business. Abbas Ali continues to explain complex events and mechanisms in a simple-to-understand way that even laypersons can comprehend. The current globalization phenomenon is most thoroughly analyzed and reformulated into an easy, enjoyable book to read. What Abbas Ali does in 300 pages is amazing. International Business Press is pushing the boundaries of knowledge in this new book *Globalization of Business.*"

Raymond A. K. Cox, PhD
Professor of Finance,
Central Michigan University,
Mt. Pleasant, Michigan

"Dr. Abbas Ali, a preeminent management scholar, has created a landmark book for those interested in world economics and global competition. He brings order and insight to central issues facing business leaders worldwide. Dr. Ali grounds his book in the realities of practice and executive thinking and explores the underlying issues by integrating the work of leading scholars. Some of the landmark characteristics of the book are: going beyond global and thus positioning globalization as a choice, not a destiny; connecting global business to the more fundamental social and political issues of our times; precisely defining what it means to be a global business and a citizen of the world; and avoiding one-sided advocacy and an ethnocentric orientation. Dr. Ali has created more than a comprehensive book on global business, he has established a framework for inquiry about major global concerns.

Despite the depth and breath of analysis and the volume of information, this book is both engaging and easy to comprehend. It speaks eloquently and clearly to both practitioners and scholars describing the current global landscape and framing the challenges for business organizations. Here is unconventional thinking about the reality of today for those who wish to make a difference in the world of tomorrow."

Daniel F. Twomey, DBA
Professor of Management
and Director,
Center for Human Resource
Management Studies,
Fairleigh Dickinson University,
Madison, New Jersey

More pre-publication
REVIEWS, COMMENTARIES, EVALUATIONS . . .

"This book provides a comprehensive survey of the corporate and academic literature on globalization. It will be a useful addition to the library of anyone who is interested in globalization and its implications."

Rosalie L. Tung, PhD, FRSC
The Ming and Stella Wong Professor of International Business,
Simon Fraser University,
Burnaby, British Columbia,
Canada

International Business Press®
An Imprint of The Haworth Press, Inc.

NOTES FOR PROFESSIONAL LIBRARIANS AND LIBRARY USERS

This is an original book title published by International Business Press®, an imprint of The Haworth Press, Inc. Unless otherwise noted in specific chapters with attribution, materials in this book have not been previously published elsewhere in any format or language.

CONSERVATION AND PRESERVATION NOTES

All books published by The Haworth Press, Inc. and its imprints are printed on certified pH neutral, acid free book grade paper. This paper meets the minimum requirements of American National Standard for Information Sciences-Permanence of Paper for Printed Material, ANSI Z39.48-1984.

Globalization of Business
Practice and Theory

INTERNATIONAL BUSINESS PRESS

Erdener Kaynak, PhD
Executive Editor

New, Recent, and Forthcoming Titles:

How to Manage for International Competitiveness edited by Abbas J. Ali

International Business Expansion into Less-Developed Countries: The International Finance Corporation and Its Operations by James C. Baker

Product-Country Images: Impact and Role in International Marketing edited by Nicolas Papadopoulos and Louise A. Heslop

The Global Business: Four Key Marketing Strategies edited by Erdener Kaynak

Multinational Strategic Alliances edited by Refik Culpan

Market Evolution in Developing Countries: The Unfolding of the Indian Market by Subhash C. Jain

A Guide to Successful Business Relations with the Chinese: Opening the Great Wall's Gate by Huang Quanyu, Richard Andrulis, and Chen Tong

Industrial Products: A Guide to the International Marketing Economics Model by Hans Jansson

Euromarketing: Effective Strategies for International Trade and Export edited by Salah S. Hassan and Erdener Kaynak

How to Utilize New Information Technology in the Global Marketplace: A Basic Guide edited by Fahri Karakaya and Erdener Kaynak

International Negotiating: A Primer for American Business Professionals by Michael Kublin

The Eight Core Values of the Japanese Businessman: Toward an Understanding of Japanese Management by Yasutaka Sai

Implementation of Total Quality Management: A Comprehensive Training Program by Rolf E. Rogers

An International Accounting Practice Set: The Karissa Jean's Simulation by David R. Peterson and Nancy Schendel

Privatization and Entrepreneurship: The Managerial Challenge in Central and Eastern Europe by Arieh Ullmann and Alfred Lewis

U.S. Trade, Foreign Direct Investments, and Global Competitiveness by Rolf Hackmann

Business Decision Making in China by Huang Quanyu, Joseph Leonard, and Chen Tong

International Management Leadership: The Primary Competitive Advantage by Raimo W. Nurmi and John R. Darling

The Trans-Oceanic Marketing Channel: A New Tool for Understanding Tropical Africa's Export Agriculture by H. Laurens van der Laan

Handbook of Cross-Cultural Marketing by Paul A. Herbig

Guide to Software Export: A Handbook for International Software Sales by Roger Philips

Executive Development and Organizational Learning for Global Business edited by J. Bernard Keys and Robert M. Fulmer

Contextual Management: A Global Perspective by Raghbir (Raj) S. Basi

Japan and China: The Meeting of Asia's Economic Giants by Kazua John Fukuda

Export Savvy: From Basics to Strategy by Zak Karamally

Strategic Networks: The Art of Japanese Interfirm Cooperation by Frank-Jürgen Richter

Export-Import Theory, Practices, and Procedures by Belay Seyoum

Internationalization of Companies from Developing Countries by John Kuada and Olav Jull Sørensen

Globalization of Business: Practice and Theory by Abbas J. Ali

Globalization of Business
Practice and Theory

Abbas J. Ali

International Business Press®
An Imprint of The Haworth Press, Inc.
New York • London • Oxford

[redacted]

Published by

International Business Press®, an imprint of The Haworth Press, Inc., 10 Alice Street, Binghamton, NY 13904-1580

Cover design by Marylouise E. Doyle.

Library of Congress Cataloging-in-Publication Data

Ali, Abbas.
Globalization of business : practice and theory / Abbas J. Ali.
p. cm.
Includes bibliographical references and index.
ISBN 0-7890-0412-7 (hd)
1. International business enterprises. I. Title.

HD2755.5 .A523 2000
658'.049—dc21 99-056499

[redacted]

CONTENTS

ABOUT THE AUTHOR

Abbas J. Ali, PhD, is Professor and Director of the School of International Management in the Eberly College of Business at Indiana University of Pennsylvania. He is also the Executive Director of The American Society for Competitiveness. Dr. Ali has extensively written on the subject of business and management environments. He is the author of seventy-five journal articles that have been published in scholarly journals, including *Business Horizons, Journal of Global Marketing, Leadership and Organizational Development,* and *The Academy of Management Executive,* among others. In addition, Dr. Ali is the editor of the *International Journal of Commerce and Management* and *Advances in Competitiveness Research* and is the executive editor of the *Competitiveness Review.* Furthermore, he serves on the editorial boards of several journals. Currently, Dr. Ali's research interests include global business leadership, strategy, foreign policy, comparative management, competitiveness issues, organizational politics, and international management.

Preface and Acknowledgments

Globalization, a cornerstone of the unending human journey, symbolizes commitment and desire for a better future. It conveys the perception of a world that is fully connected and finite in its geographical space, and yet offers infinite possibilities for growth, renewal, and revitalization. Advances in information technology and unprecedented growth in business and trade make globalization a fact of life. In the business context, globalization embraces both cooperation and competitiveness. The idea of cooperation represents a deep understanding of interdependence and joint responsibility at work, across firms and national boundaries. The idea of competitiveness conveys the perception that cooperation without motivation is doomed to failure and that only through practical inducement can continuous improvement and progress become a normal way of life. Put another way, globalization represents the best that human beings can offer in the age of information, as it reinforces a sense of responsibility toward ourselves as partners and competitors, as beneficiaries and custodians of our organizations and environment. It is this understanding that encouraged me to write this book. The concepts and ideas presented here attempt to capture the best in the existing literature and offer an eclectic view that helps managers and students of international business and organization to understand globalization and its significance, challenges, and implications for today's organizations.

The first three chapters of the book present a discussion of the theories, discourse, and environment of globalization. These chapters provide the most comprehensive coverage of the subject to date, thereby enabling readers to grasp the essence of globalization and common pitfalls in the treatment of the subject in the literature. They set the stage for analyzing global matters at the level of the firm in the later chapters. In this analysis, readers will come to recognize the role of firms and global executives in world affairs and their potential not only to contribute more but to steer globalization onto a path that spreads benefits and fosters the participation of the world's communities in rewarding, promising, and spirit-lifting activities. Furthermore, both the destructive and constructive consequences of globalization are covered, and related issues are integrated smoothly throughout the book.

In the course of preparing this book, I reviewed both corporate publications and academic literature. I was surprised to discover that business executives are well ahead of scholars and politicians, not only in embracing globalization but also in understanding its essence and real meaning. Global executives, compared to other groups, appear to have, in general, a clearer understanding of globalization, its principles, and its challenges. This realization enriched the book, illuminated the linkage between theory and practice, and oriented the text to serve the needs of executives and future managers in conducting their affairs. Indeed, this book offers new perspectives and approaches seldom presented in the existing academic literature. Therefore, its utility for executives, students of globalization, and policymakers, will continue for years to come.

It is unfortunate that in the literature, the role of global executives and firms in spreading and maximizing globalization benefits has been either dismissed, underestimated, or ignored. In fact, executives and business corporations have been mistakenly and unjustly accused of generating most of the world's existing ills (e.g., poverty, environmental problems). It is neither adequate nor practical to deny that some of the existing problems are the result of irresponsible behavior on the part of certain corporations. However, attributing all the negative consequences of globalization to business executives and their corporations is a dangerous obsession. Such attitudes have contributed unnecessarily to perpetuating myths and illusions. Fruitful opportunities, therefore, are often missed. Global executives have vested interests in multiplying worldwide benefits and in steering the path of globalization toward serving all populations. Moreover, building civil institutions on a global scale is one of global executives' top priorities, because global executives consider citizens all around the globe as customers and stakeholders. Meeting their needs, including a safe environment, is good business practice—and a competitive advantage. Indeed, globalization creates the need for leaders with worldwide perspectives. Global executives, with their practical judgment and sensitivity to global concerns, are more qualified than any other leaders to assume new roles that ultimately will contribute to building a better world.

There are certain outlooks and strategies that global executives need, which existing theories and strategies fail to adequately identify or address. This book provides an in-depth look at what it means to be a global executive, and what strategies set global corporations apart from other business organizations, by identifying their competitive and innovative practices and their networks and alliances. In short, the pivotal roles of global executives are highlighted, and their orientations are clarified, along with an extensive analysis of economic, social, technological, and political trends on a global scale. In fact, the book is written for those who are not afraid to confront myths and challenge existing approaches, and who yearn for unorthodox thinking and practical yet intellectual perspectives. The book should appeal to those who want to be global actors and are not intimidated by competition and ever-unfolding realities.

In preparing this book I had to consult with and seek assistance from several individuals. All have been very cooperative and supportive. My deepest appreciation goes to Robert C. Camp, Dean, Eberly College of Business, Indiana University of Pennsylvania. He provided unlimited support and created an environment conducive to intellectual activities. He and Paul Swiercz contributed useful comments and suggestions. Erdener Kaynak, Executive Editor for the International Business Press at The Haworth Press, is a friend and scholar who is always ready to provide assistance and moral support. In addition, I am thankful to Bill Palmer, Peg Marr, Andrew R. Roy, Karen Fisher, and Melissa Devendorf at The Haworth Press for their cooperation and understanding.

Furthermore, I would like to thank Nancy Corbett for editing the manuscript. My graduate assistants Liliana Perez, Brian Williams, Bharat Das, and Haiyan Zheng did a fantastic job helping me finish the book, and I am grateful for their exceptional enthusiasm in arranging and organizing references. Liliana, in particular, did an outstanding job of typing and retyping several drafts of the manuscript. In addition, I extend my sincere appreciation to the many

CEOs who provided materials related to their organizations and to those scholars who participated in the Delphi study.

Finally, my children Fadil, Aziz, and Yasmin, along with their mother, Huda, have given me incentive to work hard and make life an enjoyable journey. To all of them go my heartfelt thanks and appreciation.

Chapter 1

The Theory and Practice of Globalization

We are a corporate citizen of Germany, so we are also a corporate citizen wherever we have major plants and investments.

Jurgen E. Schrempp
Chairman of the Board, Daimler-Benz, 1990

Globalization has special meaning within Procter & Gamble. It means that we will continue to change from a United States-based business . . . into a truly world company. A company that thinks of everything it does . . . in terms of the entire world.

Edwin Artzt
Chairman and CEO, Procter & Gamble, 1990

As the world becomes smaller, economic boundaries become less and less important.

Jack Schofield
CEO, Airbus—North America

In today's business environment, most of an organization's activities are becoming global in nature. Firms across the world have recognized that globalization is a reality that creates unlimited opportunities while intensifying competition and threats. Many organizations, such as Exxon and GM, have been engaged in cross-border activities and functions for several decades. This, however, does not mean that, in the past, these organizations were pursuing globalization as a strategy and a way of life. Pursuing globalization and living it differ from mere involvement in international business activities. The differences are qualitative and include issues of scope, depth, commitment, and orientation. In the past, as Ohmae (1995) has argued, most multinational corporations (MNCs) behaved as extensions of colonial powers. MNCs were able to use their home government's influence to get concessions from host countries. In the meantime, they were expected to follow the political dictates of their host governments. According to some critics (e.g., Barnet and Cavanagh, 1995; Vernon, 1997), this hindered otherwise normal business relations and gave undue influence to political considerations.

Recent political and business developments (e.g., the abatement of ideological conflicts, the end of the Cold War, the ascension of free market movement, the rise of regionalism) have cultivated new aspects and strengthened business dimensions that have long been ignored or given low priority. Cooperation, alliances, and the need for free movement of goods and capital have profoundly affected business dealings and interactions. More important, the rise of global thinking and practice has made business interests and orientations more necessary than ever.

GLOBALIZATION ASPECTS

Adelman (1997) believes that the globalization of the world economy started about 1600 A.D. Global trade expanded rapidly from 1600 to 1800. *Forbes* magazine (see Lee and Foster, 1997) indicates that between 1870 and 1910 the free flow of labor was impressive, and capital moved freely among major countries. "National boundaries did not disappear. . . . But for the first time in history people, money, and goods were able to flow across them quite freely" (p. 88). *Forbes* declares that Richard Cobden—a nineteenth-century British liberal who dedicated his life to free trade—can be considered the father of globalization because Cobden's zeal helped set off a worldwide flow of people, capital, and goods similar to the recent world economic situation. In fact, "As Cobden's version of free trade spread its blessings throughout the world, investment followed it, and so did people" (Lee and Foster, 1997, p. 88). *Forbes* estimates that in the second half of the nineteenth century,

15 million people crossed the Atlantic to settle in North America. Cobden viewed free movement of trade as the grand panacea that would "serve to inoculate with the healthy and saving taste for civilization all the nations of the world" (quoted in Read, 1968, p. 110). Cobden's remarks of 1860 seem as applicable today as when he wrote them (see Morley, 1881, p. 343):

> It is an economic error to confine our view to the imports or exports of our own country. In the case of England, these are intimately connected with, and dependent upon, the great circulating system of the whole world's trade. Nobody has fully grasped the bearings of Free Trade, who does not realize what the international aspect of every commercial transaction amounts to; how the conditions of production and exchange in any one country affect, both actually and potentially, the corresponding conditions in every other country. It is not Free Trade between any two countries that is the true aim; but to remove obstacles in the way of the stream of freely exchanging commodities, that ought, like the Oceanus of primitive geography, to encircle the whole habitable world. In this circulating system every tariff is an obstruction, and the free circulation of commodities is in the long run as much impeded by an obstruction at one frontier as at another.

Nevertheless, most scholars seem to agree that the use of the term "globalization" is a recent phenomenon. Robertson (1992), for example, argues that in academic circles globalization was not recognized as a significant concept until the 1980s. Waters (1995) finds that "overall, the number of publications which use the word 'global' in their titles have now probably reached five figures, but the procedural term 'globalization' is still relatively rare" (p. 2). He acknowledges, however, that globalization is key to understanding the transition of human society into the third millennium. James Laxer (1993) posits that the concept of globalization has arisen at a very particular historical moment—the ascension of the Anglo-Saxon business elite. Despite these various characterizations, there seems to be a general agreement that "globalization," as a term, began to have wide appeal after McLuhan's (1960) popularization of the term "global village."

In the business world there is a consensus, too, that globalization is a recent development. For example, John Pepper (1991), president of Procter & Gamble (P&G) indicates that globalization is still a relatively new concept. These days, he points out, we see comments about it and there is not an annual report of "any self-respecting multinational company that doesn't talk about globalization as a foundation strategy" (p. 2). Similarly, Merrill Lynch, in its *1997 Annual Review,* stated, "Rapid convergence of the global markets is the cumulative result of the potent forces of globalization and deregulation . . . combined with advances in information technology that demolish time and distance as barriers to doing business" (p. 9). For Richard Grasso (1997, p. 216), chairman and CEO of the New York Stock Exchange, "globalization, perhaps for some . . . remains a buzzword that suffers from overuse. In fact, we in the financial community have used it for a quarter of a century. But, for us, globalization is no longer a mere buzzword, a utopian vision never to be realized."

In their quest for an adequate conceptualization and workable terminologies in international business, researchers and practitioners alike have encountered numerous problems. Nevertheless, developments in the behavioral sciences and in general research methodology, coupled with the persistent search for new meanings and perspectives, have enabled scholars and practitioners to overcome many obstacles. Still, in trade and international business, competitiveness and globalization are common. Globalization, in particular, is often misunderstood because the use of the term "globalization" attracts the attention of ordinary citizens and intellectuals alike. In addition, the term has undiminished utility for policymakers and business people who wish to project the image of a cultivated, well-rounded individual.

What complicates the issue even further is that the concept of globalization is not only interdisciplinary, but its utility and aspects have far-reaching implications for the business and policymaking communities at the national and international levels. In addition, the forces that advocate, resist, or are influenced by globalization are numerous and espouse dissimilar orientations, objectives, and strategies. For example, environmentalists, labor unions, social planners, and human rights advocates have expectations, fears, and needs that differ from those of managers and policymakers. Likewise, nongovernment organizations, academic and research institutions, MNCs, and supernational entities (e.g., the European Union) are all involved in the globalization process but follow different paths in pursuing their global goals.

DEFINITION OF GLOBALIZATION

The study of globalization has never been the exclusive concern of any scholarly circle. Unlike cross-cultural or competitiveness studies of the past, globalization studies appeal to a wide range of scholars and practitioners. It is no wonder, then, that different perceptions and approaches have developed for addressing globalization. This diversity accentuates the importance of globalization in the lives of individuals and societies and has contributed to the ever-continuing enrichment and refinement of discourse about it. As the participants and the actors of this discourse are not situated in any particular locality, nation, or field of study, the hope is that the benefits of globalization, both spiritual and material, will reach a wider range of the world's populations.

Globalization has often been debated in the fields of economics, international relations, management, and sociology. In all these fields, the meaning, approaches to, and consequences of globalization have been given a high priority in the past two decades. Reflection on the definition of globalization in these fields and in business practice is imperative for understanding its scope and foundation. In economics, Harris (1993, p. 755) defines globalization as "the increasing internationalization of the production, distribution, and marketing of goods and services." Similarly, Rhodes (1996) views globalization as "the functional integration of national economies within the circuits of industrial and financial capital" (p. 161).

Globalization in international relations and politics has become a new area of interest that rivals the well-established traditional political areas. McGrew and Lewis (1992, p. 319) define globalization as "a set of processes which embrace most of the globe or which operate worldwide; the concept therefore has a spatial connotation. . . . On the other hand it also implies an intensification in the levels of interaction, interconnectedness or interdependence between the states and societies which constitute the world community." For Naim (1997, p. 5), globalization "represents a profound redefinition of roles, possibilities, and risks around the world that is altering the very nature of international relations and, therefore, the nature of foreign policy." On the other hand, Boutros-Ghali (1996, p. 87) believes that globalization is creating "a world that is increasingly interconnected in which national boundaries are less important, and it is generating both possibilities and problems."

In the field of management, globalization has often been used interchangeably with internationalization. For example, Pearce and Robinson used the term internationalization in their 1988 edition, but in 1997 changed it to globalization. Rugman (1997) notes that globalization "means regionalization," while Lodge (1995, p. 1) provides a more general definition: "Globalization is the process whereby the world's people are becoming increasingly interconnected in all facets of their lives—cultural, economic, political, technological, and environmental."

In their treatment of globalization, sociologists place emphasis on the scope and intensity of interactions among people living as a single world entity. Waters (1995) defines globalization as "A social process in which the constraints of geography on social and cultural arrangements recede and in which people become increasingly aware that they are receding" (p. 3). Similarly, Robertson (1992, p. 8) refers to globalization as both the "compression of the world and the intensification of consciousness of the world as a whole."

For managers, globalization is not only a curiosity, but also an actuality that has to be dealt with on a daily basis. Managers, like scholars, however, are also diverse in their thinking and attitudes toward globalization. Christopher Rodrigues (1994), CEO of Thomas Cook Group, views globalization in a very narrow way—"running a global business from a global center." Similarly, Richard Grasso (1997, p. 216), chairman and CEO of the New York Stock Exchange, treats globalization as an economic trend: "Global markets when they are realized in their entirety, are the ultimate result of a trend now underway . . . called globalization." Peter Hellman (1997, p. 57), president and CEO of TRW, sees globalization as "an opportunity for prosperity that is equal to any in our history. It can be a force for positive change, if we manage it skillfully as an industry."

Percy Barnevik (1994), CEO of Asea Brown Boveri, goes further in his view of globalization: "What I mean by globalization is not only that you export to other markets and compete with people there—but also that you have a presence in [product] development and indeed, in manufacturing in many markets" (p. 20). Harry Stonecipher (1996), president and CEO of McDonnell Douglas, views globalization as "the whole movement toward a single world economy and a single world society" (p. 251). Previously, Edwin Artzt (1990), chairman and CEO, P&G, provided a more comprehensive definition of globalization in the business world:

> Globalization means doing a better job than your competitors at satisfying consumers' needs and their demand for quality, no matter where they live. It means creating the network and infrastructure to efficiently compete in the increasingly homogeneous worldwide marketplace. Globalization has special meaning with Procter & Gamble. It means that we will continue to change from a United States-based business that sells some of its products in international markets into a truly world company. A company that thinks of everything it does—including the development of products—in terms of the entire world. (p. 1)

The United Nations, on the other hand, defines globalization as a concept that "refers both to an increasing flow of goods and resources across national borders and to the emergence of a complementary set of organizational structures to manage the expanding network of international economic activities and transactions" (UNCTAD, 1997a, p. 70). Many observers, however, consider the emergence of international organizations such as the World Trade Organization and the World Bank as consequences of world interdependence and interconnectedness. It is obvious that in the academic disciplines two major treatments of globalization have emerged. The first considers globalization in terms of internalization and integration of activities and functions on a global basis (economics). The second orientation, generally, views it in terms of an interconnected world and intensification and awareness of the scope of interactions as the constraints of time, geography, and culture recede (international relations, management, and sociology). Practitioners, on the other hand, stress meeting customers' needs and doing a better job than competitors in the global marketplace. They view globalization as an opportunity to enhance their presence in every significant market in the world.

Building on the academic and practical elements presented, the following definition of globalization is adopted. Globalization is a process that is built on collective understanding of the need to establish a world community that is prosperous and tolerant, and on respect for and equitable treatment of people across the globe. It is a process that enhances and strengthens global understanding and improves the quality and effectiveness of business, professional, and personal interactions through unrestricted access to world commodities, technology, and information. As a concept, globalization is defined as a set of beliefs that foster a sense of connectivity, interdependence, and integration in the world community. It highlights commonalties without overlooking differences, and it extends benefits and responsibilities on a global scale. At the firm level, globalization should mean the ability of a corporation to conduct business across borders in an open market, maximizing organizational benefits, without inflicting social damage or violating the rights of people from other cultures.

The underlying assumption of this definition is that there is an urgent need to rethink globalization, its meaning, and its scope, in terms that convey and capture its spirit and virtue. In today's business environment, global corporations must stress objectivity in the treatment of issues across the globe and have the courage to confront biases and prejudices. They should not behave like a "colonial entity" that is interested only in making profits and reinvesting them in the "home market." Global corporations should treat globalization as a view and outlook that broadens and energizes human minds and perspectives. Practically and spiritually, globalization must be an inclusive, rather than an exclusive, endeavor.

It is important, however, to recognize that in the near future financial and trade activities will still be the dominant forces and features of globalization. Nevertheless, it is essential to point out that trade is only one of a myriad of worldwide activities related to globalization. Free movement of capital, goods, and labor and the establishment of a civil society, where cultural and political tolerance are the norm, are the foundations for true globalization.

In other words, the pillars of globalization are open trade and vital civil and legal institutions that uphold individual and group rights while facilitating social and economic integration. The benefits of economic activities, especially international trade, are numerous, including job creation, improving customer welfare, stimulating economic growth, and so on. Nevertheless, limiting globalization only to trade and the profits associated with increasing trade volume does an injustice to growing beliefs and practices that aim at establishing a prosperous and stable world. Globalization is not synonymous with trade volume and export profits. It is an orientation that seeks to enhance and strengthen global understanding and effective business, professional, and personal interactions. The focus on trade volume and on export limits the ability and capacity of people to become involved in activities that release energy and stimulate global thinking and behavior. In addition, focusing on trade volume alone may prevent individuals and organizations alike from moving forward in advancing causes and programs that are not profit-oriented. While it is a misjudgment to discount the importance of profit-oriented activities in furthering globalization aims, it is equally a mistake to disregard nonbusiness activities. These activities are expected to be crucial for strengthening global thinking and practice in the decades to come.

APPROACHES TO GLOBALIZATION

Levy-Livermore (1998) claims that the world between 1820 and 1913 was more borderless than it is today. He argues that the Industrial Revolution helped to connect European and overseas economies in complementary development patterns that transmitted changes in the rhythm of economic growth in the industrial world overseas. Nevertheless, evidence indicates that the world is shrinking and that the scope of trade and financial activities is no longer the monopoly of the United Kingdom and the United States. That is, today's world economy differs significantly from that of a century ago for at least three reasons (Kobrin, 1997a): the world economy is broader in terms of the number of national markets that are engaged; it is deeper in terms of the density and velocity of interaction and flows of trade and finance; and the dominant mode of organization of world economic transactions has changed significantly from the market (trade and portfolio investment) to internationalization of production through MNCs. In addition, today's world economy is more integrated than ever. Joan Spero (1996), U.S. Under Secretary of State for Economic, Business, and Agricultural Affairs, furnished the following as evidence of business globalization:

- Capital now moves with startling speed around the world. Each day over $1 trillion is traded in a global foreign exchange market that never closes.
- Technological advances in computers and telecommunications are paving the way for a new information-based economy.
- Even small- and medium-sized companies recognize that the competition for market share is global, and that participating in the global economy is no longer a choice but a necessity.

Several forces are solidifying the transformation to the age of globalization. These forces are diverse but their impacts are wide, immediate, and intense. Chief among them are the following:

1. *Trends toward regionalism* (e.g., NAFTA and the European Union). Such trends have boosted the argument that open trade has more advantages than disadvantages, and the world is better off with few or no trade restrictions.

2. *Abatement of ideological conflicts and the end of the Cold War.* These developments accelerated the adoption of free trade systems by various countries as vital economic regimes. This development has induced governments not only to restructure their economies through liberalization and privatization but also to invest in productive sectors. Likewise, governments have become more inclined than ever to solve international problems through constructive engagement and dialogue.

3. *Rising influence of nongovernment organizations (NGOs) in addressing and regulating a wide range of international problems and issues.* NGOs such as Amnesty International and Greenpeace, along with many organizations affiliated with the UN, have done marvelous jobs of dealing with complex and urgent international

issues. The ascendancy of such organizations contributes significantly to world economic, social, and technological integration. NGOs such as the International Standards Organization (ISO), World Business Council for Sustainable Development, and International Securities Markets Association (ISMA) set widely observed standards in the global marketplace. At a time of rapid change, NGOs are quicker than governments to respond to new demands and opportunities (Mathews, 1997).

4. *Mobility of capital across the globe.* It is estimated that each day over $1 trillion is traded in the global foreign exchange market, where investors search to expand their markets and seize better financial opportunities. Furthermore, the emergence of electronic cash and a digitally networked global economy raise vital concerns about the very idea of domestic and international "as meaningful and distinct concepts" (Kobrin, 1997). Traditionally, increased flows of financial capital were complementary to trade. In recent years, however, "the role of international finance has extended well beyond the coordination of international trade and investment. It has gained a life of its own independent of the international flow of goods and investment" (UNCTAD, 1997a, p. 94).

5. *Expanding the role of international corporations in the global marketplace.* Traditionally, most MNCs were U.S. based. In recent years the situation has changed dramatically. UNCTAD (1999b) estimates that there are some 60,000 MNCs with about 500,000 affiliates. Over 3,470 of them are U.S. based, with 18,608 affiliates. These corporations have established production sites abroad and engaged in interfirm cooperation and alliances. In fact, the 1997-1998 period has witnessed a phenomenal increase in mergers and acquisitions. Chief among them are the acquisitions by Daimler-Benz of Chrysler Corporation; Merrill Lynch's acquisition of fifty branch offices in Japan of Yamaichi Securities; Worldcom's merger with MCI Communications; Bertelsmann AG's takeover of Random House; and British Petroleum's merger with Amoco. U.S.- and European-based firms dominated cross-border acquistions in the first nine months of 1999. For example, the major purchasers, in deals worth $202 billion, $113 billion, $74 billion, and $45 billion are British-, U.S.-, French-, and German-based firms respectively (KPMG, 1999). KMPG reported that for the same period the vol-

ume of cross-border mergers and acquisitions reached $608 billion, already exceeding the total value of 1998 ($544 billion). Cross-border mergers and acquisitions are methods of integrating world markets.

6. *Ease of flow of foreign direct investment (FDI) and of labor across the globe.* In 1998, FDI flows set a record as international corporations responded to economic liberalization in various countries. Inflows increased by 39 percent, to $644 billion, while outflows rose 37 percent, to $649 billion. Increases in FDI inflows in 1998 exceeded the growth in the nominal value of world gross domestic product (GDP) and international trade, which grew by 2.5 percent and 3.6 percent respectively (IMF, 1999). About fifty-four countries were the recipients of FDI, and twenty countries were the sources of the FDI flows. The liberalization and restructuring of world economies have induced international corporations to pursue a wide range of investment activities. This allows MNCs to integrate both their global portfolios of ownership and locational assets and, in the process, still integrate the economies of the host and home countries (Gray, 1998). Furthermore, the liberalization of much of the world economy and the active engagement of international corporations facilitate not only knowledge transfer but also labor movement and integration among countries. Many nations, especially in the West, have designed a more liberal immigration policy to attract skilled labor. For example, the U.S. Senate passed a bill on May 18, 1998, that allowed 30,000 more skilled foreign workers to enter the country in 1998 and increases quotas for the following five years. In addition, international corporations have become major world employers. Nestlé, for instance, employs more than 206,125 workers overseas. Unilever and GM employ 273,000 and 221,313 workers overseas respectively (UNCTAD, 1998a). Trade liberalization, however, has contributed to increased wage inequality in some countries (UNCTAD, 1997a). Nevertheless, as Koudal (1998) found, workers' wages in MNCs are generally higher, more equal, and converge faster across economies than those of the total manufacturing sectors. This development by itself is a force for accelerating economic integration.

7. *Expanding the role of the service sector in the world economy stimulates people to rethink priorities, and be aware of erasing*

national borders and of the intensity and speed of global interactions. Certainly, the liberalization of services produces a profound change in orientations among the parties involved. In fact, according to UNCTAD (1996), the liberalization of services and of trade in services fosters the application of new management techniques, facilitates relations between various stages of design, production, and marketing of products and services, and generates greater economies of scale.

8. *Advanced technological breakthroughs* in recent years, which have created a new dynamic that makes it possible to get more worldwide information and make major decisions in a short time. In addition, technological advancement eases communication, knowledge transfer, and transportation. Geographical space and time have lost, therefore, their utility as a serious barrier for people and business interactions. The Internet revolution has made universal connectivity a reality. People across the globe converse with one another. Likewise, the spread of the "Internet Population" to almost every corner of the world, along with instant sharing of information related to the availability and quality of goods and services, has induced the homogenization of taste. While cultural homogenization is far from being a reality, cultural integration and cross-cultural familiarity are advancing quickly.

9. *Worldwide appeal of democratic transformation and principles.* Worldwide development intensifies the search for commonly accepted norms of conduct on a global basis. Most world governments seem to agree that building social institutions and establishing a foundation for civil society enhance their respective country's status in the global community and improve living standards. Such trends encourage worldwide economic, political, and social integration and speed knowledge transfer across nations. Therefore, nations have become more accepting of convergence around the effective techniques that ensure their vitality and competitiveness.

These forces, individually and collectively, facilitate the globalization of production and consumption, thereby creating new opportunities for international actors, especially MNCs. Various approaches have been utilized by MNCs to globalize their operations and to respond to globalization's challenges. The following is a brief discussion of select distinct approaches employed by some MNCs in specific industries. In the auto industry, Toyota, for example, adopted two methods:

- Localize far-flung activities further by integrating operations by region
- Establish presence in every major market and focus on products designed for local needs, produced locally (Toyota, 1996).

Similarly, Honda (1997d) organized its operations into four regions—the Americas, Europe/Middle East/Africa, Asia/Oceania, and Japan and introduced products that met the needs of each unique market. In addition, Honda is committed to making more efficient use of its existing resources by providing more autonomy for regional operations.

Siemens and Emerson, in the electric capital goods industry, place emphasis on building a global presence in each business and on strategic partnerships and acquisitions. In its *1996 Annual Report,* Siemens (1996), for example, states, "When markets go global and competition gets faster and tougher, when innovation alone isn't enough and partnerships with customers are decisive, it's time to thoroughly revamp the way we think and work" (p. 8).

In the food and consumer product industry, P&G and Nestlé have unique approaches. Nestlé's approach to globalization centers on two elements:

- Establishing a proper balance between regional and global conditions and decentralizing operations and global connections, as well as coordination.
- Producing locally and regionally as well as raising the added value of each product. Create products that employ local raw materials and correspond to local eating habits, and sell them at affordable prices (see Maucher, 1994).

In contrast, P&G has devised plans to succeed globally by doing the following (see Wehling, 1997):

- Restructuring its business into four major geographic regions along with eleven Global Category Teams

- Understanding the consumer and what is universal and what is unique in each category
- Defining brand's equity (e.g., freshness, resealability)
- Testing success models—the ability to create and reapply success models by institutionalizing them—and deploying them globally
- Expanding the best model around the world as fast as possible
- Continuing to experiment so that future improvements and innovations are created with the whole world in mind

P&G attempts to provide the right balance between standardization and localization of its products. That is, P&G strongly believes that "you can't standardize everything" and that there are significant regional differences in consumer habits and culture. It is important to note, however, that many business organizations still do not differentiate between globalization and internationalization, a point that will be addressed in Chapter 5.

THEORIES OF GLOBALIZATION

In academia as in the business world, various approaches have evolved for treating globalization. In general, there are two historical approaches—open pluralism and structured pluralism (Wilkin, 1996). In open pluralism, globalization represents a qualitative shift in the world system as various "autonomous forms and sites of political, ideological, cultural, economic and military power conflict and transform the world-system with no form of social power possessing primary importance" (Wilkin, 1996, p. 229). Under this view there are not only multiple conflicting power centers, but also no unique and straightforward relationship can be delineated to understand current and future processes of globalization.

Under structured pluralism there is agreement that the driving mechanisms for globalization are founded in the capitalist system. The world system is viewed as "a totality of social relations rather than a series of autonomous spheres that have become independent" (Wilkin, 1996, p. 230). According to Wilkin, globalization is understood as "the necessary relations that exist between a series of mechanisms that are capable of generating a range of cultural, social, and ideological responses, which, in turn, reflect the prevailing power of conflictual social groups" (p. 230). Most of the globalization theories briefly discussed below come under this approach. Nevertheless, some of them dispute the claim that globalization necessarily involves exploitation.

Barnet and Cavanagh (1995) claim that, in conducting their operations, MNCs are the major force that is integrating the planet. These corporations are powerful and dynamic and tend to demand concessions from governments relative to regulations, taxes, laws, and facilities. In pursuit of their world goals, MNCs manage to undermine the effectiveness of national governments in performing activities on behalf of their people. MNCs, because of the nature of their global production and alliances, assume enormous power that can be used to control and bypass traditional national and economic borders, political systems, and other power centers. While hundreds of millions of people across the globe contribute to creating the ties that connect across great distances, MNCs control the human energy, technology, and capital that make it happen. The motives and interests of the corporate leaders are "global but parochial" as their eyes are on the global market even though most of the people remain invisible. Therefore, global economic integration may stimulate political and social disintegration.

Robinson (1996) views transnational capital as the pivotal factor for globalization. He advances the idea that in the last few decades there has been a phenomenal dominance of transnational capital in the world economy, which in turn induces the transnationalization of social classes. Elite classes in the industrial societies establish alliances with elites in developing economies. The latter, as the local contingents of the transnational elite, focus their energies on creating the best local conditions for transnational capital within the new world division of labor. In this new world division of labor, global class structure is superimposed on national class structures and "both dominant and subordinate classes are involved in global class formation" (p. 382). The formation and acceptance of transnational elites weaken the nation-state system and all its relative frames of reference. Therefore, the prospect for world order is strengthened by a greater worldwide unity of goals and interests of the transnational elite and by the declining threat of social conflict.

Robertson (1992) also stresses that globalization is not a new development. Rather, its roots go back to the emergence of state communities in Europe (1400-1750), and it has been strengthened through successive historical stages. However, globalization has accelerated in recent decades. He argues that the world gradually has become more and more united, and this has manifested itself in a holistic consciousness. Robertson identifies four elements: individual self, national society, an international system of societies, and humanity in general. He maintains that globalization places less emphasis on the individual and national components than on the last two elements.

Waters (1995) proposes that the theory of globalization centers on the relationship between social organization and territoriality. Several types of exchange predominate in social relationships: material exchange (e.g., trade, capital accumulations); political supports of security, coercion, surveillance, and authority; legitimacy and obedience; and symbolic exchange by means of all types of communication, publication, and information transfer mechanisms. He argues that material exchanges localize, political exchanges internationalize, and symbolic exchanges globalize. That is, the degree of the economy and polity to be globalized depends on the extent to which the exchanges that take place within them are achieved culturally (symbolically). In other words, the degree of globalization is greater in the cultural arena than in either the political or economic arenas. Waters believes that the world's populations experience a phase of "cultural economy." In this cultural economy, markets move beyond the capacity of governments to manage them, and the leading actors in the globalization process are those whose products are themselves symbols—mass media and entertainment and the postindustrialized service industries. Therefore, the economy "becomes so subordinate to individual taste and choice that it becomes reflexively marketized and, because tokenized systems do not succumb to physical boundaries, [the economy becomes] reflexively globalized" (p. 95). Stated differently, there is a global unification of cultural orientations that breaks down the boundaries between national politics and local economies and makes it possible to develop transnational practices. This global unification is facilitated by electronic communication and rapid transportation.

In the field of international business, Dunning (1997) has been the leading advocate of globalization. He postulates that world economic events and technological advances are deepening the structural interdependence between nations and that the diamonds of competitive advantage of these nations become clearly connected in such a way that MNCs find it beneficial to locate some of their home bases from their country of ownership to other countries. MNCs will locate new product-line bases in the country that offers the most attractive location-bound endowments for their innovation. Furthermore, MNC subsidiaries specialize in activities in which they have a competitive advantage and market their outputs to regional and global markets. The increasing mobility of various intangible assets, specifically knowledge and information, influences a government's ability to manage its internal affairs. This mobility, coupled with interfirm alliances and corporate networks, paves the way for world economic integration and globalization.

In this book, I take the basic position that in today's marketplace, firms tend to engage directly and indirectly in complex trade, economic, technological, political, and social alliances globally. That is, firms seek to sustain their competitiveness by establishing a set of worldwide relationships and alliances with competitors, suppliers, customers, politicians, and social and environmental actors. Such involvements, along with advanced information technology and the worldwide appeal of the principles of civil society, facilitate free movement of trade, capital, and eventually people across the globe, thereby strengthening world interdependence and elevating peoples' consciousness of the unity and vitality of our planet. This theoretical proposal is based on the following assumptions:

1. The widespread appeal of the free market system induces a firm to act as a citizen of the market in which it operates. The issue of a home country is still important in the firm's conduct, but it will gradually fade.
2. Corporate alliances and networking circle the globe and eventually render corporate boundaries obsolete. The center for ultimate decision making no longer resides in the headquarters.

3. The ascendancy of international production and consumption systems reinforces the belief and practice among corporate managers that suppliers and customers are their partners regardless of where they are located. Furthermore, managers eventually recognize that every person, even in a remote corner of the world, is a potential customer.
4. Corporate involvement in societal and environmental issues is a good business practice and a source of competitive advantage.
5. Governments have a stake in seeing that corporations are less restricted in their operations and that these corporations are cooperating with local communities on a range of issues related to business practice, environment, and civic activities. Therefore, they tend to develop relations with other governments to minimize negative aspects while maximizing positive conduct.
6. Instant transmission of information to most of the world's regions sensitizes people to issues that are global in nature and induces them to demand no less than the best quality, price, and service. Furthermore, individuals will be more inclined than ever to question coercion, corruption, and abuse, regardless of their sources.
7. NGOs' involvement in solving social, economic, and political problems compels governments and business organizations to cooperate and tackle issues that seem to be local but often have consequences beyond national borders.
8. The nation-state as an entity is not in danger of collapsing in the near future; rather, it is assuming new functions that are in line with globalization trends and the principles of civil society.
9. Intellectual, political, and cultural elites, especially in industrial countries, have a vested interest in advancing their conceptual designs for the world. In doing so they ally themselves with the elite of the developing countries. In the process, people become more aware of the global interdependence of thought and action.
10. There are no inherent contradictions between global integration and increasing awareness of social, ethnic, and religious identity among many segments of the world's populations. Globalization has cultural, political, and business dimensions.

Chapter 2

Global Business Environment

Changes in the international economy are opening up opportunities to every part of BP's business. To maintain competitive success we are developing our "global reach"—the ability to grasp the best opportunities whenever and where ever they arise.

British Petroleum, 1997

We are living in a world of rapid and profound change, altering the expectations and our vision of the future.

Alex Krauer
Chairman, Novartis, 1996

In a dynamic global business environment, there is always a shift in the power and influence of the forces that shape market functions and structures. While this might be the case in many situations, it is the world economy that is driving today's profound changes, changes so sweeping that they have altered certain market and government fundamentals. Assumptions related to the role of the nation-state and corporations have been radically revised. In addition, because of world interdependence, economic downturns and crises that were traditionally treated as isolated phenomena have come to require urgent international solutions. Their impact has been immediate and far-reaching: for example, the financial crisis that originated in Thailand in July 1997 triggered an unforeseeable economic, political, and social upheaval in both nearby and remote countries. Indeed, the spillover effects on Indonesia and Malaysia were more than economic. The International Monetary Fund (IMF), in its September 1998 *World Economic Outlook,* warned that international economic and financial conditions have deteriorated considerably as recessions have deepened in many of Asia's emerging markets and Japan, and Russia's financial crisis has expanded the spectrum of default. It states (p. 1):

> Negative spillovers have been felt in world stock markets, emerging market interest spreads, acute pressures on several currencies, and further drops in already weak commodity prices. Among the industrial countries of North America and Europe, the effects on activity of the crisis have been small so far but are beginning to be felt, especially in the industrial sector. World growth of only 2 percent is now projected for 1998, a full percentage point less than expected in the May 1998 *World Economic Outlook* and well below trend growth. Chances of any significant improvement in 1999 have also diminished and the risks of a deeper, wider, and more prolonged downturn have escalated.

This means that the global business environment is complex and interconnected. Furthermore, today's environment has acquired additional new characteristics. First, recent forces and events have influence that goes beyond national boundaries and operates in sudden and sometimes mysterious ways that surpass even the wild anticipations of governmental and international institutions. Second, most of the forces originate in geographically distant places but appear to be linked together in their impacts and consequences. Third, actions needed to limit these consequences must be regional or international, and such actions demand plans and policies that are well coordinated, thoughtful, and practical. Last, the forces that shape global business are numerous and uncontrollable, and they simultaneously stimulate integration and differentiation. It is this very nature of global business that makes it qualitatively different from previous historical and economic developments. What happens in other parts of the world is no longer an object of mere curiosity or a luxury in which to indulge. These realities necessitate that issues vital for global business environments be addressed. In this chapter, therefore, trade and economic matters, along with subjects that are normally considered the domain of political economy and sociology (e.g., functions of the nation-state, cultural activities, wealth and poverty, etc.), are clarified.

LIBERALIZATION

One of the most important trends leading to world integration in recent years is liberalization. Governments in developing, transition, and market economies have accelerated the liberalization process. The scope of liberalization, however, differs in speed and depth among these economies. In market economies, such as those of the United States and Britain, liberalization becomes an urgent matter. The Reagan and Thatcher governments initiated a widespread program to deregulate economies and to reform regulations in the areas of environment, health, banking, and insurance. In addition, tax reductions and partnerships with the private sector have been intensified. In societies in transition (e.g., the Czech Republic and Poland), governments initiated privatization programs and enacted laws and regulations to attract foreign investors and to establish environments conducive to economic growth. Developing countries differ in their liberalization initiatives. Countries such as Egypt, Turkey, and Argentina have dismantled many state enterprises and deregulated their economies while encouraging private enterprises to play significant roles in economic development. Other countries such as India, Syria, Iran, and Tanzania have been cautious about liberalization. Nevertheless, they are opening their economies to the world. According to United Nations data, between 1991 and 1997, governments made 750 changes in regulatory regimes relating to FDI; 94 percent were in the direction of liberalization. The number of countries that introduced changes in their investment regimes rose to seventy-six in 1997, compared to thirty-five in 1991 (UNCTAD, 1998a). The financial crisis that erupted in 1997 had been thought to slow the march for liberalization, especially in the financial market. This, however, did not materialize. Only Malaysia imposed strict capital control measures (e.g., suspending trading in and fixing its local currency exchange rate). Still, the Malaysian government had to relax them in 1999. In his testimony to the U.S. Congress in September 1998, George Soros warned that the global capitalist system "is coming apart at the seams," and that "financial markets have recently acted more like a wrecking ball, knocking over one country after another" (p. 1).

Liberalization was reinforced by the conclusion, in 1994, of the Uruguay Round of multilateral trade negotiation and the establishment of the World Trade Organization and as nations and investors alike have acquired confidence in and are motivated by its mission, objectives, and procedures. The expansion of regional integration efforts also stimulates the trend toward liberalization. Liberalization policies have significantly widened the effective economic space available to producers and investors. That is, producers and investors behave more than ever as if the world economy consisted of a single market and production platforms with regional or national subsections, rather than as a set of national economies linked by trade and investment flows (UNCTAD, 1996). Nevertheless, liberalization is endangered by the rise of national protectionism and the use of economic sanctions by the leading economic powers. James Perrella, president and CEO of Ingersoll-Rand, maintains that even though economic and trade sanctions have become outdated tools of the Cold War era, the United States, during the Clinton administration alone, imposed more than sixty of them on other countries. He has said that "whether they are used as a diplomatic weapon to help isolate an adversarial nation, or as an economic tool to protect a sector of the U.S. economy from foreign competition, trade restrictions are almost invariably ineffective and self-defeating" (Perrella, 1998, p. 683).

TRADE

Since the 1950s, trade has been expanding faster than world output. In fact, world GDP and trade grew at ostentatious rates in 1997 despite the Asian financial crisis. Merchandise exports grew at 9.5 percent, and this is the highest rate of trade growth in more than two decades (WTO, 1998). Merchandise exports increased from $4,915 billion in 1995 to $5,295 billion in 1997. For the same years, commercial services increased from $1,200 billion to $1,295 billion. The annual percentage change rate for world exports increased from an average of 6 percent for 1995-1996 to 9.5 percent in 1997.

The major regional exporters (see Table 2.1) in 1997 were Western Europe ($2,269 billion), Asia ($1,380 billion), North America

TABLE 2.1. Growth in the Value of World Merchandise Trade by Region, 1990-1997 (in Billions of Dollars)

Exports (f.o.b.) Value		Exports (f.o.b.) Annual percentage change				Imports (c.i.f.) Value		Imports (c.i.f.) Annual percentage change		
1997	1990-1995	1995	1996	1997		1997	1990-1995	1995	1996	1997
5295	7.5	20.0	4.0	3.0	World	5435	7.5	19.5	4.5	3.0
904	8.5	14.5	6.5	9.5	North America	1100	8.0	11.0	6.0	10.5
280	9.0	22.0	12.0	11.0	Latin America	319	14.5	11.5	12.5	17.5
110	14.0	31.0	21.0	14.5	Mexico	113	12.5	−10.5	25.5	22.5
170	7.0	17.5	7.5	9.0	Other Latin America	207	15.5	25.0	6.5	15.0
2269	6.0	23.0	3.5	−1.0	Western Europe	2236	5.5	22.5	2.5	−1.0
2100	6.5	23.5	3.5	−1.0	European Union (15)	2045	5.5	22.0	2.0	−1.0
179	7.0	27.0	7.5	4.0	Transition economies	192	5.0	26.0	15.5	7.5
89	7.5	26.5	5.5	6.5	Central/Eastern Europe	115	11.5	28.0	16.5	4.0
120	0.5	13.5	11.5	3.0	Africa	127	5.5	21.5	−1.0	5.0
30	3.5	10.5	2.5	6.0	South Africa	32	10.5	30.5	−1.5	5.0
163	1.5	13.5	14.0	0	Middle East	144	6.0	14.0	6.0	1.5
1380	12.0	18.0	0.5	5.5	Asia	1317	12.0	23.0	5.0	0
421	9.0	11.5	−7.5	2.0	Japan	338	7.5	22.0	4.0	−3.0
183	19.0	23.0	1.5	21.0	China	142	20.0	14.0	5.0	2.5
548	14.0	23.0	3.0	3.0	Six East Asian traders*	581	15.0	26.0	3.5	0

Source: WTO, 1998.

*Chinese Taipei; Hong Kong, China; the Republic of Korea; Malaysia, Singapore, and Thailand

($904 billion), and the Middle East ($163 billion). The United States, Germany, Japan, France, and the United Kingdom were ranked as the top five leading exporting nations (WTO, 1998). In terms of imports, the world average increased from 6.5 percent in 1990-1995 to 9 percent in 1997. The leading regional importers again were Western Europe, Asia, North America, and the Middle East. The United States, Germany, Japan, United Kingdom, and France were the leading importing nations. Most trade activities take place among the most advanced industrial countries. Nevertheless, since 1996 there has been growth in output and trade in almost all regions of the world. The acceleration in trade growth, especially in 1997 (9 percent), was shared between the advanced and developing countries (IMF, 1998). For instance, in Africa, the growth of regional output accelerated to 3.9 percent from 2.8 percent in 1995. About 120 out of 143 economies registered positive per capita growth in 1997. Similarly, the value of merchandise exports for North America rose by 9.5 percent in 1997, three times faster than world trade. Exports to Latin American countries and intra-North American trade expanded at double-digit rates (WTO, 1998).

The collapse of the financial market (1997-1998) induced recessions in many countries and regions, especially in Asia, Latin America, and Russia, resulting in a fall in the import demand of many concerned countries, with certain negative impacts on the economies of their export suppliers. In fact, the crisis resulted in the reemergence of major trade imbalances in the global economy not experienced since the 1980s, the slowdown of world trade, and in the sudden and widespread fall in commodity prices (UNCTAD, 1999a).

FOREIGN DIRECT INVESTMENT

Watkins (1997) argues that FDI flows have grown since the 1960s and have overtaken foreign trade as an engine of world growth. As seen in Table 2.2, inflows in 1998 increased by about 40 percent, to $644 billion. Outflows in 1998 increased by 37 percent, to $649 billion (see Table 2.3). The share of advanced industrial countries in world FDI inflows and outflows was about 72 and 92 percent respectively. This is similar to trade flows and patterns and may suggest that international corporations are the most important instruments for global

TABLE 2.2. FDI Inflows, 1987-1998 ($U.S. millions)

Region/Economy	1987-1992 (annual avg.)	1993	1994	1995	1996	1997	1998
World	173,530	219,421	253,506	328,862	358,869	464,341	643,879
Developed Countries	136,628	133,850	146,379	206,372	211,120	273,276	460,431
Western Europe	75,507	78,684	84,345	121,522	115,346	134,915	237,425
North America	52,110	48,283	53,299	68,031	85,864	120,729	209,875
Other Developed Countries	9,011	6,884	8,735	18,819	9,910	17,632	13,130
Developing Countries	35,326	78,813	101,196	106,224	135,343	172,533	165,936
Africa	3,010	3,469	5,313	4,145	5,907	7,657	7,931
North Africa	1,214	1,518	2,330	1,180	1,888	3,048	2,643
Other Africa	1,797	1,950	2,984	2,965	4,021	4,609	5,288
Latin America and the Caribbean	12,400	20,009	31,451	32,921	46,162	68,255	71,652
South America	5,510	7,974	14,999	18,950	31,711	46,686	49,973
Other Latin America and the Caribbean	6,890	12,036	16,452	13,970	14,450	21,569	21,680
Developing Europe	82	274	417	470	1,060	970	1,297
Central and Eastern Europe	1,576	6,757	5,932	14,266	12,406	16,532	17,513
Asia	19,613	54,835	63,844	68,126	82,035	95,505	84,880
West Asia	1,019	3,710	1,562	−416	621	4,638	4,579
Central Asia	25	1,327	697	1,479	2,017	3,032	3,023
South, East, and Southeast Asia	18,569	49,798	61,386	67,065	79,397	87,835	77,277
The Pacific	220	226	170	562	180	146	175

Source: Based on UNCTAD, 1999b.

TABLE 2.3. FDI Outflows, 1987-1998 ($U.S. millions)

Region/Economy	1987-1992 (annual avg.)	1993	1994	1995	1996	1997	1998
World	198,670	247,425	284,915	358,573	379,872	475,125	684,920
Developed Countries	184,680	207,378	242,029	306,025	319,820	406,668	594,699
Western Europe	110,957	108,295	136,018	175,511	203,942	240,238	406,220
North America	35,384	80,548	82,545	103,540	87,718	131,999	1159,406
Canada	5,545	5,711	9,293	11,466	12,885	22,044	26,577
United States	29,839	74,837	73,252	92,074	74,833	109,955	132,829
Other Developed Countries	38,340	18,534	23,465	26,974	28,161	34,432	29,073
Developing Countries	13,946	39,756	42,600	52,089	58,947	65,031	52,318
Africa	1,118	654	453	454	−26	1,418	511
North Africa	113	23	73	100	33	144	115
Other Africa	1,005	631	380	355	−59	1,274	386
Latin America and the Caribbean	1,309	7,575	6,255	7,510	7,202	15,598	15,455
South America	714	2,900	3,301	3,984	4,091	8,174	.8,037
Other Latin America and the Caribbean	595	4,574	2,954	3,526	3,111	7,423	7,418
Central and Eastern Europe	44	292	286	460	1,105	3,425	1,903
Asia	11,495	31,476	35,886	44,060	51,681	47,741	36,182
West Asia	849	777	−1,315	−884	2,114	2,087	1,861
Central Asia	--	--	--	--	--	1	8
South, East and Southeast Asia	10,646	30,700	37,201	44,944	49,567	45,653	34,312
The Pacific	14	29	--	–3	--	22	25

Source: Based on UNCTAD, 1999b.

trade and investment. Furthermore, it suggests that the dominance of advanced industrial countries in world economic activities reflects historical patterns initiated since the industrial revolution and that these countries offer competitive conditions for firms to expand and grow. FDI inflows to other regions have not been even or consistent over the years. Inflows to Central and Eastern Europe in 1998 increased by 1,000 percent over the 1987-1992 period. This was followed by an increase by 353 and 478 percent for Asia and Latin America and the Caribbean, respectively, for the same period. The regions that attract the smallest increases for the same period are Africa (63 percent) and the Pacific (−20 percent).

FDI outflows for developing nations increased by 275 percent in 1998 over the 1987-1992 period; other regions had a positive increase—Asia (214 percent); Central and Eastern Europe (4,225 percent); and Latin America and the Caribbean (1,080 percent). Africa has negative outflows (−54 percent). Again, it appears that both Africa and the Pacific (78 percent increase) are neither attractive hosts nor homes for FDI inflows and outflows. This may indicate that there are economic and political factors preventing the development of attractive environments for trade and investment. Furthermore, it may indicate that these regions are not inviting sites for rising or well-established international corporations. In addition, it suggests that world trade growth accelerated in 1997, despite turmoil in some Asian financial markets.

According to UN data, world FDI flows continued to expand in 1998 and are expected to increase further in 1999. Advanced industrial countries invested $595 billion globally and were the host for $460 billion. FDI inflows and outflows to developing countries in 1998 declined relative to 1997 (−4 and −20 percent respectively).

FINANCIAL MARKET

One of the most volatile forces in the past two decades has been capital flows. By the end of the 1980s many governments abandoned capital controls, and fixed currency rates were determined more by markets than by states. Capital flows roam the globe searching for better returns and opportunities. Meanwhile, governments appear unwilling if not unable, to a large extent, to regulate capital movements.

Private currency traders, accountable only to their financial results, now trade $1.3 trillion a day, 100 times the volume of world trade (Mathews, 1997). International bank lending increased from $604 billion in 1996 to $1,190 billion in 1997. For example, the Bank for International Settlements (BIS, 1998) reports that international debt to the private sector increased from $127 billion in 1990 for Asia and $108 billion for Latin America to $408 and $440 billion in 1997 respectively. Net long-term private capital flows to developing countries rose from $42 billion in 1990 to $256 billion in 1997. At the same time, official flows, for the same period, drifted down from $56 billion to $44 billion. That is, substantial capital flows, in recent years, have reached more countries and come in more diverse forms and instruments than ever before (Stiglitz, 1998). Because of the Asian crisis, however, investors have become more risk averse. Markets in all but the safest securities have become much less liquid, and firms that rely on markets for capital have found difficulty in acquiring it. Therefore, these firms have to seek loans instead (*The Economist*, 1998a). Investors and lenders all over the world felt the pressures and feared the possibility of a global recession. International institutions (e.g., the World Bank, IMF, and WTO) devised serious programs and policies to reverse the downturn of the world economy. Japan's parliament approved landmark legislation on October 12, 1998, to revive the banking system. The government was allowed to inject more than $500 billion into the nation's banks. In the United States, the Federal Reserve (Fed) announced lower interest rates twice in about two weeks (September 30 and October 16, 1998). The World Bank, IMF, and WTO issued a joint statement on October 3, 1998, that called for pursuing policies that facilitate a return to more "orderly financial markets and exchange rate stability" as immediate requirements for recovery.

Some experts argue that the 1997-1998 financial crisis does not differ from earlier crises, such as the one that the United States experienced in 1842. At that time the United States was a developing country. It was blacklisted and scorned in international markets, and the Rothschilds declared that America would be unable "to borrow a dollar, not a dollar" (see Kristof, 1998). Nevertheless, the 1997-1998 economic crisis is different from previous ones both in its scope and depth. James Wolfensohn (1998b), of the World Bank, sheds light on the nature of the current crisis. He identifies four waves of international financial systems. The first was the 1870-1914 crisis. During that time, the United Kingdom was the single source of financial flows to Australia, Argentina, Brazil, and the United States. The second was the debt crisis in the 1920s. The United States was the center of the financial market, and money in bonds and in equities went to Latin America and to Southern and Eastern Europe as the debt crisis induced many countries to turn inward. For about forty years, the flow of international investing did not resume. The Marshall plan was introduced and the Bretton Woods agreement created the World Bank and the IMF to enhance development and stabilize the crisis. This was followed by the creation of the Eurodollar markets, which led to more liquidity in the international system. The increase in oil prices in 1973 set the stage for the third wave. Huge amounts of petrodollars were available for banks to lend. Thus, there was a significant increase in lending to developing countries and an immense expansion of the Euromarket. The large accumulation of debt led to the Mexican crisis of 1982. Other countries, too, experienced serious debt crises.

The 1997-1998 crisis represents the fourth wave. It started in South Asia and caused investors to panic and abruptly move their money out of that region. The spread of the crisis to Russia and Latin America caused default in the former and a recession in the latter. An editorial in *The New York Times* (October 11, 1998) sounded an alarming note: "the world's economic situation is perilous, and there is little doubt that there will be pain and suffering in many countries during the next few years. But the problems need not lead to world recession, let alone depression."

The chief characteristics of this wave are as follows:

1. Bankers and investors showed, in the last decade, a sudden interest in the developing countries. The external debt of these countries reached $1,774 billion in 1997, an increase of 47 percent over the 1990s (IMF, 1998). Most of the investors poured their capital into developing countries without adequate concern for risk. Once the financial crisis started, however, there was an exodus of foreign investors.

2. Ease and speed in the movement of funds by green screens. Availability of financial information enables people to trade huge amounts of short-term flows.
3. Most of the loans were short term in nature (up to one year). The proportion of short-term loans increased from 45 percent in 1990 to 55 percent in 1997 (see Table 2.4). The proportion of short-term loans has been highest in Asia and the Middle East (52.5 and 60.9 in 1998 respectively).
4. Most of the loans come from the private sector. There has been a gradual decline in the share of the public sector in total loans. In 1988 the official funding was roughly $40 billion, and private sector funding was close to $20 billion. In 1997, $44 billion came from official funding and $256 billion came from the private sector (Wolfensohn, 1998b). Likewise, there was an increase in the proportion of loans to private nonbank borrowers (from 31 percent in 1990 to 47 percent in 1997). In fact, direct credit to the nonbank private sector is now "predominantly in Asia and Latin America" (BIS, 1998, p. 40). Among the most important players in funding are the hedge-fund firms such as Tiger, Quantum, and Long-Term Capital Management (LTCM). These firms, along with other hedge-fund groups, have been active in currency speculation, and any big swing in any market is often, right or wrong, attributed to these firms. What makes the problem worse is that the hedge-funds industry "operate[s] largely outside the scope of traditional bank and security regulators, and relies on money borrowed from a variety of sources, including commercial banks . . ." (Stevenson, 1998). Many of these firms, however, have been victims, too, of the current crisis. LTCM had to be rescued by the Federal Reserve. Tiger lost nearly $2 billion in 24 hours as the dollar plunged against the yen (*The Economist*, 1998b).
5. Commercial banking in the major industrial countries was under pressure, due to deregulation, to find alternative sources of business to increase return. Deregulation, therefore, has been an important cause of increased international financial instability. Furthermore, the financial instability in the industrial world has centered either on banking or currency prob-

TABLE 2.4. Main Features of Consolidated International Banking Statistics

Positions vis-à-vis	Consolidated cross-border claims in all currencies and local claims in non-local currencies					
		Distribution by maturity		Distribution by sector		
	Total	Up to and including one year	Over one year	Banks	Public Sector	Non-bank Private Sector
	In billions of U.S. dollars			As a percentage of total consolidated claims		
All Countries						
End-1990........	664.8	45.0	50.2	35.6	30.8	31.0
End-1995........	873.6	55.3	36.8	40.7	18.7	39.7
End-1996........	991.4	55.1	35.8	40.2	16.3	42.6
End-1997........	1,120.1	54.9	35.9	37.7	14.2	47.2
End-1998........	1,083.5	50.3	38.7	34.8	14.6	49.8
Of which:						
Developed Countries						
End-1990........	146.5	49.0	43.0	35.6	19.2	40.6
End-1995........	152.5	53.6	34.7	39.6	15.3	44.3
End-1996........	171.0	53.2	32.0	40.5	14.6	43.9
End-1997........	195.7	53.5	29.7	40.3	14.5	44.1
End-1998	228.0	53.8	28.3	39.7	13.8	46.3
Eastern Europe						
End-1990........	92.5	26.4	70.8	67.5	20.0	10.1
End-1995........	90.6	39.1	55.2	70.0	14.6	15.3
End-1996........	103.0	44.2	49.9	64.2	15.1	20.4
End-1997........	123.0	43.4	49.3	52.7	12.8	34.4
End-1998........	121.6	36.0	55.0	56.0	8.9	34.8
Developing Countries						
End-1990........	422.0	47.6	48.6	28.6	37.4	32.3
End-1995........	622.7	58.4	34.9	37.0	20.3	42.3
End-1996........	708.2	57.7	35.1	36.7	17.1	46.0
End-1997.......	774.6	58.1	35.4	35.1	14.0	50.8
End-1998.......	705.9	52.8	39.3	29.4	16.2	54.3

TABLE 2.4 *(continued)*

Positions vis-à-vis	Consolidated cross-border claims in all currencies and local claims in nonlocal currencies					
		Distribution by maturity		Distribution by sector		
	Total	Up to and including one year	Over one year	Banks	Public sector	Nonbank private sector
	In billions of U.S. dollars			As a percentage of total consolidated claims		
Of which:						
Asia						
End-1990........	135.4	54.8	39.8	33.8	28.8	36.0
End-1995........	306.9	63.5	29.8	43.4	11.5	45.0
End-1996........	367.0	61.5	30.7	43.3	9.0	47.6
End-1997........	381.3	60.6	31.9	40.7	7.4	51.8
End-1998........	297.9	52.5	38.7	34.7	9.8	55.5
Latin America						
End-1990........	184.8	36.9	60.1	21.0	52.0	25.9
End-1995........	212.2	52.3	39.6	24.6	32.2	43.0
End-1996........	242.4	53.7	37.9	24.2	27.9	47.7
End-1997........	283.1	54.8	38.6	26.0	21.2	52.6
End-1998........	288.5	51.8	40.1	21.2	22.0	56.6
Middle East						
End-1990........	42.6	72.1	25.8	43.9	17.4	34.7
End-1995........	51.2	59.1	38.9	46.0	23.8	29.4
End-1996........	48.6	56.7	40.9	47.3	20.1	32.6
End-1997........	52.2	60.0	37.6	45.8	19.2	35.0
End-1998........	63.1	60.9	35.9	39.8	20.2	39.9
Africa						
End-1990........	59.2	47.0	49.3	29.6	25.8	42.1
End-1995........	52.4	53.1	42.5	41.2	20.3	37.3
End-1996........	50.2	49.8	47.2	39.1	21.4	38.7
End-1997........	58.0	56.3	40.1	33.1	17.4	49.4
End-1998........	56.4	50.9	41.7	31.7	15.5	52.7

Source: BIS 1998 and 1999 consolidated international banking statistics.

lems. In developing countries it has typically been a combination of the two (UNCTAD, 1998c).

BEYOND THE ECONOMIC CRISIS

Economic and financial crises in 1997 and 1998 stirred up unsettled debate relative to the validity of globalization assumptions and the vitality of capitalist institutions. Pfaff (1998) argues that the globalist economic philosophy's attribution of a divine design to the unregulated play of the market is not a rationally defensible position. Reich (1998), on the other hand, claims that most financial institutions are staffed by economists who have no particular knowledge of politics or sociology and no special insights into what arrangements may be considered appropriate in places around the world. Alarmed by the depth and seriousness of the crises, many experts have sought strategies to cope with them. The consequences of these crises are far-reaching and usually incite passions. Therefore various proposals have been advanced to deal with them. Some of these proposals are detailed in the following sections.

Revitalization of the Asian Economy

The proposal to revitalize the Asian economy was suggested by the Japanese government. It is based on the assumption that the Asian economy is highly interlinked with other economic regions and that stimulating it will contribute to worldwide economic growth. Japan's finance minister, Kiichi Miyazawa, announced at the International Monetary Fund and World Bank annual 1998 meeting that a $40 billion program would be allocated to aid economies throughout Asia. The program includes government loans and the purchase of bonds issued by Asian countries, and guarantees that private bank loans will be repaid. Likewise, the Japanese Parliament passed a relief bill for ailing banks. This program allows the government to deal with urgent bank crises in Japan. The government can nationalize failing banks, liquidate them, or transform them into publicly owned enterprises, which take over good loans while collecting bad loans. Furthermore, the Japanese government suggests that other countries must meet their commitments to the IMF and in the short run, "capital controls" may be necessary to prevent immediate outflows of capital from countries facing potential financial crises.

Global Architecture

A proposal for a global architecture was advocated by the Clinton administration and was endorsed by members of G7 on October 30, 1998. The proposal focused on long-term mechanisms to make the world economy less vulnerable to shocks. Specifically, it calls on the IMF to intervene earlier to prop up economies that are at risk of "financial contagion." In addition, the proposal requires private financial institutions to disclose adequate and reliable information about their loans around the world. Private investors are expected to pay a larger share of bailouts. This is aimed at creating additional risks for investors that may make them cautious about pouring capital into troubled economies.

In particular, the proposal advocates the following measures (Rubin, 1998):

A. Providing better information through improved disclosure and transparency. This is facilitated by following four steps:
   1. An expansion in the types of economic and financial data available. It is essential to get adequate information on the external liabilities of both the public and private sectors.
   2. Obtain and publicize a broader range of qualitative descriptive information on financial sector matters that affect the risk of investing in emerging markets.
   3. Make the IMF's analyses and lending conditions transparent.
   4. Increase incentives for countries to be more transparent.

B. Building strong financial sectors. This can be achieved through specific actions in the following areas:
   1. Develop a more complete range of global standards to guide individual governments' efforts.
   2. Develop a mechanism to provide for international surveillance of countries' financial, regulatory, and supervisory systems.
   3. Access to markets of major financial centers by banks from other countries is contingent upon a strong home country

supervisory regime (e.g., adherence to the Basle Core Principles plus whatever relevant additional standards are developed).

C. Building effective mechanisms for creditors and investors to more fully bear the consequences of their actions. This can be met through promotion of flexible forms of debt agreements and indentures that facilitate direct negotiations between creditors and investors through the establishment of an international bankruptcy regime. The latter covers debtor-creditor relations, allowing business failures a better chance of being resolved on time with less impact on the broader economy.

The Austerity Program

A proposal for an austerity program reflects the deep conviction of the IMF policymakers. It encompasses two elements: stabilizing currencies by increasing interest rates and balancing budgets to cover the costs of needed financial restructuring and to reduce current account deficits. Specifically, the program calls for (IMF, 1998): strengthening the robustness of financial institutions in both debtor and creditor countries; enhancing the transparency of the financial health of corporations and countries; fostering a realistic privacy of risks in the face of market volatility; and finding means to cooperate more effectively among debtors, creditors, and the international community to prevent defaults in situations of stress.

The Greater Equity and Social Justice Program

The World Bank advocates a program of greater equity and social justice. It is based on the assumption that without political stability even soundly designed financial packages will not ensure financial stability. It stresses that widespread poverty and abuses are sources of political turmoil. James Wolfensohn (1998a), president of the World Bank, states, "while we talk of financial crisis across the world, 1.3 billion people live on less than $1 a day; 3 billion live on under $2 a day; 1-3 billion have no access to clean water; 3 billion have no access to sanitation; 2 billion have no access to power." He accentuates the need for getting macroeconomic rights, building sound infrastructures, empowering the people, writing fair and effective laws, recognizing and educating women, eliminating corruption, building banking systems, protecting the environment, and inoculating children.

Other approaches call for fundamental reform in World Bank and IMF missions and operations. Some, such as Garten (1998), assert that neither the IMF nor the World Bank is capable of dealing with international crises. The first, he argues, cannot deal with an international phenomenon in which all countries' problems occur at once and are linked. The second is designed to finance big projects and alleviate poverty. Therefore, he proposes the creation of a global central bank to maintain global financial stability. Soros (1998) advances the need to establish an international credit insurance corporation (ICIC) to supplement the IMF and the World Bank. ICIC would operate as an international supervisor of the national supervisory authorities.

Most of the proposals described here have some shortcomings. Many of them are short-term oriented and ignore the vested interests of the elites in advanced and developing countries. These elites are highly sophisticated and able to manipulate or steer events in a way that ensures that their interests are safe. Eventually, this leads to irrational exuberance and then panic rather than equilibrium in the marketplace (Soros, 1998). Furthermore, existing proposals reflect the experience and orientations of those who advance them. These orientations may not mirror those of the majority of countries. Most important, however, is the fact that the market system is dynamic and solutions that appear to be sound under specific circumstances and for specific situations may prove to be inadequate in the future. A case in point is the monetary system that was established at Bretton Woods in 1944 and then collapsed on August 15, 1971, after the United States decided not to continue its commitment to buy and sell gold at $35 an ounce. Sound international financial arrangements are needed. However, such arrangements are doomed to failure without proper programs to address issues of equity and social justice. In recent years, there has been an increase in social fragmentation and marginalization of large segments of the world's populations. Financial systems alone are incapable of dealing with the destructive aspects of global financial markets. A starting point for establishing appropriate programs to cope with the financial, economic, and social crises is to enlist the contributions of NGOs and other grassroots associations that have allegiances to global causes. It is imperative that the fate of the global community not be left to any particular group or government.

POLITICAL AND SOCIAL ENVIRONMENT

The movement toward economic liberalization has produced significant changes in the world's economic structures and priorities. In addition, it opens a completely new era in which many of the hopes and dreams of humankind could finally be met. Consequently, fresh expectations and problems have emerged. These developments cannot be addressed by relying solely on economic regimes. Political and social issues are interwoven with the economic system and must be treated simultaneously to maximize the benefits of globalization. The postwar experience and the post-Cold War period demonstrate that compartmentalized and fragmented approaches to solving the world's pressing problems led to major setbacks in quests for prosperous and stable communities. Therefore, global political and social aspects need to be addressed.

POLITICAL ASPECTS

The abatement of the Cold War has profoundly changed the state of the world's politics. The United States emerged as the indispensable power broker and the hegemonic political regime. This, however, does not mean that the United States is capable of shaping the world without any challenge. The issues of sovereignty and aspirations for supremacy of other competitors render many of the U.S. world projections and designs far from realistic. Toffler and Toffler (1998) advocate a three-tiered world-power structure: the first-wave states (agriculture based; depend on one or a few other countries to buy their agricultural goods and raw materials), the second-wave states (factory-based, industrial nations that rely heavily on mass production and have more varied connections with the outside world), and the third-wave states (technology-based, high-tech countries that need the most highly interdependent relations with the outside world to sustain their advanced economies). The authors predict that the fourth wave is about to begin, which represents the colonization of space.

Ali (1992) suggests two general categories of existing nation-states: market-driven societies (MDSs—societies that are characterized by the manufacturing and consumption of high-value-added products; these countries use mass production or knowledge-based technology), and commodity-driven societies (CDSs—societies that are characterized by the production and consumption of agricultural and low-value-added products). In spite of their diverse economic and political agendas, MDSs, relative to CDSs, are more cohesive in their economic policies and often have been able to influence world events to serve their interests. Furthermore, the MDSs have difficulty coping with emergent competitors from CDSs (Hormats, 1994). The new competitors have enormous economic potential (e.g., China, India, Malaysia, and Korea). Thus, several questions are set forth pertaining to the direction and role of CDSs in the world economy. Will MDSs cooperate with CDSs to sustain an open global market order? Can CDSs integrate smoothly into the global market order? Traditionally, the MDSs have resorted to force to ensure their economic and political interests. These interests have been the driving force for colonial expansion and military/political domination. In recent years, powerful nations have relied on coercive seduction in pursuing their "vital interests." To suggest that MDSs will not resort to force to maintain their interests is not realistic in the immediate future. Recent events (e.g., the Gulf War, the invasions of Panama and Grenada) are a reminder. In the United States, for example, policymakers are not shy about advocating the use of force to maintain U.S. interests abroad. For example, Richard Haass (1994), a senior director on the National Security Council (1989-1993), states: "The United States, liberated from the danger of military action leading to a confrontation with a rival superpower, is now free to intervene. Moreover, only the United States possesses the means to intervene in many situations, particularly in those that are more demanding militarily" (p. 21). Haass suggests that if a rebellion in Egypt took place, for example, the right response "might be a larger scale indirect aid for government forces coupled with selective strikes by U.S. and Egyptian forces against rebels. But the time to consider acting is when coups or insurrections are still in their early phases" (p. 30). Nevertheless, he advocates that a popular uprising in the Arabian Gulf, especially in Saudi Arabia, would need to be crushed by U.S. forces immediately. President Nixon (1991) made a similar argument regarding intervention: "We should not apologize for defending our vital economic interests" (p. 186).

The relevant issue, however, is not defending a vital national economic interest. Rather, it is the position of CDSs in the power equation, because they are the weakest part of the equation. Therefore, their vital interests are often ignored in the international arena, as Ken Roth (1995, p. 121) has argued:

> There is some sense of community among the liberal democratic countries, but for the most part the phrase "international community" is a platitude, trotted out by the powerful when they want to legitimize a particular action. The "international community" label of the G7 global protection racket is by no means the worst international order imaginable, but it falls far short of the idea of a "community." The latter is a term of hypocrisy when attached to a situation in which the powerful in the G7 prosper beyond historic dreams, while tens of millions elsewhere live utterly wretched lives. The cozy phrase "international community" often represents the diplomatic equivalent of honor among thieves.

Since the interests of the CDSs are often ignored, it is difficult to determine where the interests of the MDSs begin and end. What complicates these issues is that in international relations, these interests are contingent upon various forces (domestic politics, international balances of powers, clashes of interests among powerful rivals, etc.). French (1997, p. A3) indicates that in France many people have come "to see the turmoil in central Africa as a reckless, American-led drive to rearrange the political map of the region at the expense of strong French influence." Likewise, the Clinton administration is advancing its interests in the Caspian Sea and is ardently against a project by eleven big oil companies to build a pipeline that will pass through Iran or Russia. The U.S. Secretary of Energy, Bill Richardson, has said that "We're trying to move these newly independent countries toward the

West. . . . We've made a substantial political investment in the Caspian, and its very important to the U.S. that both the pipeline map and the politics come out right" (quoted in Kinzer, 1998). All these political pressures and designs are justified in the name of national interests. These interests, however, are not specified and are often stated in nationalistic/emotional terms, such as "threats to our vital interests," "stopping naked aggression," or "protection of our friends."

Many hoped that the post-Cold War era would open the door for peaceful coexistence and a prosperous world. However, such hopes have collapsed as the cold trade war started between former allies (e.g., United States, Japan) and as a clash of civilizations moved to center stage. J. Orstrom Moller (1991), the state secretary of Denmark's Ministry of Foreign Affairs, argued that the world moved from economic and possible technological competition between countries toward a competition between ideas and values. Recently, Huntington (1993) argued that the West would not hesitate to use force against other civilizations to maintain its access to economic resources. He asserts that the Gulf War was not only about oil, but was also a clash between Western and Islamic civilizations. Nixon (1994) urged that the United States not let the "clash of civilizations" become the dominant characteristic of the post-Cold War era. He conceded, however, that "if we continue to ignore conflicts in which Muslim nations are victims, we will invite a clash between the Western and Muslim worlds" (p. 153). The theory of a clash of civilizations predicts that a conflict between Western and Confucian civilizations is a possibility in the near future. Japan and East Asian countries may be the next target on the Western agenda. This fear has been echoed by Kazua Ogura (1991), the Director General of Economic Affairs at Japan's Foreign Ministry. He has declared that "Asia has been exploited before" and "Asians do not want to see Asia used as a means for American ambition" (p. E17). Similarly, Ishihara (1991), in *The Japan That Can Say No,* identified racial prejudice and hostility toward nonwhites as the greatest source of friction between the United States and Japan.

The second question raised is, "Can CDSs integrate smoothly into the global market order?" The answer to this question is tied to the previous one. As was previously argued, the current global political/economic environment is not yet conducive to just and fair international relationships. The abatement of nuclear war and the disappearance of the Cold War have produced a transitional period, a period of adjustment, realignment, and rethinking. The strategies that cover the relations among nations are not stable. While we believe that this period is transitional, its time horizon is not yet clear. Nevertheless, as the obsession with security issues and nationalistic games gives way to realistic thinking and to the supremacy of global economic integration, a new global vision and new strategies will emerge. Consequently, global free trade goals and open market policies will dictate relations among global partners, regardless of their economic or military status.

Toffler and Toffler (1993) predict that most of the CDSs, or what they call "peasant based societies," would hardly be connected to the global system. These societies are assumed to provide food and raw materials, perform unskilled menial jobs, and provide markets for the knowledge and industrial societies. Chomsky (1993) believes that most of the CDSs will remain in a service role. He believes that the knowledge-based and industrial societies are intentionally marginalizing the role of CDSs in the global marketplace and that their dependency on the MDSs will increase rather than decrease. In fact, the prospects of the twenty-first century appear gloomy for the poorest countries among the CDSs (Nelan, 1992). If this is the case, few strategies will be available for most of the CDSs to get out of their misery. Unable to meet the threat and domination of MDSs, the CDSs are left with the options of continuing their service roles or energetically engaging in bilateral relationships and informal relations among themselves and with selected members of MDSs. This latter option could give them the chance to build vital institutions while strengthening their involvement in international trade, thereby creating the conditions for building mature economies and eventually participating in multilateral agreements.

GLOBALIZATION AND THE NATION-STATE

The issue of sovereignty complicates discourse about globalization. As a concept that originated in the early modern period, it was the product of the contradictions between the universalistic claims of the Church and the Holy Roman Empire and the apparent particularism of aspiring political-territorial jurisdictions in the later years of the medieval era (Cox, 1997). In fact, the emergence of the nation-state represented the highest form of sovereignty and national identity in early Western political thought. The state has evolved to perform various functions (e.g., security, economics, international relations and politics, social relations). The quest to colonize the rest of the world by the new Western nation-states (e.g., Holland, Belgium, Spain, and Britain) gave the state a new function of domination and control of other nations' resources. Therefore, the state facilitated its national business expansion overseas. During the mercantilism era (1500-1800 A.D.), the colonial states used their military might to intervene on behalf of national business companies. The rise of nationalism and liberation movements among the CDSs and increasing worldwide awareness of the extent of the damage that had been inflicted upon CDSs forced many colonial countries to change their courses of action.

The emergence of the Soviet Union and the strengthening of socialist movements reinforced state economic and social functions. The collapse of the Soviet Union, however, prompted many countries to de-emphasize government involvement in economic and social activities. This trend is expected to continue as countries that previously espoused socialism and planned economies initiated privatization and liberalization programs. Some nations, however, among the MDSs still cling to the old colonizing function of the state. For example, William Cohen (1998a), the U.S. Secretary of Defense, stated in a speech to businesspeople:

> As American business and the American military move about the world, we are relearning the old wisdom that "business follows the flag." Our efforts to build security and your efforts to build prosperity have become increasingly synergistic—to the benefit of millions around the globe. When our diplomats and military forces combine to help create stability and security in a nation or region, that same stability and security attracts investment. That investment, in turn, generates prosperity. . . . In short, peace brings prosperity which reinforces peace. It is what I like to call a virtuous circle of security and prosperity.

Scholars and practitioners agree that globalization has caused dramatic changes and altered the functions of nation-states. Sauer-Thompson and Smith (1996, p. 102) assert that the nation-state is currently being "tossed around by the forces of globalization like a ship in a storm." Forces such as the speed of capital and information transfer on a global scale, cross-border business alliances and mergers, and globalization of production networks compel states to rethink their functions and strategies. Various orientations relative to the impact of globalization on the nation-state have been advanced by experts. Three orientations stand out:

1. *The declining role of the nation-state.* Strange (1997) argues that globalization has created six problems for the nation-state: counter-cyclical economic management, financial stability, financing state budgets, industrial and competition policy, managing labor relations, and preventing crime. Consequently, the state has found it difficult to monitor or control activities associated with these problems. Sassen (1993) and Sauer-Thompson and Smith (1996) maintain that globalization weakens national boundaries and the power of national and subnational communities.
2. *The changing role of the nation-state.* The major assumption here is that the state still has considerable scope of influence on micro- and macroeconomic levels (Rhodes, 1996; Dunning, 1997). Dunning argues that the role of national administrations may begin to become more important, as in the early stages of capitalism. Globalization is inducing changes in the actions of nation-states quite independently of the ownership of the firms that operate within their jurisdictions. Governmental policies and priorities are likely to remain differentiated from each other. As such, states may assume new roles in conducting their affairs.
3. *The end of the nation-state.* Some scholars, such as Evans (1997), feel that the intensified development of cross-border economic transactions has undermined the power of the state, leaving it marginalized as an economic actor. Evans, however, does not foresee the eclipse of the state. Others (e.g., Ohmae, 1995) predict the end of the nation-state. For Ohmae, today's borderless-world economic activity does not follow either the political boundary lines of the nation-state or the cultural

> boundary lines of "civilization." Rather, he argues that economic activities follow information-driven efforts to engage in the global economy. He bases his theory of falling national borders and the demise of the traditional nation-states on four premises: access to cash for investment in the MDSs that needs to be invested in other parts of the world (investment is no longer geographically constrained); industry is far more global in orientation today than it was a decade ago (MNCs are no longer shaped and conditioned by state interests); information technology makes it possible for MNCs to operate in different parts of the world without having to establish an entire business system where they operate; and individual consumers have better access to information about lifestyles around the globe and therefore are less conditioned by government restrictions to buying products that are produced within a country.

The first two orientations appear to have substantial support in the literature. The third one seems to be unrealistic in the near future. Furthermore, while globalization is weakening some state functions and inducing reprioritization of other functions, globalization, ironically, is progressing forward through multilateral agreements and other facilities that are initiated by states. These agreements and the perceived benefits of globalization have brought to the international stage a postsovereign system (e.g., European Union) and global organizations (e.g., IMF, World Bank, WTO), and hybrid authorities that regulate matters ranging from environment, child labor, and energy, to the Internet. Globalization influences nation-states profoundly, and as a result states are competing to attract investment. The objective is to create wealth through sound microeconomic policies, thereby stimulating firms to operate within state territories. Put differently, there is a shift in the functions of states stemming from the globalization process. In addition, many of the states have found it advantageous to engage in bilateral and multilateral agreements to perform their traditional functions (e.g., security, economics, defense, etc.). Most important is the increasing emphasis on a microeconomic business environment as instrumental in enhancing a competitive advantage. This does not mean that macroeconomic policies are no longer vital. Rather, it indicates a shift in the function of the state from a regulating force that is limited to a specific territory to a motivating factor that espouses international openness and collaboration.

In addition, emerging global organizations have been gradually displacing and assuming some functions of the sovereign state. This is especially true in policy and standards development and in management on a global scale. Such development has reinforced the shift in state functions toward enhancing opportunities for wealth and job creation. Furthermore, there is a change among nations in their nationalistic conduct. Most of the CDSs are under pressure by various internal and external forces to downplay national sentiments. In contrast, the MDSs, especially the United States, have displayed in recent years a more nationalistic tone in international affairs and trade. For example, Maynes (1998) indicates that even in its relations with friends, the United States has begun to command more and listen less. It demands national legal protection "for its citizens, diplomats, and soldiers who are subject to criminal prosecution, while insisting other states forego their right" (p. 44). That is, in the early stage of economic globalization, many CDSs may abandon their right to exercise independent political will in order to attract FDI and participate in multilateral trade and economic agreements. There is a strong belief among influential actors in CDSs that globalization offers a better way of life and they should not be left out of the global future.

POPULATION, POVERTY, AND HEALTH

Population is considered the key factor in determining and influencing the globalization process. Over the last fifty years, serious population problems such as poverty and health have become critical and often fuel unrest in many countries. According to the UN's medium fertility scenario, the world population will grow from 5.7 billion persons in 1995 to 9.4 billion in 2050. The scenario predicts that there will be a continued geographical shift in the distribution of the world population as the share living in the currently more advanced regions will decrease from 19 to 10 percent between 1995 and 2150. For the same period, the share ages sixty years or above will increase from 10 to 31 percent of the world's population (UNDESA, 1998).

The United Nations Commission on Population and Development (1998) reports the following astonishing facts:

- In 1990-1995, about 11 million children died annually before reaching age 5, and 8.2 million of them did not reach their first birthday. About 98 percent of those deaths occurred in CDSs.
- Developed market economies have an estimated 75 nurses and midwives per 100,000 population, and the economies in transition report an estimated 800; the least developed countries have only 20 per 100,000.
- It is estimated that over 30 million people worldwide were living with HIV or AIDS at the end of 1997, around 1.1 million of whom were children. More than 90 percent of cases were to be found in CDSs.
- Of the estimated 17.2 million communicable disease deaths in 1990, 96 percent were estimated to have occurred in CDSs.

The 1998 Human Development Index (HDI) published by the UN, which measured the average achievements in a country in three basic dimensions—longevity, knowledge, and a decent standard of living—revealed the following:

- Public and private consumption expenditures were estimated to top $24 trillion in 1998, twice the 1975 level and six times that of 1950.
- The twentieth century's growth in consumption has been phenomenal but unevenly distributed. Globally, the 20 percent of the world's people in the highest-income countries:

  1. consume 45 percent of all meat and fish, the poorest fifth 5 percent;
  2. consume 58 percent of total energy, the poorest fifth less than 4 percent;
  3. have 74 percent of all telephone lines, the poorest fifth 1.5 percent;
  4. consume 84 percent of all paper, the poorest fifth 1.1 percent; and
  5. own 87 percent of the world's vehicle fleet, the poorest fifth less than 1 percent.

- More than a billion people are deprived of basic consumption needs. Of the 4.4 billion people in CDSs, about three-fifths lack basic sanitation. Furthermore, a third have no access to clean water; a quarter do not have adequate housing; and about a fifth do not get enough dietary calories and protein.
- About 7 to 17 percent of the population in MDSs is poor. A country's average income does not ensure an end to deprivation.
- A child born in an MDS contributes more to consumption and pollution over his or her lifetime than do thirty to fifty children from CDSs.
- Since 1950, MDSs have accounted for more than half the increase in resource use.
- A fifth of the world's people in MDSs contribute 53 percent of carbon dioxide emissions, the poorest fifth 3 percent.
- Millions of people in CDSs live in water-stressed areas. Other countries, especially Latin America and the Caribbean, suffer from deforestation.
- More and more new products with higher chemical content are being introduced into the market. Advertising is increasing on a global scale, faster than population or incomes.

Table 2.5 presents the extreme gap in HDI between MDSs that are part of G7 and seven selected poorest countries from CDSs. G7 countries have similar per capita GDP, enjoy life expectancies of 78, have an average adult literacy rate of 99 percent, and an average .92 HDI. In contrast, the seven poorest CDSs have dim futures, as all of them are ranked well below the world average. On average, people in these countries have a life expectancy of 47.40 years; adult literacy is 49 percent, with a surprisingly low ratio in second- and third-level gross enrollment of 30.4 percent; per capita GDP is $669, and .37 HDI. It appears from these indicators that the CDSs must go a long way before they can achieve even minimum levels of development. More important, it means globalization has created opportunities for the well-established communities, but many are left behind. It is for this very reason that the gap between the wealthiest and poorest countries has been widening. Sustained efforts, therefore, are needed to engage CDSs in the globalization process and its fruition.

TABLE 2.5. Human Development Index

MDSs G7	Life expectancy at birth (years) 1997	Adult literacy	Combined first-, second- and third-level gross enrollment ratio % 1997	Real GDP per capita (PPP$) 1997	Life expectancy index	Education index	GDP index	Human development index (HDI) value 1997	Real GDP per capita (PPP$) rank minus HDI rank*
1. Canada	79.0	99.0	99.0	22,480	.90	.990	.90	.932	12
2. France	78.1	99.0	92.0	22,030	.89	.970	.90	.918	4
3. USA	76.7	99.0	94.0	29,010	.86	.970	.95	.927	0
4. Japan	80.0	99.0	85.0	24,070	.92	.940	.92	.924	5
5. United Kingdom	77.2	99.0	100.0	20,730	.87	.990	.89	.918	9
6. Germany	77.2	99.0	88.0	21,260	.87	.950	.89	.906	2
7. Italy	78.2	98.3	82.0	20,290	.89	.093	.89	.900	2
Avg.	78.0	99.0	91.4	22,839	.86	.960	.91	.92	—
CDSs (Poorest)									
1. Dem Rep of the Congo	50.8	77.0	39.0	880	.43	.64	.36	.479	21
2. Tanzania, U. Rep. of	47.9	71.6	33.0	580	.38	.59	.29	.421	16
3. Madagascar	57.5	47.0	39.0	930	.54	.44	.37	.453	13
4. Ethiopia	43.3	43.3	24.0	510	.31	.32	.27	.298	1
5. Burundi	42.4	42.4	23.0	630	.29	.37	.31	.324	1
6. Mali	53.31	35.5	25.0	740	.47	.32	.33	.375	1
7. Sierra Leone	37.2	33.3	30.0	410	.20	.32	.24	.254	0
Average	47.4	49.0	34.9	669	.37	.41	.31	.370	—
World	66.7	78.0	63.0	6,332	.69	.73	.69	.706	—

Source: Based on United Nations,1999.

* A positive figure indicates that the HDI rank is better than the real GDP per capita (PPP$) rank, a negative the opposite.

Chapter 3

Globalization Discourse

Powerful minorities seeking to take full advantage of the market economy will want total control of their resources and will come to view the collective democratic decisions of poor majorities as intolerable burdens.

Jacques Attali
President, Attali and Associates, 1997

I am not convinced that we are truly globalizing the world marketplace. Some regions are prospering and growing; others are lagging, and some haven't caught on at all.

Alex Trotman
CEO, Ford Motor Co., 1996

The restructuring of American industry has been painful for the hundreds of thousands of workers who were laid off. But it did what it was supposed to. It restored the ability of our companies to compete. As a result, the U.S. economy is incredibly robust, and most of the people laid off are working again.

Larry Bossidy
CEO, Allied Signal, 1997

The debate about and the use of the term "globalization" is in a state of flux. In the business world, globalization has become the fashionable term among CEOs in presentations and annual reports. In academia, the globalization concept has attracted the attention of both eminent and emerging scholars and has become a focal point for serious research and theory development. Furthermore, the intense focus of the media on globalization has made it a part of both popular culture and world consciousness. The growing interest in the concept of globalization among scholars, policymakers, and businesspeople, however, increases the probability that the term will be used in contradictory ways and, more important, that it will be misused in the service of the dominant forces in a given society. This may induce bias in the discourse on globalization, thereby turning it to the service of special interest groups instead of the entire global community. One comforting reality is that those who are participating in the pursuit of globalization come from various fields, backgrounds, and interests. While this fact may prevent any single group from gaining a total intellectual monopoly over the term "globalization," it does not mean that globalization is immune to contradictions or exclusive interpretations. Robertson (1992, p. 49) cautions that there is a danger that globalization "will become an intellectual 'play zone,' a site for the expression of residual social theoretical interests, interpretive indulgence, or the display of world ideological preferences." Rodrik (1997a) argues that as the globalization debate expands, confusion about the term increases and that there should be serious concern about the quality of discourse on globalization.

Rodrik (1997a) maintains that, at best, the debate about globalization resembles "a dialogue of the deaf." His assertion is misleading and does an injustice to the growing awareness of and interest in the nature and process of globalization. His frustration may reflect a dissatisfaction with the general direction of the current globalization debate and the lack of concrete, collective actions to solve pressing global issues (e.g., poverty, hunger, displacement of workers, lower living standards for some population segments, etc.). In addition, the nature of the discourse on globalization may complicate matters. The discourse has three characteristics—intensity, variety, and complexity. It is intense, as suddenly there is a large amount of literature focused on vital and urgent issues of the world community. Decisions related to these issues clearly have global ramifications. Second, the discourse is filled with diverse topics and concerns that manifest novelty and heterogeneity in origin and interest on a global scale. Last, the discourse is complex, not only in terms of the number of interest groups and forces involved, but also in terms of the uncertainty of outcomes resulting from the globalization process and its progress.

TYPOLOGY OF THE CURRENT DISCOURSE

The constant stream of literature pertaining to globalization in the last fifteen years or so is a healthy trend. It ensures continuity and refinement while addressing challenges and easing transition. As indicated in the preceding discussion, however, the general discourse is filled with contradictions and confusing terminology.

Three terms are often confused with or compared to globalization: globalism, internationalization, and universalism. Ritchie (1996) argues that globalism manifests a strong sense of international solidarity and a quest for world peace while globalization denotes a process for the "exploitation" of world resources "by giant corporations beyond the reach of the democratic process" (p. 2). Albrow (1990) holds that globalism is just one of the forces which facilitates the development of globalization. That is, globalization is broader in its meaning and scope than globalism. It is a comprehensive process "by which the peoples of the world are incorporated into a single—global society." Robertson (1992), however, suggests that globalism conveys negative connotations and is usually described in ideological terms to indicate "one-worldism" or cosmopolitanism. In contrast, globalization refers to "the idea of the world being 'for-itself'" (p. 10). Attiga (1997, p. 1) refers to globalism as "a new kind of empire." Likewise, Al-Jabiri (1998) advances the proposition that globalism is "an ideology that represents the will to hegemony over the world" (p. 3).

Albrow (1990) indicates that internationalism was initially espoused by socialist nations to promote Marxist ideology. Later, however, it came to represent the worldwide penetration of Western ideas. Rothkopf (1997) suggests that globalization has economic roots and political consequences. He implies that the political consequences represent "internationalism." For him, internationalism means specifically that the United States assumes the responsibility for encouraging "the development of a world in which the fault lines separating nations are bridged by shared interests. And it is in the economic and political interests of the United States to ensure that if the world is moving toward a common language, it is English; that if the world is moving toward common telecommunications, safety, and quality standards, they be American . . . ; and that if common values are being developed, they be values with which Americans are comfortable" (p. 45). Similarly, Kagan (1998) views internationalism as a means of preserving U.S. world dominance. To this end he asserts the need for a New World hegemony and advocates that "the benevolent hegemony exercised by the United States is good for a vast portion of the world's population" (p. 26). Gardner (1989, p. 830) views internationalism as the ability to utilize "multilateral diplomacy and international organizations" to advance national interests, particularly in cases where a nation cannot perform "as well by acting alone."

Internationalism should be differentiated from internationalization. The latter is often used in the business world to mean expanding business activities beyond national borders, conducting business across two or more nations, or exposure to and engagement in international activities and processes. It is not surprising, therefore, that in the business world and in business disciplines, globalization and internationalization are often used interchangeably. For example, the *World of DuPont* (DuPont, n.d.) states:

> The globalization trend continued vigorously in the 1990s, with new plants opening in Spain, Singapore, Korea, Taiwan, and China, and a major technical service center opening in Japan. (p. 6)

Similarly, Danfoss (1978), in its *1997 Annual Report,* states:

> Our growth can be especially attributed to the Danfoss globalization strategy. We have, for example, doubled our sales in Africa. In Latin America we achieved a growth of 28 percent and in North America, including Mexico, 21 percent. (p. 2)

Likewise, in academia, business scholars have a tendency to equate internationalization and globalization. For example, a booklet published by the Center for International Business Studies, Texas A & M University (1998, p. 3), states that, "Companies operating in purely domestic markets are experiencing ever greater competition as foreign firms enter their markets. Thus many domestic companies are having to expand into international markets to achieve economies of scale and scope in order to maintain or develop their competitive advantage. . . . Increasing globalization . . . has produced a new competitive landscape." The 1970s and 1980s witnessed a phenomenal increase in published materials addressing internationalization—its meaning, objectives, processes, and benefits. This, however, changed dramatically in the early 1990s. The intellectual focus shifted to globalization and its adjective "global." Printed materials dealing with both subjects have become common in almost all business and related disciplines. This stream of publications is in great flux. As one might expect, some of the publications lack academic precision and rigor.

Scholars generally view universalism positively relative to internationalism. Robertson (1992) highlights the human aspects of universalism as being "concerned directly with humanity as a whole." Similarly, Albrow (1990, p. 8) argues that universalism refers to "those values which take humanity, at any time or place, hypothetically or actually, as the subject." That is, universalism is deeper in its origin and broader as a concept than globalization. Al-Jabiri (1998) views globalization negatively but attributes positive qualities to universalism. Table 3.1 presents his contrast between globalization and universalism. He views universalism as a civilized cultural system that focuses on dialogue, receptiveness, understanding, and inclusion. Globalization, on the other hand, represents hegemony and the will to control others.

The preceding analysis affirms the prevailing contradictions and misunderstandings in the discourse on globalization. It accentuates the necessity for continued dialogue and for refinements in thinking and approaches. But overall, it asserts the necessity for a common understanding of the principles and pillars of globalization.

Existing literature on globalization can be classified into three typologies: factor driven, motive driven, and consequence driven (see Figure 3.1). The following description of each typology seeks to encompass the extensive literature, allowing researchers and practitioners alike to clarify the direction and the forces of change in order to develop a better appreciation of the nature of the discourse on global-

TABLE 3.1. Globalization and Universalism

Attributes	Globalization	Universalism
Orientation	Denial of the other and replacement of ideological struggle with cultural uniformity	Openness to world cultures; retention of ideological divisions
Means	Uses political and cultural domination and the global market to weaken or disturb the status of national states with regard to systems, special programs, and social protections	Uses dialogue and give-and-take relationship with the other
Domain	Culture, politics, military, technology, and economics that repress uniqueness	Culture, technology, economics, and diplomacy that acknowledge diversity and appreciate specificity
Degree of inclusion	Exclusive reliance on global networks with a hegemonic will to redraw the contours of choice and taste in thought and behavior	Inclusive; reliance on open dialogue, cultural and ideological exchange, and belief in the potential of others to contribute to world civilizations

Source: Based on Al-Jabiri, 1998.

ization and to help map the relationships among various elements and concepts, motives, and forces.

Factor-Driven Discourse

The discourse in terms of factors that drive globalization can be divided into three categories—capital and market, elite driven, and bottom up.

Market-Driven Discourse

Back in 1899, A. W. Flux observed that the industrial nations of Western Europe and the United States were increasingly conscious

FIGURE 3.1. Categorization of Globalization Literature

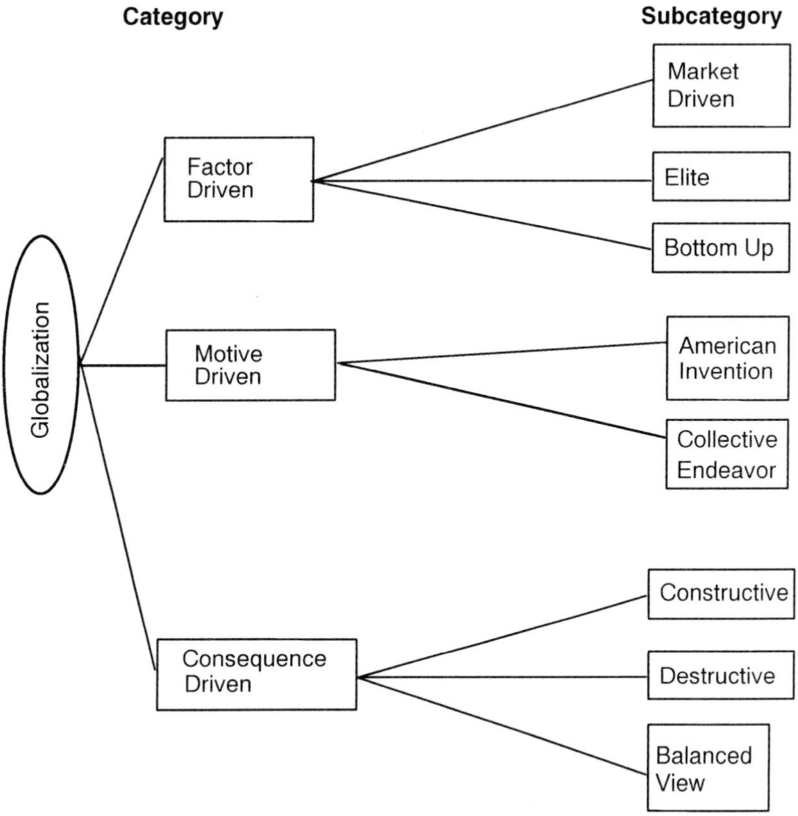

of the extent to which the continued development of their industries involved a search for new markets for their commodities. Williamson (1998) calls that era the first epoch of globalization. During that time, capital and labor flowed across nations in unprecedented quantities. Against this background and because of rapid world economic integration in the last few decades, the vast majority of globalization experts believe that globalization is largely driven by the free movement of capital and the desire of MNCs to integrate the global marketplace (e.g., Barnet and Cavanagh, 1995; Dunning,

1997; Haass and Litan, 1998; Ohmae, 1995; Sachs, 1998). The global stock market crash of 1987 and the Asian crisis of 1997, and their aftermaths, demonstrate that national economies are no longer immune to instability in other parts of the world.

Robinson (1996) argues that the emergence of a global economy brings with it the material basis for the development of a single global society. He suggests that in today's environment the central dynamic is globalization, and the pivotal tendency is the supremacy of transnational capital. Total mobility of capital in search of the cheapest labor and the most congenial conditions brings with it a tendency toward uniformity in production systems and in civil and political superstructures. Alliances between global corporations and the hypermobility of capital diminish the regulatory power of nation-states (Cox, 1997; Higgott, 1996; Milner, 1998). In fact, in the era of globalization, nation-states have ostensibly lost the power to manage the process of wealth creation and redistribution while MNCs have become the leading force in integrating national economies (Rhodes, 1996).

Elite-Driven Discourse

The major assumption under this type of discourse is that elites (groups of powerful and influential persons) are the key players in advancing globalization. Elites are viewed as the designers and shapers of world events. Influential elites assume the function of integration at the global level. They are situated in the world powers and bound by a similar culture and lifestyle and have convergent solidarities (Modelski, 1987). They take advantage of the market economy, control resources, and influence the behavior of the majority, thus deepening doubt about the vitality of political and democratic values (Attali, 1997). George Soros (1997), a leading capitalist, admits that a global community exists, but thinks its interests are subordinated to those of the elites. In an era of globalization, however, elites have become more precise in their strategic intentions and are not shy about advocating them. For example, Madeleine Albright, the U.S. Secretary of State, in a speech at Harvard University in June 1997, stated:

> Because we are entering a century in which there will be many interconnected centers of population, power and wealth, we cannot limit our focus. . . . Our vision must encompass not one, but every continent. . . . Today I say that no nation in the world needs to be left out of the global system we are constructing.

Elites in MDSs (the North) have control over the worldwide distribution of productive resources and the management of these resources (Robinson, 1996). The political behavior and outlook of these elites are disposed to a global logic rather than local accumulation. Therefore, these elites are called transnational. They are inclined to enter partnerships with other elites from CDSs (the South). The latter perform the role of agents or junior partners to transnational elites (Robinson, 1996). Both elites, however, share more common global interests and identities between themselves than with their respective countrymen (Mathews, 1997). Solidarity and alliances bind these elites, both in MDSs and CDSs, into the social infrastructure of the global system (Modelski, 1987).

Bottom Up-Driven Discourse

This discourse focuses on the positive aspects of "globalization from below" by addressing the pressing issues faced by communities across the globe. Issues of labor displacement, immigration policy, civil society, child labor, globalization of culture, the environment, and other social concerns are addressed. Two conferences on "globalization from below" took place at the University of Chicago and Duke University in 1998. While most of the literature in this category highlights the role and vitality of local communities in globalization and the necessity of engagement at all levels and of all processes, there are some who focus on the threat of globalization and on its negative consequences. Korten (1997) and Burbach, Nunez, and Kagarlitsky (1997) argue that all globalization benefits serve the interests of MNCs. In addition, globalization produces inequality and poverty by harming localities (Greider, 1993; Kirdar, 1992; Laxer, 1993; Morris, 1993). Specifically, Greider (1993) calls for Americans to create democratic alliances across national borders with less prosperous people who are affected by globalization processes to counter the power of MNCs.

Motive-Driven Discourse

This type of discourse can be divided into two general categories—globalization as an American invention and as a worldwide collective endeavor.

American Invention

The essence of this discourse is that globalization is simply the projection of the interests of the strongest nation. Kagan (1998) argues that the United States' share of the world economy and the overwhelming superiority of its military capacity allow it the option of pursuing any number of global ambitions. Therefore, some experts believe that globalization is a uniquely American invention, a very American phenomenon (Evans, 1997; Friedman, 1996; Milner, 1998). As such, the real authority for managing the global economy is concentrated in the United States (Friedman, 1996). Friedman (1998a) further suggests that the hidden hand of the global market would not work without the hidden fist: "The hidden fist that keeps the world safe for the Silicon Valley's technologies to flourish is called the United States Army, Air Force, Navy, and Marine Corps" (p. A27).

Collective Endeavor

Globalization is viewed mostly as a cultural phenomenon that engulfs the world. Waters (1995) asserts that terms such as "McDonaldization," "Americanization," and "Cocacolonization," are misleading in their popular use and are value-laden. They refer to the consumer culture that grew in the United States and has been mass marketed to the rest of the world. He argues that although consumer culture, in its original form, was probably intentionally created, under "postmodernized conditions, it is 'hypersimulated,' having a life of its own that is beyond the control of any particular group" (p. 140).

Others view globalization as a collective consciousness of the world as a single entity. Martti Ahtisaari (1997), president of Finland, indicates that globalization provides for more effective participation in order to ensure that its benefits are distributed more equitably among various segments of the world's population. Similarly, Johnson (1991) underscores the belief that in true globalization, there are no pockets of stagnant growth where disciplined work forces and/or natural resources are underutilized.

Consequence-Driven Discourse

A large segment of the globalization literature focuses on economic consequences. Some scholars warn of both constructive and destructive consequences of globalization. Rodrik (1997b) focuses on the opportunities available to those who are skilled and mobile enough to flourish in the global marketplace. Simultaneously, he highlights the downward pressure exerted by globalization on the wages of unskilled workers in MDSs. Schwab and Smadja (1996), the most renowned advocates of globalization, identify the unpleasant consequences of globalization and the tendencies to abuse trade relations when a balance is not maintained between the quest for profits and moral responsibilities toward individuals, communities, or nations. They indicate that the benefits of globalization are multiple and far-reaching at individual, corporate, and societal levels. Nevertheless, benefits should not be taken for granted because social and economic structural adjustments eventually multiply "the human and social costs of the globalization process to a level that tests the social fabric of democracies in an unprecedented way" (p. 4). A balanced view of the consequences of globalization is hardly common. Indeed, the existing discourse is highly compartmentalized. On one hand are those who focus mostly on the benefits of globalization (constructive view), especially in terms of economic growth, wealth, and job creation (e.g., Dunning, 1997; Fischer, 1998; Kobrin, 1998; Bergsten, 1996; Ohmae, 1995; Sachs, 1998). The antiglobalization camp encompasses individuals and organizations on both the right and the left of the political spectrum (e.g., AFL-CIO and Liberty Lobby). Antiglobalization experts cite threats to the environment, sovereignty, economic stability, and human rights in support of their arguments (Burbach, Nunez, and Kagarlitsky, 1997;

Greider, 1993; Nader, 1993; Sauer-Thompson and Smith, 1996; Teeple, 1995).

BEYOND SELF-DELUSION

In Chapter 1, it was suggested that globalization should be viewed not only in economic, but also intellectual, cultural, and moral contexts. Instant transmission of information to most of the world's population sensitizes people to global issues and has increased awareness of the nature and principles of a civil society. Perhaps intellectual elites should play a crucial role today in promoting the quality of true globalization and in advocating for civility in conduct at personal, organizational, and societal levels. At present, many intellectuals, intentionally or unintentionally, ignore crucial issues that stem from economic or political decisions at home and abroad. Robertson (1992, p. 55), for example, argues for a position that recognizes the moral and cultural implications of globalization:

> While I do not subscribe to the view that social theorists should at all costs attempt to be neutral about these (globalization, civilization, imperialism) and other matters, I am committed to the argument that one's moral stance should be realistic and that one should have no intrinsically vested interest in the attempt to map this or any other area of the human condition. More precisely, I argue that systematic comprehension of the structuration of world order is essential to the viability of any form of contemporary theory and that such comprehension must involve analytical separation of the factors that have facilitated the shift toward a single world—for example the spread of capitalism, Western imperialism and the development of a global media system—from the general and global agency-structure (and/or culture) theme.

Hobson (1919) long ago acknowledged that the rise of capitalism allowed some classes to gain more than others and imposed "injustice and oppression in a hundred different ways upon society" (p. 397). The rising middle classes, he noted, were incapable of providing justifications for the prevailing inequality and had to rely on intellectual elites to defend the system. These elites furnished the middle class with "intellectual spiritual defenses" and "comfort[ed] them with the conviction that prosperity was the natural reward of virtue" (p. 397). While some intellectuals, over the years, have not abandoned their duty to enlighten societies, others have vigorously defended their preferred economic systems and completely overlooked political, social, and economic injustices. Blind ideological preferences may prompt intellectuals to relinquish responsibility toward disadvantaged segments of the population. The fact that these segments are not powerful should be a motive for intellectuals to address their concerns. Those who have power and access to economic opportunities also have the means to defend and articulate their positions. Barrington Moore (quoted in Robinson, 1996, p. 1) states:

> In any society the dominant groups are the ones with the most to hide about the way society works. Very often, therefore, truthful analyses are bound to have a critical ring, to seem like exposures rather than objective statements. For all students of human society, sympathy with the victims of historical processes and skepticism about the victors' claims provide essential safeguards against being taken in by the dominant mythology. A scholar who tries to be objective needs these feelings as part of his working equipment.

Certainly, addressing the benefits of globalization and commending the institutions that facilitate its processes are essential for enhancing world integration. This, however, does not imply that one should be uncritical of the globalization process. Indeed, it is essential for the vitality of the discourse that both the destructive and the constructive views of globalization be debated.

For the purposes of this book, elites are divided into four categories. These categories are general in nature and are intended to focus attention on the players that have much to contribute to shaping and influencing the direction and output of globalization.

Business Elites

Business elites include industrial, financial, and media/entertainment elites along with other leading managers in other economic sectors. Elites in the media industries, in finance, and in the weapons industry have acquired undeniable power in recent years. Thompson (1981, p. 51) points out that in the United States "big law, banking, and investment firms accounted for 36 percent of key positions" in the federal government. Similarly, Bhagwati (1998) argues that Wall Street has exceptional clout with Washington for the simple reason that there is "a definite networking of like-minded luminaries among the powerful institutions—Wall Street, the Treasury Department, the State Department, the IMF, and the World Bank most prominent among them" (p. 11). He asserts that elites in this network are unable to look beyond the interests of "Wall Street, which it equates with the good of the world" (p. 12). Contrary to prevailing convictions, managers in leading industrial and commercial companies have displayed an interest in and a commitment to broader societal and global issues (e.g., human rights, child labor, economic sanctions, and the environment). Global corporations including Nestlé, Shell, and Mobil have aggressively promoted human rights and displayed dismay at using economic sanctions as a political tool.

Political Elites

Political elites are those who publicly advocate and implement policies and plans that directly or indirectly influence the lives of people at home and abroad. These elites generally espouse, especially in MDSs, distinct openness, inclusion, and democratic civil institutions. In recent years, however, the events in Brazil, Indonesia, Korea, and other nations demonstrate that the political elites not only oppose any solution that is not promoted by them but also fear democratic debate.

Intellectual Elites

Intellectual elites include scholars in various fields of the social sciences, humanities, management, and organizations, and other academic areas. The emphasis here is on management and organizational intellectuals. The latter, despite their potential, have not been able, in general, to view things beyond the narrow definitions of corporate performance, productivity, and competition. In today's rapid climate of global changes, management and organization scholars should become actively involved in shaping the course of events and in defining the discourse on globalization. As intellectuals, their responsibilities are not confined to classrooms, and their outlooks must be inclusive and global.

Think-Tank Intellectuals and Politically Oriented Intellectuals (Ideologists)

In recent decades these elites, in conjunction with political elites and some elites in finance, the weapons industry, and media/entertainment have come to exercise subtle influences far beyond any of the other elites. Blumenthal (1988, p. 53) describes these elites as "micro-planners, who think not in terms of particular firms but particular policies; and they are macro-planners, who think of the political economy as a whole." They play three major roles: creators of ideas for corporations, developers of plans and policies for politicians, and intermediaries between corporations and public policymakers. In fact, think-tank intellectuals provide access for corporations to leading public policymakers (Birnbaum, 1998; Blumenthal, 1986).

DOMINANT ISSUES

In the course of the dialogue on globalization, two issues often surface: the increasingly powerful role of intellectual elites and the abilities of existing superpowers, notably the United States, to shape the course of globalization. From the early days of the Industrial Revolution to World War I, industrial elites exercised unlimited privileges in dictating foreign and economic policies. Industrial elites were the rising stars, and both the state and the society relied on their ingenuity. During this period, therefore, the intellectual elites provided the needed theoretical bases for the expansion of business activities. With the exception of leftist intellectuals, the rest rendered their services to the "rising star." The situation changed, however, after the war. The state, in both socialist and capitalist-oriented countries, became more intrusive and assertive. Politicians, at the national level, acquired additional expertise in managing economic and international affairs and allied themselves more with media and financial elites. The industrial elites gradually lost some of their power. This era continued until the mid-1970s when some restructuring took place among the elites. Political leaders, along with media and financial elites, had accumulated a wealth of knowledge (mostly in G7). These elites, however, were the subject of constant criticism from left- and right-wing groups. The emergence of think tanks was seen as an attempt by these elites to provide organized, intelligent, and well-articulated defenses of their positions, polish their images, and furnish theoretical and conceptual models to legitimize their actions and sustain their roles.

Since the mid-1970s, the think-tank elites have found that their services are increasingly in demand by political, media, and financial elites. For example, in 1995 the number of think-tank citations in the media in the United States was 13,919 and that number increased to 14,623 in 1997 (see Table 3.2). The intellectual elites at the Brookings Institute, for example, who see themselves "as sort of interdisciplinary philosopher-King technocrats, eye the task of building global structure. . . . [T]hey are so often parroting the conventional wisdom, fearing that they are outmatched in the media by the right-wing Heritage Foundation, that they are sidetracked from doing the strategic planning for elites that has made Brookings so influential" (Husseini, 1998, p. 23). Think-tank intellectuals present themselves as the indispensable "strategic mind" that neither CEOs nor leading politicians can manage without. Societal and economic restructuring, along with the political circumstances in most of the G7 countries, have permitted think-tank intellectuals to strengthen their positions of influence. That is, the intellectual elites in think-tanks and other associated research institutions have become the thought creators and shapers of major events, especially in the United States. In the 1970s, for example, Brookings pushed for the creation of the Congressional Budget Office. Furthermore, in 1998 it teamed up with the American Enterprise Institute to form

TABLE 3.2. Think-Tank Media Visibility

	Political Orientation	**Number of Media Citations**		
		1997	1996	1995
Brookings Institution	Centrist	2,296	2,196	1,951
Heritage Foundation	Conservative	1,813	1,779	2,284
American Enterprise Institute	Conservative	1,323	1,401	1,324
Cato Institute	Conservative/ Libertarian	1,286	1,136	1,202
RAND Corporation	Center-right	865	826	813
Council on Foreign Relations	Centrist	755	727	763
Center for Strategic and International Studies	Conservative	668	586	623
Urban Institute	Center-left	610	655	
Economic Policy Institute	Progressive	576	452	390
Freedom Forum	Centrist	531	625	
Hudson Institute	Conservative	481	396	366
Institute for International Economics	Centrist	438	288	442
Center on Budget and Policy Priorities	Progressive	425	359	—
Hoover Institution	Conservative	355	350	484
Carnegie Endowment	Centrist	352	502	524
Competitive Enterprise Institute	Conservative	290	205	299
Manhattan Institute	Conservative	261	227	255
Progressive Policy Institute	Centrist	251	279	462
International Institute for Strategic Studies	Conservative	177	145	171
Institute for Policy Studies	Progressive	172	110	160
Worldwatch Institute	Progressive	168	186	183
Center for Defense Information	Progressive	158	187	136
Joint Center for Political and Economic Studies	Center-left	158	228	257
Progress and Freedom Foundation	Conservative	122	234	562
Reason Foundation	Conservative/ Libertarian	92	133	268
Total		14,623	14,212	13,919

Source: Dolny, 1996, 1998.

the Joint Center for Regulatory Studies (Husseini, 1998). The director of the Center declared that "the real purpose is to keep the regulators—and the legislators who regulate the regulators—on their toes" (quoted in Husseini, 1998, p. 22). That is, intellectual elites affiliated with think tanks have become a power to reckon with, having garnered the confidence of government agencies and officials to such a degree as to leave their imprint on events. Abrams (1995, p. 24) argues that the test America faces in the coming years is whether its democratic institutions have the capability to reverse the destructive policies that are advocated by elites: "In their long march toward victory in remaking American culture, their successes have been great." Similarly, Zbigniew Brzezinski (1995) indicates that the new elites, mostly TV-Hollywood-mass media cartels and think-tank intellectuals, have produced in the United States a new, dominant, and style-setting culture. This elite group, Brzezinski (p. 38) argues:

> Quite deliberately promotes the worship of celebrities as a substitute for the role previously played by the established elite and moral leaders. These celebrities, through their highly publicized conduct, by and large, foster the values of greed and encourage the illusion of a permissive cornucopia as the ideal definition of social reality. To make matters worse, some of our top political leaders are happy to play the role of supporting cast in this demoralizing social deception.

Therefore, some think-tank intellectuals, along with financial and political elites positioning themselves at higher societal places of influence, have begun to believe that their designs and policies are valid on a global scale. Despite worldwide crisis and the spread of misery in many countries, these think-tank intellectuals resist rethinking their approaches and theories. By contrast, in terms of the Asian crisis and its aftermath, James Wolfensohn (1998a) of the World Bank asserts that economic policies must not be designed without regard to human needs and realities: "We cannot close our eyes to the fact that the crisis has exposed weaknesses and vulnerabilities that we must address. . . . [T]he notion that development involves a totality of effort—a balanced economic and social program—is not revolutionary, but the fact remains that it is not the approach that we in the international community have been taking" (pp. 3, 5). In the era of globalization and world economic integration, economic matters, world prosperity, and the welfare of the less fortunate segments in the world should take on added value in practice and discourse. However, this is not the case, especially with regard to the role played by the superpowers in global affairs. The contradiction appears to stem from the nature of the political and cultural systems prevailing in MDSs. In these systems, there has been a gradual transformation toward an elite-led society and away from wider public participation in designing major domestic and foreign policies. Rothenberg (1996) has argued that, in the case of the United States, the public has not had direct access to decision making in many areas of life, "so its consent was unnecessary." In fact, in the United States there is what Phillips (1994) calls a "reversal of fortune"; "the grass roots of America have been losing national influence to permanent political-interest groups and financial elites located in Washington, New York, and other centers of power" (p. xii). Think-tank elites have been able, in recent years, to reshape foreign policy and define the discourse on globalization. Their objectives are to maintain domination, hegemony, and limit the spread of globalization's benefits. Warder (1994), vice president of the Rockford Institute, an Illinois-based think-tank focused on political and cultural issues, is of the opinion that today politicians are good at getting elected, but do not know what to do once they are in power. Therefore, he argues, it has become quite natural "in this century for political leaders to turn to thinkers who know the most about a subject and to ask them what they would do" (p. 435). Similarly, Edwin Faulner, president of the Heritage Foundation, holds that "ideas are always ahead of the politicians. Ideas are refined through organizations like ours" (quoted in Blumenthal, 1988, p. 36).

These elites have played significant roles in redesigning and shaping realities. Morse (1997) looks at how the elites in think tanks and the defense establishment shifted their focus, after the election of President Clinton, away from Japan and the European Union as adversarial trade and protectionists toward "the fine tuning of a Democratic Party Industrial Policy agenda that aimed at giving coherence to a public private trade and technology strategy" (p. 49).

Previously, Blumenthal (1986) has shown how the idea of Star Wars was developed by elites at the Heritage Foundation, which on March 23, 1983, President Reagan presented and defended as nothing less than "our ultimate goal." Elites from the most prominent think-tanks (e.g., Brookings Institute, Rand Corporation, Heritage Foundation, American Enterprise Institute, Washington Institute for Near Eastern Policy, etc.) have been able to move in and out of the most influential federal government agencies. Reese (1997) asserts that there is a constant circulation of more or less "the same elite who, in fact, determine U.S. policy." The names of present and former members of think tanks have become familiar. These include: Baker, Eagleberger, Haass, Albright, Brzezinski, Kissinger, Schultz, Kantor, Kirkpatrick, Indyk, Ross, Perle, and Haig among others. During their time in think tanks, they not only cement their work with other elites, but also articulate visions about what the government should do. Once they are in power, they are in a position to translate their visions into policy. A case in point is Martin Indyk. When he was the director of the Washington Institute for Near Eastern Policy, he advocated, among other things, trade sanctions against Iran and "dual containment" of Iran and Iraq. Once he was appointed a national security officer, trade sanctions against Iran and "dual containment" policies were enacted as hallmarks of the Clinton administration's foreign policy. Likewise, sanctions enacted against Iran, Libya, Cuba, and Burma are all examples of how members of think-tank institutes align with other politically motivated groups to use their influence to subordinate commercial relations to their political agendas, thereby subverting the free movement of goods and capital. For example, the Burma sanction was not endorsed by either the American business community or foreign governments (Barth, 1997). Nevertheless, the National Endowment for Democracy and the Burma Foundation used their influence and connections to introduce legislation that kept American-based firms from investing in Burma.

FACING THE CHALLENGE

Intellectuals in the social sciences, especially those involved in cross-cultural studies, have been more engaged in globalization discourse than scholars in management and organization studies. This was understandable twenty or thirty years ago when management and organization fields were emerging and there were strong motivations for addressing immediate concerns (e.g., organizational performance, development, and environment, along with personal career considerations). But these should not continue to be real roadblocks. Globalization and competitiveness have rendered many of these concerns obsolete and accentuated a broader global view of the organization—its vision, commitment, and involvement. In addition, executives have shown an interest in debating issues beyond their "narrow" business affairs. Dominic Tarantino (1998), chairman of the Board of Directors of Pricewaterhouse, World Firm, for example, has called on business leaders in and out of academe to face up to the consequences of their practices:

> We have not been especially good pupils. We have supported open trade and investment policies when they suited us, and pressured our governments to invoke national sovereignty when they did not. We have done our share to perpetuate corrupt practices in other countries by acquiescing to them. We have behaved irresponsibly toward the environment. Our record on labor practice is far from spotless. Publicly owned corporations have not always been responsive to demands for increased financial disclosure. (p. 559)

Similarly, John Wolf (1994, p. 437), the executive vice president of McDonnell Douglas, argues that globalization is "the key to promoting the welfare of the world community as a whole through revitalizing economies and bettering the standard of living of people worldwide." These examples vividly reveal that executives are sensitive to the state of the world around them—economic, social, political, and otherwise. Furthermore, they do not hesitate to acknowledge wrongdoing. This should encourage intellectuals in organization and management to confront biases and prejudices in the globalization discourse. The situation, in general, however is not promising. Anita Roddick (1995), a global manager and CEO of the Body Shop, argues:

> Political awareness and activism must be incorporated into global management education. In a global world, there are no value-free or politically disentangled actions; the very act of organizing on a global basis is political because of culture, geography, and differing value systems. There aren't many motivating forces more potent than giving people an opportunity to exercise and express their idealism to influence change: locally, nationally, and globally. Management education needs to realize that this must be the way forward; the personal becomes the political, which becomes the global. (p. 3)

Likewise, Ian Mitroff (1995, p. 750) asserts that ethical and moral issues, at the national or global level, are seldom adequately covered in the management and organization literature:

> It [management literature] contains virtually no mention of the deeply ethical, moral, and spiritual "variables" that exert such a profound influence in the lives of people and organizations. How then can we pretend to have a "theory" of organizations? We are so far from a theory of organizations that the claims to have produced them are pitiful. I don't believe I exaggerate. Open any of the current journals and one finds all kinds of "hypotheses" as to how such and such a structural variable is supposed to affect others. But where are the "variables" that affect humans at the deepest core of their existence?

Some of the intellectual elites in the management and organization fields, instead of taking the lead in clarifying the human aspects of globalization, tend to subscribe to a meaning of globalization that prevails among political elites and think-tank intellectuals. These elites, who dominate the global stage, seem to have little interest in optimizing the welfare of global customers and certainly no interest in promoting a form of globalization that encourages cultural understanding and worldwide prosperity. For example, Rothkopf (1997, pp. 48-49) affirms a message that conveys extreme nationalism and total disregard of other cultures:

> Americans should not shy away from doing that which is so clearly in their economic, political, and security interests—and

> so clearly in the interests of the world at large. . . . Americans should not deny the fact that of all the nations in the history of the world, theirs is the most just . . . and the best model for the future.

Management and organization scholars should not discount the power of the mind in pursuing a broader agenda for humanity. That is, we should not utter terms and concepts that are advanced by other political and politically oriented intellectuals without thinking and evaluating them intelligently and without examining the motives behind them. More important, we should not be instruments of propaganda that are drained of the capacity for critical thinking and assessment. A case in point is a speech given by Richard Cooper of Harvard University. The speech, "Considerations for the Future of the World Economy," was given at the Academy of International Business Conference in Boston (November 4, 1994). The speaker was eloquent and provided definitive projections regarding the consequences of population growth, higher per capita income, and increased international mobility. In terms of globalization, however, the speaker provided false premises and biased Western judgments. First, he stated that the notion that the primary role of government is to "enhance the power and dominance of its power" is held by "leaders in many developing counties." Second, he pointed out that military coercion "will be nonexistent among rich democratic countries." Third, he said that power is seldom used by Western nations. In fact, power "has no useful meaning in today's world systems except with respect to governments that are physically aggressive against their neighbors or, increasingly, against their own population." Cooper further held that "political dominance among rich countries is not likely, and it is increasingly rare between rich and poor countries without substantial financial inducements." And, finally, he argued that conflicts result from religious or other ideological differences and thus, "the historical basis for wars—conflict over resources—is gone." The message is that Western nations do not use power or force in their relations with others and that oppression is found only in what the speaker called "developing nations." The danger of such thinking stems from the fact that it ignores the reality that the Western colonial powers have created and still maintain dysfunctional systems in the societies that were colonized. Shenon (1995) explains how Western colonialization of the Pacific island of Nauru stripped it of everything. After ninety years of strip mining, nothing is left for the islanders, who are plagued by bad diet and short life expectancies and may have to evacuate the island. He indicates that during the German occupation of the island from 1888 until World War I, the Germans "banned native dancing as pagan, and today only a handful of elderly Nauruans have even the barest recollection of how the sacred dances should be performed." Subsequent colonizers made the situation worse. Current evidence indicates that the Western nations, especially the United States, resort to or withhold the use of force whenever and wherever they wish (e.g., the immediate use of force in the case of Iraq, years of tolerance of Serbian aggression and genocide in Bosnia, and preventing the implementation of sixty-nine UN Security Council resolutions in the case of Israel). Likewise, the use of power and influence by the United States and Europe is evident in the case of Algeria and the rest of Africa. The recent events in the Congo and Rwanda are a vivid reminder. *The Wall Street Journal* (1997a), in its editorial "The Virtual Empire" (January 10, 1997, p. A10), suggests that the French government sent troops to its former African colonies not to restore or establish democracy but to protect its economic interests. Official justifications for intervention seldom reflect reality. It argues:

> Rather, the combination of substantial business interests and the grandeur afforded by having a "virtual empire" more often appear to be the main drivers of French policy.

Two years before, *The Wall Street Journal* (June 12, 1995) had stated that during January through May 1995, Bahrain had witnessed instability as the prodemocracy movement demanded freedom and respect for human rights. The ruling elite, supported by the United States, "responded by unleashing their foreign mercenaries, who have pulled young people off streets at random, beaten and jailed them." Using power and influence is common not only between "rich and poor countries" but also among "rich nations." This point was made clearly on December 20, 1998, by Tony Blair, the British prime minister. He termed that use of force a "global reality." Relations between the United States and Japan offer yet another example of utilizing intimidation and influence among "rich nations." Washington has often resorted to tough statements to the "point of rudeness" as "the only mechanism that has ever worked in Japan" (Kristof, 1998, p. 3). Additionally, *The Wall Street Journal* editorial (1997b, p. A14) indicates that even Japan may resort to political domination: "Now, it is an unalterable fact of Asian politics that the victims of Japan's wartime aggression are made nervous by any sign that the economic superpower may be gearing up to take a leading role in regional security arrangements." Britain, too, is an example of a rich country that still yearns to dominate others. In the early twentieth century it colonized most of the Arab world and South Asia. In 1920, when the Iraqis rebelled against British rule, the Royal Air Force asked the Secretary of State for War, Winston Churchill, for permission to use chemical weapons "against recalcitrant Arabs as an experiment." Churchill ordered the use of chemicals, saying, "I do not understand this squeamishness about the use of gas. I am strongly in favor of using it against uncivilized tribes" (*Middle East Report,* 1998, p. 7). Margaret Thatcher, British prime minister from 1979 to 1990, communicated a similar message, though the language was different. In 1990, she asserted that it was not enough for Iraq to withdraw from Kuwait. Rather, its economic and industrial infrastructure must be destroyed. In 1993 Thatcher voiced regret for giving the eastern Arab states political semi-independence:

> I regretted, even at the time, the decision of Ted Heath's government not to reverse the Wilson Government's withdrawal of our forces and the severing of many of our responsibilities east of the Suez. Repeatedly, events have demonstrated that the West cannot pursue a policy of total disengagement in this strategically vital area. Britain has, however, continued to supply equipment, training and advice. (p. 162)

On the subject of Western colonization of many CDSs (developing nations), William Pfaff (1995) noted that the European colonial powers in Africa, for example, uprooted ancient laws and gave in exchange Western justice, whose precepts negatively influenced the indigenous culture by striking at the roots of time-honored traditions and norms. He argued that "colonialism lasted long enough to destroy the preexisting social and political institutions, but not long enough to put anything solid and lasting in their place" (p. 4). Similarly, Koopman (1994, p. 64) asserts that "[i]t is not hard to understand, that given the fact that nothing human appeared to be worthy of respect on the African continent, the colonialists proceeded with the mass violation of human rights by destroying dignity." Truly, there is no desire to justify the existence of ills in many CDSs or to gain comfort by blaming Western colonialism. It is essential, nonetheless, to engage in an honest discourse and accurately depict the reality of CDSs. In this regard, it is not accurate to state that "political dominance among rich countries is not likely." In the last five years, threats have been directed at Japan. The "trade war" between the United States and Japan highlights and underlies motives to influence political and economic world events. The use of power and influence in relations with other countries is vividly summarized by Anthony Lake (1994, p. A35), then Clinton's national security advisor: "effective diplomacy depends not only on the skills of our diplomats but also on power. . . . Because we fight on so many fronts at once, we make progress only over time, in small victories, through persistence and pragmatism." Similarly, James Fallows (1993) has argued that the United States must maintain its military presence in East Asia: "Surely America can use this and other forms of leverage for better-balanced economic relations, starting with Japan." U.S. Secretary of Defense, William Cohen (1998b), in remarks to the Foreign Policy Association, was not apologetic in his pronouncement that the United States influences the political, cultural, and economic lives of the peoples of other nations. He proudly and eloquently expressed the virtue of shaping events:

> We have to be forward deployed in Europe and in Asia in order to shape people's opinions about us in ways that are favorable to us. To shape events that will affect our livelihood and our security. And we can do that when people see us, they see our power, they see our professionalism, they see our patriotism, and they say that's a country that we want to be with. So we are shaping events on a daily basis in ways that are favorable to our interests. (p. 3)

This evidence reveals that politically and intellectually elite groups, with intellectual-sounding propaganda, have taken the lead in shaping events domestically and internationally. Their agendas are often based on political or cultural motives rather than business motives (e.g., the embargoes against Cuba and Iran have been resented by the business community in the U.S. and much of the rest of the world). Some critics point out that scholars in the field of business and organization are not adequately addressing many issues at the heart of globalization, which is the human element. That is, business and organization scholars have to move beyond the narrow view of corporations as economic actors only. Corporations are social and political actors too. Ignoring this reality does an injustice to the growing practice and development associated with globalization. Management and organization scholars have a broader responsibility than those in other academic fields because the focus of their work is on both individuals and groups in an organized setting. Indeed, our studies revolve around employees and corporations—two of the most important forces in the globalization era. Their goals and activities intertwine with the aspirations and future of humankind as a whole. Consequently, our writing should enrich humanity by not abandoning our intellectual responsibility and by not keeping silent about actions that marginalize other people or their cultures, vilify and enslave them, or strip them of their present and future. That is, our writing should enlighten, rather than alienate and peripheralize, the less fortunate.

Claiming neutrality while using the justification of being apolitical is an attempt to escape reality and evade intellectual responsibility. The Academy of Management, a leading professional organization, in the last decade has focused its annual meetings' themes on critical human and organizational issues. These themes, however, have not become an integral part of intellectual discourse. This can be attributed to the habit of many scholars of minimizing the importance of human interactions and activities that lie at the core of globalization discourse. Focusing solely on economic and technological activities reinforces the belief that human factors are less significant for corporations and for global development.

ISSUES FOR CONCERN

Placing the globalization discourse in a truly global perspective certainly requires that scholars focus on, but not limit themselves to, the following topics: economic sanctions; political corruption; the AIDS epidemic; global warming; weapons sales; hunger; child labor; superpower discrimination against small countries; the meaning and limits of legitimate national interests; and the universal mistreatment of minorities. These issues are not abstractions, but rather problems that should be of concern to any scholar who engages in organizational studies and competition. To put it another way, neither organizations nor competition can take place without human involvement. It is a misjudgment to include individuals as customers and employees in the globalization discourse, but exclude them when they are victims of mistreatment and organized aggression.

The most urgent and crucial issues for inclusion in the management and organization discourse are national interests, economic sanctions, and hunger. All have a potentially devastating impact on the human quest for a peaceful and prosperous world. One of the most abused concepts/terms used by political elites and their apologists in academia is the "national interest." This term is often utilized to mislead the public and divert attention from the real aim of a particular policy. During the Cold War era, the two existing superpowers drew their areas of domain and had an understanding of where each stood. The collapse of the Soviet Union left one country (the United States) in a position to pursue its interests unrestrained by any countervailing force. Given worldwide military hegemony, the United States (it had 275,383 members of its armed forces overseas in 1998) has gone beyond defining its own national interest and now makes a habit of defining the "national interest" of other countries. For example, President Clinton in his remarks to the Arab world on December 19, 1998, regarding the attack on Iraq (December 16), stated, "We believe this action is in the interests of the Iraqi people and all the people of the Middle East." Likewise, Lloyd Axworthy, Canada's Foreign Minister, was called anti-American by some political elites in Washington because he visited Cuba, and was instrumental in advancing the establishment of an international criminal court and getting the international treaty to ban land mines signed in Ottawa in 1997, against the U.S. government's wishes (see DePalma, 1999). Domestic politics and power maneuvering among contesting forces have always played a major role in packaging and promoting what is considered the national interest. President Reagan extended the proposition of national security to include the defense of U.S. "national interests" in any part of the world (McGrew, 1992).

Pursuing national interests aggressively and often without regard to the interests of other parties reflects a sense of superiority and disregard of the "insignificant" others. This usually creates problems in international negotiations and competition, as the national interests of others are marginalized or discredited. International opportunities for compromise and mutual understanding may be sacrificed. A case in point is the U.S. rejection of any role for the World Court in solving a trade dispute with the European Union over the legality of certain American sanctions against Cuba (Greenberger, 1997). The Clinton administration claims that the WTO "has no competence to proceed" in a matter that is important to American "national interests." This attitude is surprising since many experts in international trade consider this a major setback for those who believe in a free market economy and in a role for the WTO in solving trade disputes. The United States was the major player in establishing the WTO. In addition, the United States "files far more complaints about foreign trade practices at the WTO than are filed against it" (Sanger, 1997, p. A1). These examples provide additional evidence that scholars should give more attention to issues that have major consequences for humans and organizations.

Economic sanctions constitute a major problem for free trade and for societies that are subjected to them. They punish the innocent in the countries where they are imposed, denying their citizens a better quality of life (Mobil, 1997). Economic sanctions are not only in violation of article 25, #1 of the UN's Universal Declaration of Human Rights but also constitute a crime against humanity (Clarke, 1996). For example, according to the UN's own agencies (UNICEF, EHO, FAO), the U.S.-led sanctions against the Iraqi people have already killed more than 1.5 million people, and it is estimated that as a result of the sanctions, more than 6,000 children die each month in Iraq. Denis Halliday, former UN assistant secretary general and head of the UN humanitarian mission in Iraq, in a speech delivered on Capitol Hill on October 6, 1998, stated:

> After eight years of sanctions, high levels of malnutrition and child morbidity and mortality continue. These victims are innocent civilians who had no part whatsoever in the decisions that led to the events that brought on United Nations sanctions in the first place. The World Health Organization (WHO) confirmed to me that the monthly rate of sanctions-related child mortality for children under five years of age is from five to six thousand per month. They believe this is an underestimate, since in rural parts of Iraq children are not registered at birth, and if they die within six weeks of birth, they are never registered. . . . We see a tragic incompatibility between sanctions that are harming the innocent children and people of Iraq, and the United Nations charter, specifically the Convention on Human Rights and the Rights of the Child. The incompatibility with the spirit and letter of the charter constitutes a tragedy for the United Nations itself, and severely threatens to undermine the UN's credibility and legitimacy as a benign force for peace and human well being throughout the world. (p. 3)

Hunger and starvation should be a major concern of scholarly debate. Starvation has inflected unimaginable damage on large segments of the populations of CDSs. For example, the UN Food and Agriculture Organization (FAO, 1998) released a report (98/70) stating that "more than 800 million people in developing countries are chronically undernourished. In addition, some two billion people are estimated to be affected by micronutrient deficiencies of vitamin A, iron, and iodine." Researchers from the World Food Program, UNICEF, and the European Union found that in North Korea because of long-term food shortages, about 62 percent of children under the age of seven suffer from stunted growth. In fact, this situation has "left an entire generation of children physically and mentally impaired" (Rosenthal, 1998).

Studies conducted by the FAO indicate that there are ample supplies of food and medicine in the world, but many do not have access to them. Basically, the problem stems from politically and culturally oriented designs and priorities set by leading political elites in both CDSs and MDSs. These elites understand neither globalization nor the triumph of independent minds; they do not understand globalization as an evolution that offers great potential to serve humanity. Rather, they view it as an evolving economic/political structure that can be used to coerce the submission of others to their ideas. Often they place more emphasis on global bleach (instability and conflict) than on global reach, and on global pillage rather than a global village. By contrast, business organizations, in recent years, and consequently global managers and enlightened business scholars, have begun to promote understanding and to maximize stakeholders' interests. Their allegiance to customers across the globe and their interests stem from innovatively maximizing their welfare. Children in North Korea, Iraq, Canada, or the United States are humans first and potential customers second. Their welfare and futures, today and tomorrow, are important for organizations wherever they operate.

Chapter 4

Globalization Dimensions

Six decades after Charles E. Merrill founded the modern Merrill Lynch, our job is still to make the free market system work—for our clients and for people every where. The difference today is that the opportunities and the responsibilities are global.

David H. Komansky and Herbert Allison
President and Chairman of the Board
Merrill Lynch, 1998

Those who possess know-how have an obligation to take the lead in sustainable development. We believe in a future with economic growth, while we strive to ensure that none of our activities will place undue burdens on the environment and natural resources. A desire for globalization is a major imperative behind our decisions and actions. This desire, our relationship with other people, the environment and technology, form the pillars that uphold the values we see as significant reasons for our existence.

Danfoss, *Annual Report,* 1998

Pushing for more flexibility in the workplace and fostering personal initiative, [permit] top focuses on unleashing the full potential and creativity of our people. It promotes international experience and calls for the dismantling of outdated hierarchies to help nurture a true team spirit.

Siemens, *Annual Report 96,* 1996

Globalization is often debated in cultural, political, business, and environmental terms. Despite its interdisciplinary nature, there has been no serious attempt to focus on globalization's dimensions coherently and in totality. Consequently, rigorous treatments of these dimensions are seldom found in the literature. Robinson (1996) and Waters (1995), among others, focus on the economic, political, and cultural dimensions of globalization. This focus needs to be advanced further to encompass other concerns such as the environment and technology. A cornerstone of globalization thinking is the commonality among peoples across cultures and borders. This commonality is not confined to relations among governments or firms; rather it must be the foundation for all activities among states, firms, localities, and individuals across the globe. Globalization has induced realignment in relationships among various actors in terms of the structuring of power, collaborations, and prioritization. The most noticeable structured integration and change, however, is taking place in the world economy (Dunning, 1997) and in world culture (Waters, 1995).

In Chapter 1, globalization is viewed as a process that encompasses and intensifies the interaction and integration among cultural, political, business, and intellectual elements on a single planet. In conducting their affairs, organizations assume various roles and pursue diverse activities. Globalization intensifies and widens such involvement. It is not only that the area for operating is wider, but that most players are unfamiliar with one another's strategies and more sophisticated in their approaches and strategies than traditional competitors. In addition, the globalization process encourages noneconomic global players to voice their concerns globally and to question business practices and contributions. Walter E. Hoadley (1998), former executive vice president of Bank America, argues that in a global economy the distinction between economic and noneconomic forces is not clear. He proclaims:

> Greater recognition will have to be given to the effects of non-economic, e.g., social, political psychological, technological, ethical, etc., forces shaping the future. The distinction between economic and non-economic cannot be precise. Some blending frequently occurs, but public interest will place more emphasis on the human emotional aspects of life. Failure to

recognize this change can be costly, invite more tensions, and generate disruptive social unrest.

The challenges that firms face come from business and nonbusiness rivals alike. Such development highlights the importance of understanding globalization dimensions in the context of business organizations. In fact, there is an urgent need to develop a coherent and comprehensive framework for viewing globalization in the context of firms' role and conduct.

An extensive review of the literature points out that the trade dimension is considerably discussed in business and nonbusiness circles. This is because many experts believe that globalization is largely a business concern (e.g., Boutros-Ghali, 1996; Dunning, 1997; Grant-Wisdom, 1995). Therefore, other nontrade aspects of globalization are sparsely treated. This is by no means an indication that other dimensions are not significant. On the contrary, the other dimensions are vital and need to be properly integrated in the globalization discourse. Several dimensions related to organizational conduct and involvement can be identified: trade (business), international relations, organizational, intellectual, and moral. Though these dimensions appear to be distinct in practice, they are interrelated. Firms are engaged in a chain of activities in the global marketplace. These activities have business and nonbusiness aspects and consequences. Traditionally, companies were viewed primarily as economic actors who focused on purely business activities. This view is unrealistic. In today's global environment it is impossible for any global firm to perform its economic tasks without involving social, political, and other nonbusiness functions. Firms have always engaged in nonbusiness activities as prerequisites or necessary functions for optimal performance. The difference is that in the globalization era these functions have become more important than ever. Firms that seek to attain or maintain a competitive advantage and enhance their public image must be actively involved in nonbusiness activities. It is for this very reason that globalization dimensions, from a firm's perspective, should be harmoniously integrated into globalization discourse.

THE STATE OF THE LITERATURE

Soros (1997) asserts that while laissez-faire capitalism holds that the common good is best served by the uninhibited pursuit of self-interest, the system is liable to break down unless it recognizes that common interests ought to take precedence over particular interests. In the context of firms, this assertion may indicate that firms should no longer be viewed as purely economic national actors. Firms are global actors who assume multiple functions on local, national, and international scales, and the performance of these functions has broad and deep effects that go far beyond economic concerns. Illuminating globalization's dimensions, therefore, becomes a necessary task for both practitioners and scholars. Following is a brief discussion of each.

TRADE DIMENSION

As the most obvious manifestation of a globalizing economy, trade has been the focus of the majority of the globalization debate (*The Economist*, 1997). In fact, it is one of the most valuable aspects of globalization (Mobil, 1998b) because the process of globalization has been boosted over the last few years by a shift in favor of market forces, deregulation, and economic liberalization (Dunn, 1995). Other scholars, while accentuating the centrality of trade in the globalization process, attribute current growth in international trade to the role of the United States in opening up new markets to itself and laying the groundwork for a single world economy of competitive capitals (Khor, 1993; Teeple, 1995). This thinking was expressed in 1946 by U.S. Assistant Secretary of State William Clayton:

> So, let us admit right off that our objective has as its background the needs and interests of the people of the United States. . . . We need markets—big markets—around the world in which to buy and sell. We are today net importers of practically all the important metals and minerals except two—coal and oil. Who knows how long we can go without importing oil? (quoted in Thompson, 1981, p. 48)

This by no means signifies that other countries were passive followers or had no interest in pursuing a free trade system (e.g., Britain, Japan, Germany). Rather, it indicates that the United States was resolute in advancing its worldview.

INTERNATIONAL RELATIONS

Ali (1992) argues that one of the most important functions that executives have come to assume in recent years is international relations. He indicates that in a global setting, international cooperation and relations take on added value as important functions for any competitive firm. A case in point is Daimler-Benz. In its 1997 corporate structure, the function of international relations and corporate business was performed by the chair of the board. In conducting their affairs, firms acquire greater expertise over the years in dealing with various subjects and issues. They have been able to ponder critical social, political, and cultural concerns. Mobil, for example, has an advocacy program and issues several op-eds a month that discuss issues ranging from the environment to education (e.g., Mobil, 1997b, 1997c, 1998a). In its "Nigeria: A Lesson for Investors" (Mobil, 1998d), for example, it states:

> We are pleased with the changes occurring today in Nigeria. Committed to progress for all Nigerians, General Abubakar is undertaking political and economic reforms that its people have long sought. A key element is ensuring that local communities receive a greater share of revenues from the development of the country's resources. Signs of openness and transparency are evident; local and state elections are on the horizon, and the prospect of a freely elected civilian president seems within reach. Our experiences in Nigeria demonstrate that patient responsible partners with a shared commitment can win out. And that is a good deal for everyone.

Similarly, the Body Shop works closely with NGOs, especially Amnesty International, to defend human rights and environmental issues. In the context of Nigeria, the Body Shop for over five years engaged actively in an international campaign to release Ogoni political prisoners. The Body Shop claims that defending human rights around the globe "embodies our conviction that business should be about social responsibility as well as profit" (Roddick, 1998, p. 3).

Higgott (1996) argues that firms have recently begun to play significant roles in the interrelationship between states and markets. That is, firms, contrary to international relations theory, are not merely instruments of a state policy; they are actors in their own right, and with their own diplomatic skills and power. Similarly, Dicken (1994) suggests that firms usually utilize diverse competitive strategies that are the result of contested power relations between and within firms, between and within governments, and between firms and states.

Organizational Functions and Activities

In terms of structuring organizational functions and activities, globalization induces a profound realignment. The ever-growing rush for strategic alliances, acquisitions, and cross-border mergers, along with an interest in maintaining organizational flexibility and agility, manifest globalization's imperative. Certain challenges and opportunities have been created, and firms have to respond to them creatively. Structural changes, therefore, are necessary to preserve a firm's vitality and valuability. Firms, however, have responded differently. For example, Xerox, on March 18, 1997, realigned its business structure to prepare for global changes in its document processing market. Under the new alignment, five business groups emerged: production systems, office products, document services, channels, and supplies. Unilever and Toyota have changed their structures to meet globalization's challenges. In *Unilever's Organization* (Unilever, 1996c, p. 2), it was stated:

> As our markets change, so must we. Our new organization makes the most of Unilever's greatest strength—our depth of local knowledge of consumers and countries. The people closest to each market have more power to make decisions, as part of a clearer split between those who run our businesses on the ground, and the small team of people responsible for overall leadership at the top, who form the Executive Committee. . . .

> The new organization will make it easier for us to develop our brands and build on strong local businesses. It also gives us the best combination of regional scale and category focus.

Toyota (1996) handles globalization demands through a deliberate design to localize its far-flung activities by integrating operations by region. It found that "the more we built outside Japan, the more we needed a framework for managing our far-flung operations in a global context. Now, we are globalizing management" (p. 10).

Intellectual Functions and Activities

This dimension is a new and innovative resource that companies are using increasingly due to globalization's influence. It is emerging as a result of a deliberate effort to rethink firms' roles in the global marketplace. The intellectual component is a product of contradictory trends: integration and differentiation at the global "societal" level and intense competition and cooperation at the firm level. In search of productive operations, companies have accelerated idea and technology transfer to most of the world. The ascendancy of knowledge over capital and natural resources (materials) as a source of competitive advantage accentuates firms' contribution to knowledge accumulation. The World Development Report 1998/99 (World Bank, 1999, p. 28) asserts:

> Large multinational firms are global leaders in innovation, and the worldwide spread of their productive activities is an important means of disseminating their knowledge to developing countries. The size of their knowledge base is reflected in the fact that the 50 largest industrial-country multinationals accounted for 26 percent of all corporate patents granted in the United States from 1990 to 1996. The knowledge in multinationals spills over through learning by their workers and domestic suppliers and through technology sales.

In practice, firms have shown various forms of commitment to intellectual involvement. Caterpillar (1992), for example, views technology transfer as a necessary means for maintaining competitive advantage (pp. 7-12):

> We view technology transfer in a broad context. Such transfer can involve information about product and manufacturing innovations, accounting and data processing know-how, purchasing and marketing expertise—in short, all the technical and managerial knowledge needed for efficient functioning of an enterprise. . . . Free flow of information across national borders is vital to Caterpillar. We transmit a large, growing volume of business data between countries: machine and parts orders, financial and inventory information, engineering, and other data.

Siemens places strong emphasis on having a global pool of talent. Siemens (1996, p. 9) is "responding to global competition and a changing job market with *innovative training programs* tailored to specific fields like microtechnology and multimedia." Merrill Lynch in its 1997 *Annual Review* views intellectual involvement as the ability to "continually transfer ourselves—broadening our understanding of the needs and desires of those we serve, closely aligning our interests with theirs, and better harnessing our resources, experience and wisdom" (p. 3). DuPont, on the other hand, gives priority to team building and skill improvement to enhance intellectual contributions. Jack Krol, president and CEO, declares "I expect a global perspective with an understanding of how to be successful in all cultures. . . . The ability to motivate, ensure fair treatment, develop and select the right people and get results through teams is now essential" (DuPont, 1996, p. 6). Caterpillar, in its *Code of Worldwide Business Conduct* (1992), clearly states that no nation has a monopoly on intellectual contributions and that human diversity is an asset:

> As a company that manufactures and distributes on a global scale, Caterpillar recognizes it competes in a world composed of different races, religions, cultures, customs, political philosophies, languages, economic resources, geography. We respect these differences. Human pluralism is a strength, not a weakness; no nation has a monopoly on wisdom. (p. 13)

Moral Concerns

The moral dimension is second to trade in terms of its coverage by practitioners and scholars. Practitioners have always sought to enhance public image and involvement in social activities as necessary conditions for strategically positioning a firm in the marketplace. Scholars, on the other hand, have been concerned with possible negative consequences resulting from a firm's conduct. Although both views are still common, the globalization process has intensified, broadened, and deepened moral concerns. Scholars and practitioners alike have engaged in heated debate, providing theoretical reasoning for moral involvement. In fact, it is fashionable these days for CEOs to list the firm's contributions to social and environmental matters. In addition, the concern for moral involvement is not limited to any particular nation. More important, moral dimensions encompass new issues (e.g., environment, diversity, wage discrimination, worker displacement, human rights). These issues are debated at all societal levels, locally and globally. Instant transmission of information and the emergence of worldwide organizations that advocate change and accountability on a global scale have deepened moral interest.

One of the most pressing arguments is that in the global free-market economy, caring, loyalty, and moderation are not priorities as gains are privatized to the benefits of the power holders, and costs are socialized by charging them to those who have no political or economic power (Korten, 1996). Lee and Foster (1997), while asserting the benefits of globalization, acknowledge that it probably accounts for almost all of the rise in inequality in the United States and other OECD countries. Rodrik (1997b) argues that the most important challenge for the twenty-first century is to engineer a new balance between the market and society—one that will continue to foster the creative energies of private enterprises without eroding the social foundation of cooperation.

Business organizations, along with other NGOs, have taken steps to meet the above challenge and to minimize and prevent possible harm to the world community. For example, the World Business Council for Sustainable Development (WBCSD), based in Geneva, was established in 1995 by 125 major companies (e.g., 3M, AT&T, ABB, Arthur D. Little, Kodak, Johnson & Johnson, Sony, Toyota, Xerox, Danfoss). WBCSD seeks to enhance commitment to the environment and to the principles of economic growth and sustainable development. In particular, it contributes through its global network to a sustainable future for "developing nations and nations in transition." Similarly, senior business leaders from the United States, Japan, and Europe established in 1986 the Caux Round Table (CRT) to promote "principled business leadership and responsible corporate practice" based on the following principles:

- Corporations must be increasingly responsive to issues affecting the physical, social, and economic environments, not only because of their impact on business performance but also out of a proactive sense of responsibility to all constituencies served.
- Corporations need to consider the balance between the short-term interests of shareholders and the longer-term interests of the enterprise and all its stakeholders.
- The primary responsibility of the corporation is to conduct its operations proficiently, i.e., to be technologically innovative, competitive, and financially sound.
- Meeting traditional objectives and performance criteria, however, is not sufficient. Voluntary standards, which exceed the requirements of prevailing law and regulations, are necessary to the development of sustainable practices. Society's "license or franchise to operate" has to be earned.
- Corporations should lead by example through business practices that are ethical and transparent, and that reflect a commitment to human dignity, political and economic freedoms, and preservation of the planet.
- Corporations cannot act alone but should seek to address key societal issues through cooperative efforts with governments, other institutions, and local communities.

The establishment of such organizations along with active involvement of NGOs and increasing awareness by corporations of their emerging global roles will induce them to develop visions and policies to sustain their moral stands. For example, Shell Chemical, in response to pressure from NGOs and activists relative to its involvement in Nigeria and other places, revised its health, safety, and environment (HSE) policies in 1997. The new policy (Shell Chemical, 1998, p. 1) states:

> The changes came as a response to advances in global communications and increased public awareness and debate about

> HSE issues. People are less willing to accept a "trust me" attitude from industry, instead they adopt the stance of "show me" and even of "prove-to-me" that what you are doing is healthy, safe and environmentally sound.

One of the most important items in the new policy is "pursu[ing] the goal of no harm to people." Shell, in its new policy, views respect for human rights as a "critical business activity." Likewise, Nike, Inc. (1997) revised its codes on labor practice and social responsibility. In particular, the revised code seeks to make continuous improvement in:

> Management practices that recognize the dignity of the individual, the rights of free association and collective bargaining, and the right to a workplace free of harassment, abuse, or corporate punishment. (p. 1)

On the matter of child labor, Nike demands that all its contractors certify that they do not employ any person below the age of eighteen to produce footwear, or below the age of sixteen to produce apparel, accessories, or equipment, and do not employ any worker under the legal minimum age where local standards are higher. Other companies such as The Gap and Levi Strauss also have environmental and child labor guidelines. Companies such as Honda, Mobil, and Xerox consider environmental and moral issues of primary concern. Some critics, however, point out that these companies have to live up to their new policies and commitments. There is always a risk that an urge to maximize profit may lead some firms to step on common moral principles and thus endanger the lives of others. A case in point is Formosa Plastics Corp., a Taiwan-based company that in November 1998 dumped 3,000 tons of industrial waste in a village in Cambodia. The company said "it had not been able to dump it in Taiwan because of a threat of public protests" (Mydans, 1999). As a result people of the Cambodian village were evacuated and many experienced various forms of illness.

DEVELOPING AN INTEGRATED APPROACH TO GLOBALIZATION

Certainly, there is a lack of coherent treatment of globalization dimensions in both practice and theory. In addition, existing literature appears to examine each dimension individually without adequate integration with the rest. Furthermore, it seems that business leaders, rather than scholars, are taking the lead in highlighting some crucial dimensions (e.g., intellectual, international relations) in their discourses and conduct. Perhaps theoretical development lags behind events in the business world. Therefore, an urgent need exists to develop a framework for articulating and integrating dimensions that will lay the foundation for sound thinking and practice.

Constructing globalization dimensions is not an easy task. The dimensions have distinct characteristics, yet they are not exclusively independent. More important, each dimension assumes philosophical and practical qualities. Stressing both qualities involves broader insight and knowledge of organizations in a global setting. Behavioral science provides several techniques that are useful for capturing the unique qualities of these dimensions. The Delphi technique is an optimal method for soliciting opinions and expert judgments. Delphi, considered a practical approach to obtaining the required forecasts and inputs (Martino, 1972), offers a set of procedures for eliciting and refining the opinions of a group of people.

Originally, Delphi was developed by researchers at the Rand Corporation, and it involves three procedures: anonymity of the group, iteration steps with controlled feedback, and statistical group response. The Delphi procedure, however, is not a single method, but a family of methods which are all variations of the original approach developed at Rand (Martino, 1972).

METHOD

One of the most important features of Delphi is that participants are selected because of their expertise. I created a list of fifty-seven global experts from the Academy of International Business Directory, including four active executives from the American Society for Competitiveness Membership List. Experts were selected based on their functional specialization and geographical locations. The objective was to ensure broad functional and geographical participation. A letter was sent to all of the experts informing them about the nature and purpose of the research and requesting their participation. Twenty-six experts agreed to participate.

The development of globalization dimensions was achieved in four phases. In the first phase, experts were asked to generate the widest possible range of ideas and opinions belonging to each dimension. Participants were provided with definitions for each dimension, which were intended to serve as guides to statement development and allowed experts to focus on the construct that needed to be measured, thereby capturing its essence (DeVellis, 1991). Delphi panelists were informed that these dimensions were to be viewed in terms of a firm's conduct and operations in the global marketplace. A sample item for what a global organization should do under each dimension was provided to help panelists get started. The purpose in this phase was to come up with as many statements as possible without venturing beyond the bounds of the definition. A total of 468 statements were generated (see Table 4.1).

The second phase consisted of a refinement of the compiled statements. A group of four scholars from various academic backgrounds, nonmembers of the Delphi Panel, participated in the refinement stage. They were asked to review the generated statements and mark those that were similar or repeated. In addition, they were asked to point out

TABLE 4.1. Statements Generated in Each Research Phase

Dimension	Phase I	Phase II	Phases III and IV
Trade	95	57	11
International Relations	102	67	15
Organizational	99	64	21
Intellectual	68	62	21
Moral	104	60	18
Total	468	310	86

statements that were awkwardly worded. About 158 statements were deleted (see Table 4.1).

The third phase constituted the second round of Delphi procedures. The Delphi Panel (the original twenty-six experts) was asked to indicate if the refined statements under each globalization dimension belonged to that dimension. In addition, they were invited to comment on whether each item was clear or confusing. Participants were asked to rate how relevant they thought each statement was to the definition of each dimension by circling the appropriate number according to the following scale:

1. Certainly does not belong
2. Does not belong
3. Possibly does not belong
4. Provides no basis for decision on belonging
5. Possibly belongs
6. Belongs
7. Certainly belongs

The objectives at this phase were to refine and integrate perspectives that are considered important for each globalization dimension. Twenty experts sent their responses on time.

The fourth phase represents the final step. It consisted mainly of statistical procedures that would determine a cutoff point for including statements under each dimension. Six scholars who teach multivariate analysis were contacted and informed about the nature and objective of the survey. There was agreement among these experts that the cutoff point for the inclusion of any item in the measure should reflect the degree to which that item appealed to its audience (scholars versus practitioners). Two methods were suggested. The first, to be on the safe side, accepted only statements that were endorsed by at least 75 percent of the experts (the liberal attitude). The second approach was more conservative; it included statements that were endorsed by at least 90 percent of the experts. The prevailing sentiment among these scholars, however, was to consider 80 percent as a cutoff point. This was adopted.

FINDINGS

Several statements were generated and considered for inclusion under globalization dimensions. The following sections define each dimension and present a set of the most important items that emerged.

Trade Dimension

> *Business organizations should conduct business across borders, in an open market, to maximum organizational benefit, without inflicting social damage or violating the rights of people from other cultures.*

The global organization should:

- Develop marketing and/or production strategies that span nation-state borders to maximize the use of its resources and skills
- Tap the globe through trade and direct investment
- Design products with attention to unique cultural and operational needs
- Work with best suppliers to improve local organizational and technological capabilities and to improve local working conditions
- Respect the integrity and autonomy of local cultures, organizations, and practices by maintaining a proper arms-length contractual relation with local suppliers
- Minimize the impact on the affected workforce and community when dislocations occur; plan well to avoid drastic shifts in direction
- Derive maximum advantages without exploiting workers or communities when entering new markets or establishing new facilities
- Make safe products and services available to the people of the world
- Ensure that foreign operations are environmentally friendly
- Conduct business in a socially and ethically responsible manner
- Advance the idea of free and fair trade and economic operations across the globe

International Politics and Relations Dimension

Business organizations should accept and participate in the development and refinement of business practices and norms across cultures while respecting national sovereignty and cultural identities.

The global organization should:

- Be flexible in dealing with a wide range of environments and their peculiarities
- Accommodate business styles that are different from their own
- Be conscious of and plan for alternatives for political risks and upheaval throughout the globe
- Make a local network of contacts to facilitate understanding of one another's viewpoints
- Hire talented local advisors to help meet new challenges
- Join industry associations and support industry publications (or start them if they do not exist)
- Keep informed about local political affairs and regulatory changes
- Be careful and thorough in assessing political stability and risk and their potential to cause expropriation of company assets abroad
- Choose the best ideas and practices from each culture to transmit throughout the global organization
- Focus on the shifting competitive structures locally and globally
- Ascertain the standards for good corporate citizenship in each host country and comply
- Find means to operate while maintaining cultural elements that are important in the host value system
- Work with local business partners to identify "culturally sensitive" business practices
- Cope well with situations of uncertainty and/or stability; be flexible in reacting to different and changing environments
- Understand foreign environments well enough to begin to anticipate broad political, social, and cultural trends, and deal with them before they become crises

Organizational Dimension

Business organizations should have the ability to set forth organizational structures and human resource systems that can mobilize managers and employees to implement globalization visions.

The global organization should:

- Attract the best personnel globally without prejudice
- Encourage the development of global teams working collectively on projects
- Have organizational systems in place that allow input from employees globally on major functional activities and projects
- Accord the same degree and respect of organizational citizenship to all employees
- Have managers from around the world meet and interact regularly
- Obtain understanding, in both the host country and home country, of the purposes and objectives of the business or project
- Accommodate cultural differences with respect to decision making, participation, and communication
- Reward people on a combination of individual, unit, and global performance
- Have a truly globalized board of directors and executive management team
- Assign and train expatriate managers carefully so that they can adjust to local environments
- Ensure that organizational structures are flexible
- Hire and promote employees who have a global vision
- Share information about hazardous waste management, job safety, and other threatening consequences of the product presence, including risks inherent in local product or service manufacture
- Provide financial and administrative support to facilitate expatriation of talent from all sources
- Offer appropriate training, enabling employees to aspire to and compete for higher positions

- Offer promotion and advancement opportunities to best-qualified employees regardless of individual background
- Have the vision to detect the talents of its people without prejudice
- Develop the capacity to manage cultural changes that will invariably occur
- Empower local managers who are closest to the marketplace to act in a manner that is responsive to local customer groups
- Have a culture and flexible structure that respond quickly and effectively to global and local host market changes
- Identify and develop "core competencies" essential for globalization

Intellectual Dimension

> *Business organizations should treat globalization as a view and an outlook that broadens and energizes the human mind and perspective; that is, the ability to create a culture where knowledge and a sense of belonging are transmitted and embedded in organizational life.*

The global organization should:

- Create a process by which knowledge and a sense of mutual obligation are transmitted and embedded in organizational life
- Sponsor and nurture global networks of the organization's professionals in their disciplines
- Promote cross-cultural organizational transfers of employees at different levels in the company
- Create a corporate culture including strong elements of ethical and moral behavior
- Create a corporate culture that is friendly and usable to all members of all cultures, genders, religions, and ethics
- View "foreigners" simply as people
- Share ideas and knowledge with its employees and customers
- Create a community feeling among its people in the host country to break down some of the "us" versus "them" barriers
- Ensure that executive managers demonstrate in their behavior the values and visions they espouse

- Recognize that knowledge must be translated into internationally competitive products and services
- Establish and implement the principles of the learning organization to the degree that learning transcends functional, organizational, and national boundaries
- Institute policies that show respect for knowledge (such as foreign language competency)
- Be sensitive to the risks of interracial hostilities that might manifest old conflicts and be counterproductive as individuals are "imported" from neighboring nations
- Encourage expatriate managers to assimilate into the local society, to better understand local expectations and to more effectively advocate legitimate local interests in the larger corporation
- Provide expatriate managers with the means for remaining effectively integrated into the organizational life of the parent organization
- Reserve international responsibilities for those managers who have international breadth, technical and organizational competence, and the personal flexibility needed to perform effectively in an international context
- Create intrapersonnel appreciation and acceptance of international differences
- Educate employees on the benefits of acquiring and using global-based knowledge for personal and organizational purposes
- Reward innovations relating to globalization of the organization
- Create systems that facilitate the gathering and dissemination of relevant information to the interested parties
- Develop systems and structures that allow for the sharing of knowledge in a way that does not compromise proprietary technology

Moral Dimension

Business organizations should stress objectivity in treating issues across the globe and the courage to confront, on a timely basis, biases and prejudices.

The global organization should:

- Promote cross-cultural awareness (through sensitivity seminars, etc.)
- Promote an organizational culture that disdains and rejects stereotyping
- Look for similarities in cultures as well as understanding differences
- Set the standards for the organization itself and for others to follow
- Ensure environmental responsibility and safety
- Value local traditions and cultural activities and respect their importance
- Clearly understand local laws and practices with regard to human rights
- Manage the company for the benefit of all stakeholders, i.e., for long-term performance
- Include ethical performance in the evaluation of individuals
- Develop an explicit statement of corporate "global values"
- Be guided by the highest standards of conduct that are generally accepted in both the parent company's home and host societies
- Remain in compliance with the general standards of local custom or local law
- Protect consumers around the globe
- Lead on the basis of character and an ethic of fairness, honesty, and integrity
- Support due process through the law
- Create a culture whereby moral and ethical business practices are a top priority
- Develop a truly diverse but well-integrated group of global managers and critical staff
- Reduce sources of cultural conflict

The results of the Delphi panel's study reaffirm the premise that globalization dimensions have a wider scope than what is currently available in the literature. Furthermore, the results underscore the fact that global organizations engage in a wide range of economic and noneconomic activities. These activities should be dealt with simultaneously to ensure the productive and creative involvement of firms. This means that in conducting their operations, firms must integrate noneconomic dimensions into their strategic plans and decisions. Focusing on one dimension (e.g., trade) at the expense of others may deprive organizations of opportunities they cannot afford to miss. In addition, in today's global environment, placing emphasis on more economic activities may convey a message that the firm is not in line with global changes and priorities. Espousing intellectual, international, and moral dimensions is a competitive tool that strengthens and enhances a firm's position in the global marketplace. This is vividly expressed by Hewlett-Packard in its 1996 annual report:

> An active, global commitment to social progress strengthens HP's ability to conduct business as we approach the twenty-first century. During 1996, HP and its employees worked in many ways to enrich communities, improve the quality of life and promote economic development around the world. This year, the company donated approximately $72 million in cash and equipment. (Hewlett-Packard, 1996, p. 27)

Surely, statements presented under each dimension should be viewed as general guidelines for companies, policymakers, and scholars. Many of these statements are currently promoted and advocated by some global corporations (e.g., ABB, Citibank, Danfoss, DaimlerChrysler, Nestlé, Siemens, etc.). Other statements and principles need to be a part of the globalization discourse (e.g., reduce sources of cultural conflict; manage the company for the benefit of all stakeholders; create processes by which learning transcends functional, organizational, and national boundaries, etc). In fact, promoting these principles differentiates global organizations from traditional ones.

Chapter 5

Globalization and Regionalism

Regionalism . . . is not a unified concept and cannot by itself be the organizing principle for a new global economic order.

Robert Hormats
Vice Chairman
Goldman Sachs International, 1994

At the very moment the world is moving towards a global economy, countervailing forces attempt to divide it. These divisive forces, simply put, are regional trading blocs.

Louis Emmerij
President, OECD Development Center
in Paris, 1992

Is regionalism a building block for multilateral trade agreements? Does regionalism hinder progress toward a liberal world trade system? The answers to these questions depend, of course, on the nature, motives, and evolution of regionalism. Regional trade pacts (RTPs), or regionalism, can take various forms: free-trade area, customs union, common market, and economic union (see Rodgers, 1998 for details). The free trade area is the simplest form of an RTP. Under a free trade area pact, tariffs are removed among members of the pact, and each member determines its own tariff structure for nonmembers. The most sophisticated form of RTP is the economic union, in which members of the pact agree on three general principles: removing tariffs among themselves but having uniform external tariffs for outsiders, free movement of labor and capital within the pact, and establishment of common monetary and fiscal policies. It is generally accepted that as a pact evolves toward protectionism (discriminating against nonmembers) and moves to take advantage of its market size and comparative advantage, regionalism constitutes a setback to worldwide market liberalization efforts (Chichilnisky, 1998).

RTPs are assumed to either create trade (specialization and competition induce higher productivity and stimulate demands for goods and services from within or outside the pact) or divert trade (increasing intrapact trade at the expense of international trade). The first alternative is assumed to improve the welfare of consumers. The second limits consumer choices and forces consumers to buy higher-cost items that are produced by members of the pact. The challenge facing regional pacts is to translate commitment to trade liberalization and multilateral economic agreement into reality. This is a serious problem, as nationalistic attitudes and immediate national interests along with domestic political considerations take priority over principles set by the WTO and its predecessor, GATT. Emmerij (1992) argues that existing RTPs have two things in common: a tendency to structure their economies behind protectionist barriers and to have free trade within the pacts but protectionism toward nonmember countries. These tendencies, if continued, present obstacles to globalization.

REGIONALISM: CONDITIONS AND ASSUMPTIONS

RTPs should be differentiated from what Ohmae (1995) calls regional economies—a region that lies entirely within or across the borders of nations (e.g., Hong Kong and the adjacent stretch of southern China; Southern California and the adjacent Mexican territory; Lombardy in Italy and nearby areas of France and Switzerland). These are natural business units. Unlike RTPs, they do not emerge because of political decrees and legal design and structure. In addition, RTPs should be distinguished from regional approaches used by companies such as Honda, Toyota, ABB, and Unilever. These companies utilize regional strategies to underscore their market segmentation of the globe into geographic and political units (e.g., Europe, Middle East, South Asia, and Africa). Such segmentation allows companies to manage their operations and design strategies that take into account prevailing political, cultural, and economic variations.

In recent decades there has been a tendency for many countries to establish RTPs. The establishment of the European Economic Community (EEC) in 1957 stimulated the formation of RTPs. Initially, the United States was not enthusiastic about regionalism. Rather, it energetically promoted multilateral trade agreements. The United States, therefore, emphasized the roles that the World Bank, IMF, and GATT could play in the liberalization of trade (World Bank, 1992). The emergence of the EEC as an economic unit, however, induced a change in the United States's attitude toward regionalism. Other countries followed suit. In the 1960s, there were many grouping and regional agreements. Currently, there are more than thirty-three RTPs involving more than 120 countries on all continents (Frankel, 1997). Among the major RTPs are the European Union, North American Free Trade Agreement (NAFTA), Southern American Common Market (MERCOSUR), and the Association of Southeast Asian Nations (ASEAN Free Trade Area). In the 1960s and 1970s, most of the RTPs were oriented toward internal concerns. The primary motive, especially among CDSs, was to protect infant industries from international competition. There was a strong focus on regional import substitution. By the early 1980s there was a worldwide interest in trade liberalization. The collapse of the Soviet Union was instrumental in accelerating the movement toward liberal economic policies on a global scale. Furthermore, the conclusion of the Uruguay Round that replaced the GATT with the WTO increased confidence in multilateral agreements and motivated countries and RTPs to be more externally oriented in their trade policies.

CONDITIONS FOR SUCCESSFUL RTPs

Most of the existing RTPs are not effective or are only declarations or official accords that have never been translated into realities (e.g., the Arab Common Market, the East African Economic Community, etc.). The EU and, to a degree, NAFTA are considered successful by many trade observers. The first has managed to move beyond trade, capital, and free movement of labor toward establishing monetary and fiscal policies. The introduction of the Euro on January 1, 1999, as a single currency will completely replace the established national currencies of many European countries by 2002. The responsibility for EU monetary policy is placed in a new European Central Bank. This development has political and economic ramifications for EU members and for other countries and RTPs that deal with the EU. The most important implication for globalization and liberalization of world trade is that the EU, despite some concerns, is a regional success story. The following are necessary, but not sufficient, conditions for successful RTPs:

1. *Members have similar per capita incomes.* For example, the average per capita income for the EU and NAFTA in 1997 was \$22,061 and \$17,236 respectively. The dispersion within each pact, however, differs significantly. The highest per capita, for the EU, was in Germany (\$28,260) and the lowest was Greece (\$10,450). This is in sharp contrast to NAFTA, where the United States had \$28,740 per capita and Mexico had \$3,680. The utility for this factor, however, is contingent upon meeting conditions five and six below.
2. *Geographic proximity.* In today's world of instant communication and rapid knowledge transfer, along with low transportation costs, geographic proximity is not an overriding factor for ensuring the success of the RTPs. Nevertheless, proximity still plays an important role in enhancing an effective RTP. It eases and economizes capital, labor, and commodity movement. In addition, cultural differences tend to be more limited and prospects for interconnectedness and assimilation tend to be enhanced.
3. *Similarity in trading systems.* Similar outlooks and expectations regarding trade and economic systems stimulate cooperation and produce effective negotiations to deal with issues significant for RTPs. The EU, over the years, has evolved gradually, but effectively, to its current status due to similar outlooks and compatible trade systems prevailing among its members.

4. *Similarity in development strategies.* Members of a pact that emphasizes different development strategies and priorities face serious problems in achieving regional integration.
5. *Political dedication and involvement.* Successful RTPs require political openness and commitment. Countries that lack democratic institutions and the political will to make RTPs operational have failed to make reasonable progress in their quest for building sound regional trade (e.g., the Middle East, Africa, and Latin America). For example, the Gulf Cooperation Council (Bahrain, Kuwait, Oman, Qatar, Saudi Arabia, and U.A.E.) has similar per capita income and economic structure, and it is geographically connected, but it has failed to achieve its economic integration goals because of a lack of political commitment.
6. *Degree of political independence.* In the 1960s and 1970s many countries in Africa and Asia obtained official independence. Nevertheless, almost all of them have maintained close political ties with the former colonial powers. Regimes in these countries have been under tremendous popular pressure to improve standards of living. Regional integration is seen as a popular pursuit and offers these regimes an opportunity to improve their public image. The commitment to regional integration, however, is weakened by influence exercised by former colonial and other superpowers that have different priorities and designs. For example, the Gulf Cooperation Council has not been able to achieve most of its goals due to political pressures exercised by England and the United States, which have a military presence in the region coupled with substantial economic interests. These foreign powers view any move toward integration and possible unity as a threat to their vital interests. The same case is common in Africa, where the former colonial powers (e.g., Belgium, France, and England) have consistently interfered to steer economic and political events in Africa to their immediate advantage. Recently, the IMF (1999b) cautioned against a multiplicity of regional arrangements in Africa with uncoordinated and possibly inconsistent objectives.

Assumptions

RTPs have generated a heated and emotional debate. Various groups—labor, industry, environmental, religious, and intellectual—have invested tremendous amounts of time and energy to advance or hinder the formation of RTPs. Supporters and opponents of RTPs articulate certain propositions and assumptions pertaining to their vitality and benefits (see Table 5.1). Those who advance the cause of RTPs point to opportunities for creating jobs, transferring knowledge, stimulating economies, and promoting institution building and the democratic process. Critics have enumerated negative consequences such as the displacement of workers, threats to selected industries, and threats to sovereignty.

PROSPECTS FOR HEALTHY REGIONAL TRADE PACTS

Hormats (1994) raises the issue that RTPs are not a unified concept and cannot by themselves be the organizing principle for a new global economic order. Many trade experts echo this sentiment. In fact, there is a widespread fear among many specialists and concerned individuals that regionalism may induce trade wars, divide the globe into trading blocs, and reduce democracy to an empty form, so that the interests of MNCs can be pursued without interference. According to some, RTPs may be an effective tactic for expanding U.S. influence on trade issues and accelerating the division of the world economy into poor, rich, and super-rich nations, where the first are assigned the role of serving the latter (see Brecher, 1993; Chomsky, 1993; Lewis and Ebrahim, 1993; Passell, 1993). One of the most significant fears among trade observers is that though discrimination within RTPs is not permitted, it is tolerated against outsiders. In this case, RTPs "amount to the formation of cliques on the playground" (Kanter, 1998, p. A21). Nevertheless, regional trade pacts are often viewed as necessary mechanisms for trade liberalization, as driving forces that motivate members of the trade pacts to engage in global bargaining and focus on the most urgent and serious trade problems; RTPs also enhance global vision

TABLE 5.1. Pro- and Anti-RTP Positions

Proponent	Opposition
Forge a powerful bloc to compete in today's global economy	Serve the interests of big companies
Create a dynamic future of economic growth and prosperity	Abuse labor rights
Serve as a stepping stone for trade liberalism	Displace workers, especially those in high-cost or in low-value-added industries
Create jobs and stimulate exports	Threaten environmental standards
Reduce the incentive for plant location overseas	Keep competitors out of countries not members of the pact
Create economies of scale opportunities	Establish supernational agencies at the expense of democratically elected institutions
Stimulate economic growth and improve standard of living	They are not about free trade; they are about free movement of capital
Allow optimal allocation of resources	Threaten national sovereignty
Harmonize standards and regulations	Displace domestic competitors
Encourage economic and trade reforms	Eliminate any chance of national economic planning and independent development
Stimulate investment flows	Do little to promote equitable income across the pact area
Reduce the gap of income inequity and contribute to improving living standards, in the long run, for members of the pact	Threaten small- and medium-sized firms which have difficulty in relocating overseas
Enhance knowledge transfer and labor skills	Do not advance global liberalization
Promote institution building and civil conduct	Provide suboptimal alternative for world trade
Speed political reform and cooperation within the pact	Divide MDSs into at least three trading blocs: North America, the EU, and East Asia, thereby fragmenting the world economy
Strengthen the credibility and the negotiating power of the pact members relative to other countries and pacts	
Induce other countries that stay outside to join trade pacts	

by strengthening the common elements while minimizing the negative impact of ongoing trade disputes. In addition, RTPs affect the decision and timing of FDIs made by corporations whose countries are not members of the RTP. Collins (1998) argues that the European community induces these corporations to increase their FDI to capture scale, size, and specialization economies. A few steps are necessary for strengthening economic integration among and between partners of various economic pacts:

1. Placing equal emphasis on free movement of capital and labor. Most existing pacts stress free movement of capital at the expense of labor movement.
2. Encouraging corporations to invest in disadvantaged regions of the pact. This is especially important in areas where there is an urgent need to alleviate human suffering (e.g., the southern part of Mexico, especially Chiapas).
3. Inducing a member of two or more pacts to play a catalyst role for maximizing trade between the pacts (e.g., Mexico as a member of NAFTA and Latin American groups) and other nations.
4. Expanding the trade zone to include neighboring countries. For example, Chile and Argentina are potential NAFTA members.
5. Reciprocating policies among trade pacts. If a particular pact decided to lower trade barriers with other nations, other pacts should reciprocate.
6. Refraining from using economic leverage to achieve a political aim.
7. De-emphasizing "rules of origin." If a particular country is simultaneously a member of two pacts, products traded in its market that originate in another pact should be exempted from rules of origin. That is, there is a need to reduce or eliminate discrimination against nonparticipants.
8. Strengthening international rules and agreements by treating RTPs as a means of realizing multilateral rules.

FROM GLOBAL PILLAGE TO GLOBAL VILLAGE

Nelson Mandela, in his speech at the 1999 World Economic Forum, asked, "Is globalization only of benefit to the powerful and the financiers, speculators, investors and traders?" He focuses attention on a worldwide concern that the fruits of globalization must be utilized to serve the global community. A common perception exists among ordinary and intellectual individuals, especially in the CDSs, that globalization has drifted from its natural path and many have been left out. As the GATT negotiation was concluded successfully in December 1993, there were encouraging moments. *The Wall Street Journal* (1993a) hailed that development as "a fundamental decision about the direction of politics in the 21st century; . . . national borders will not become walls. Corporations will not need so many teams of lawyers and consultants." Peter Sutherland, GATT's Director General, declared, "Today, the world has chosen openness and cooperation instead of uncertainty and conflict" (Ali, Chaubey, and Camp, 1994, p. 10).

Some, however, do not share such optimism. Cavanagh, Broad, and Weiss (1993) argue that free trade gives U.S.-based firms license to bargain down wages and working conditions, and to slash workforces. Similarly, Dawkins and Muffett (1993) argue that GATT meant freedom to maximize profits with less government intervention in business affairs; weakened environmental regulations, public health and safety standards, and labor protection laws; and that GATT was given preeminence over any existing law. Likewise, Chomsky (1993) believes that GATT and other global institutions were designed to serve the interests of transnational corporations. They argue that as a result of the conclusion of GATT and the establishment of the WTO there will be a rise in new governing institutions to serve the interests of private transnational powers and a spread of the "Third World" social model, with islands of enormous privilege in a sea of misery and despair.

Brecher (1993) stresses that globalization is out of control. He specifies seven "danger signals" that reflect misery and disparity in today's globalization trend:

1. *Race to the bottom.* Wages and social environmental conditions tend to fall to the level of the most desperate.

2. *Global stagnation.* Lower wages and reduced public spending mean less buying power, leading to stagnation, recession, and unemployment. This dynamic is aggravated by the accumulation of debt as national economies in poor countries become geared to debt repayment at the expense of consumption, investment, and development.
3. *Polarization of haves and have-nots.* As a result of globalization, the gap between rich and poor is increasing both within and between countries around the globe.
4. *Loss of democratic control.* Globalization has reduced the power of individuals and communities to shape their destinies.
5. *Unfettered transnational corporations.* Corporations have become the world's most powerful economic actors, yet there are no laws that provide a degree of corporate accountability.
6. *Unaccountable global institutions.* For poor countries, foreign control is formalized in the World Bank's "structural adjustment plans," and IMF decisions and GATT rules affect the economic growth rates of all countries. The decisions of these institutions also have an enormous impact on the global ecology.
7. *Global conflict.* Economic globalization is producing chaotic and destructive rivalries. In past eras, such rivalries have ultimately led to world wars.

Brecher suggests seven prescriptions to alleviate these problems. Specifically, he calls for establishing international rights and standards; the IMF and the World Bank must replace their ruinous structural adjustment plans with policies that meet the broader goals of development; redistribution from haves to have-nots; strengthening democracy; establishing codes of conduct for international corporations; reforming international institutions; and establishing multiple-level, democratically regulated public institutions at every level from global to local.

Brecher's identification of the seven danger signals and his prescriptions carry great weight. Nevertheless, today's world is so complex that generalized or idealized prescriptions may not work. More practical prescriptions may better serve the goal of worldwide prosperity. Any progress toward realizing such a goal, especially reducing poor countries' debt problems, is a step forward. Table 5.2 provides a summary of arguments by pro- and anti-WTO groups.

The objective of GATT and subsequently of the WTO to lower or eliminate tariffs and other barriers to implementing free trade fosters not only new ideas for development but also channels the energy of

TABLE 5.2. Pro- and Anti-Multilateral Agreement Positions

Proponent	Opposition
Stimulates economy domestically and globally	Establishes faceless supernational institutions
Stimulates export	No laws are above the WTO
Ensures cohesiveness of international trade policies and procedures	Threatens sovereignty
Represents an end to law of the jungle	Gives license for U.S.-based firms to bargain down wages and working conditions
Minimizes the need for RTPs	Induces corporations to downsize
Encourages cooperation and openness among nations	Gives freedom for transnational and global corporations to maximize profits with less government intervention in business affairs
Fosters sources of growth, innovation, creativity, etc.	Weakened environmental regulations
New rules governing investment will level the playing field globally	Spreads the "Third World" social model, with an island of enormous privilege in a sea of misery and despair
National borders will not become walls	Sets the framework for a one-world government
Lessens the need for teams of lawyers and consultants	Inflicts damage upon national workers and industry
Government will find it difficult to coddle national industries	Polarization of haves and have-nots
Protects intellectual property and copyrights	Reduces the role of democratically controlled institutions at local and national levels
Strengthens international rules and norms	Limits trade and economic options for the poorest countries
Poor countries stand to gain the most from a strong multilateral trading system	

workers and nations alike in the direction of achieving effective use of existing resources. Operating in an open, competitive market is a prime vehicle for ensuring that the best producers of goods and services have access to markets and that consumers have plenty of choices, thereby maximizing their welfare. National or international political agendas, however, will not disappear as a result of the WTO. For this reason there is a need for practical prescriptions:

1. Despite Burt's (1993) claim that the Group of Seven, rather than the UN, should set the global agenda and should dictate the terms for implementing free trade, there is a strong belief among international relations experts that the UN Security Council should be expanded to achieve the representation of diverse cultural, political, and economic groups. Germany, Japan, India, Pakistan, Brazil, Egypt, Algeria, Mexico, and South Africa must serve as permanent members. Otherwise, the dominant "Western civilization" group would dictate their agenda at the expense of other cultures or nations. In addition, Security Council resolutions should be approved by the majority at the UN General Assembly to be enforceable.
2. Reduce the debt problems of CDSs through effective channels of resources to serve national economic needs and accelerate growth. Transnational and global corporations can be important forces in providing resources that upgrade human capital and skills and improve national living standards.
3. Encourage existing RTPs to advance global trade liberalization and eliminate any clauses that are inconsistent with WTO guidelines.
4. Encourage RTPs to enact laws and reforms that ensure the protection of investment and intellectual property.
5. Induce reforms in IMF and World Bank loan structures and conditions that better serve the needs of CDSs. Equally important, aid programs to these nations should be linked to the productive sectors and to the improvement of infrastructure. Many existing aid programs are military in nature and aim at serving the needs of the political elite.

6. Collectively designate some areas across the globe as "cultural regions" and ensure that these regions would not be victims of industrialization and environmental abuse.
7. Ensure equal participation in the management of the WTO and the enforcement of its objectives.
8. Avoid the temptation to allow control of the WTO by the dominant or most powerful participant.
9. Refrain from using the WTO as a tool to achieve political aims at the expense of justice and fairness.
10. Collectively, the WTO should establish general guidelines setting out the responsibilities for transnational and global corporations. Executives from these companies, along with scholars and representatives of human rights and environmental groups, should participate in designing these guidelines. The guidelines should be flexible and adaptive. In addition, guidelines should give general directions that encourage collective involvement of local communities, members of NGOs, and business corporations.

In summary, regional trade pacts may serve as a means for achieving the WTO's objectives. There are, however, practical problems that both RTPs and the WTO face. In the long term and in a world environment conducive to cooperation and understanding, far-reaching benefits can be realized. But in an environment that is characterized by mistrust and political and economic nationalism, it would be impossible to achieve the desired global benefits. That is, unless RTPs are structured to complement open markets, they could create barriers that would hinder the potential growth of the global economy (Hormats, 1994). Consequently, the world may experience, in the years to come, an economy that is dominated by three to four major regional trade pacts. Certainly, beliefs in the free trade philosophy and in the practicality and usefulness of global institutions are necessary conditions for improving the quality of life at home and abroad. The benefits of a global economy and global business participation should not be viewed in a narrow, chauvinistic sense. The unbridled ambition to control global business benefits runs counter to the spirit of globalization. The belief in a free-trade system and a commitment to its principles and to independent global institutions are the means to enhance trade benefits for all parties involved.

Chapter 6

Global Corporations

We are not homeless. We are a company with many homes.

Percy Barnevik
President and CEO, ABB, 1991

We are truly becoming global in the full sense of the word. . . . Companies must compete locally and view all major geographic markets, not as foreign markets, but as their home away from home.

Frank P. Popoff
Chairman, Dow Chemical, 1994

Autonomy at local branches and de-nationalization are the essence of a successful corporation that wants to develop a business with a global outlook.

Koh Sera
Sumitomo Corporation, 1995

Unilever is essentially a local company in all of its countries. [It is] "international," not "global."

Unilever, 1996

One of the most intriguing phenomena in the globalization of the economy is the rise and evolution of global corporations. Drucker (1994) argues that multinationals are a response to the emergence of a genuine world economy—a world in which the territorial political unit and the economic unit are no longer congruent. Amin (1997) and Modelski (1987), among others, however, believe that the modern era's multinationals are a form of innovation characteristically linked to and originally associated with world powers. Perhaps there is some truth to such a claim. For example, on the 1998 *Wall Street Journal* list of the world's 100 largest public companies, only seven firms have a base in a non-world power nation (ING, Netherlands; Ericsson, Sweden; Telefonica, Spain; and Novartis, Nestlé, UBS [Union Bank of Switzerland], and Roche, Switzerland). The rest are based in economically and/or militarily powerful countries (e.g., fifty-eight firms in the United States; twelve in the United Kingdom; nine in Germany; and three in Japan).

Nevertheless, it is possible to suggest that modern firms (e.g., transnational corporations [TNCs], or global corporations) operating across borders are different from traditional world companies, be they colonial trading or resource extraction companies (e.g., Dutch East Indies Company; Borneo Company; Hudson's Bay Company, etc.; see Table 6.1). Today's companies are not necessarily extensions of colonial powers and domination; likewise, they are not blindly motivated to control natural resources of other nations. Rather, they actively pursue access to markets and innovatively seek to meet customers' needs in these markets. Furthermore, modern firms are mostly run by professional managers and engage in a wide range of activities not limited to import/export or extraction. Their ownership, management, and employees are diverse. In addition, these firms utilize complex systems, structures, and processes and rely on a sophisticated worldwide network of alliances and relationships. Most important, allegiances and orientations may not bind these firms to any nation, and they often encompass almost all parts of the world. Indeed, their existence and future are solely determined by their ability to cope with and shape intense competition and global market reality. For practical reasons, Table 6.1 differentiates only between traditional (colonial) and modern firms (millennial—TNCs, global corporations). Many other organizations exist that cannot be classified as either colonial or modern. These firms are in service to the nation-state only incidentally and choose to operate in a single or specific market. In orientations and conduct, these firms do not display the exact characterizations identified in Table 6.1.

TABLE 6.1. Contrasting Traditional and Modern World Companies

Factor	Traditional	Modern
Management	Autocratic owners or their loyal representatives	Professionally oriented managers
Ownership	Mostly private and by limited groups from Western nations	Often publicly held, diverse ownership, possibly from various countries
Root	Colonial powers	Market competition and mechanism
Activities	Mostly import/export and extraction	A wide range of activities
Systems and Processes	Relatively simple systems and determined processes	Complex systems and processes
Structure	A rigid predetermined structure	Various structures possible
Network	Limited to ruling elites and closed circles of owners and friends	Sophisticated network of alliances among competitors, suppliers, clients, governments, and NGOs
Goal	Nation-bounded; disregard for host country needs	Not bound to any nation, strive to accommodate the demands of diverse stock-holders
Motivation	Exploitation of host countries' natural resources and reaping maximum profits in a short time	Access to markets and meeting existing and potential demand of various population segments across the globe to ensure survival and growth
FDI	Follows the flag	Follow opportunities wherever they exist
Involvement	Limited to economic activities and relations with ruling influential elites at home and abroad	Wide range of economic and noneconomic activities
International Role	Limited to maximizing profits and remittance revenue to the home country	Revolves around integrating the world economy and accelerating social and technological changes

SIGNIFICANCE OF MODERN FIRMS

Firms operating across borders play invaluable roles in economic, technological, and social development. In recent years, the well-being and welfare of world citizens have become increasingly determined by the activities and conduct of private firms, rather than by governments. As world actors, these firms assume two vital functions: integrating the world economy and facilitating the acceleration of profound social and technological changes. It is not difficult, therefore, to recognize why much attention has been given to them. The following facts are illustrative:

- At least 53,607 firms operate across borders, which have about 448,917 worldwide affiliates (see Table 6.2).
- The world's fifty largest public firms have, in 1997, a market value of $5.157 trillion and total sales of $1.96 trillion (see Table 6.3).
- Sale of goods and services by foreign affiliates estimated to be $9.5 trillion in 1997 (UNCTAD, 1998b). Available statistics indicate that foreign affiliate output amounted to 5 percent of world GDP in 1982, 6.7 percent in 1990, and 6 percent in 1994. The gross product of foreign affiliates almost tripled between 1982 and 1994 (see Table 6.4).
- Foreign affiliates worldwide generated more than $2 trillion in value added (income of employees, profits, and taxes) in 1997 (UNCTAD, 1998b).
- Export of foreign affiliates more than doubled between 1982 ($732 billion) and 1994 ($1.850 trillion, see Table 6.5). More than 40 percent of the exports by parent firms of world firms went to their foreign affiliates. According to UNCTAD (1997b), about one-third of world trade took place within infrafirm networks, and two-thirds of international transactions are associated with the international production of these firms.
- FDI flows have increased steadily over the years, especially among MDSs. The ratio of FDI stocks in 1997 to world GDP was 21 percent. In 1998, FDI flows were expected to reach a projected level of around $430-440 billion for both inflows and outflows (UNCTAD, 1997b).

- Firms have increasingly used cross-border agreements (e.g., joint ventures, licensing, franchising, etc.), in addition to FDI, to engage in international production. The number of these agreements (excluding strategic R&D partnerships) increased from 1,760 in 1990 to 4,600 in 1995. The average rate of increase remained stable at about 61 percent (UNCTAD, 1997b). Such agreements have broadened the firms' networking activities and strengthened their role as primary global actors.
- Firms operating across borders directly employ more than 73 million people in nonagricultural activities worldwide (Dunning and Sauvant, 1996). Total foreign employment of the world's fifty largest public companies amounted to 2.27 million in 1997. The ratio of foreign-to-total employment was 39 percent (see Table 6.3). ABB, Nestlé, and GE, for example, employ overseas respectively.
- Cross-border mergers and acquisitions (M&A) have become a major mode of investment by major corporations. Mergers and acquisitions in 1998 surpassed $2.4 trillion, 5 percent above 1997's total. About one fourth of M&As were cross-border.
- Service firms have become increasingly involved in the globalization of the word economy. In entertainment, food, services, securities, banking, and telecommunications, firms such as Disney, McDonald's, Merrill Lynch, Citicorp, and AT&T have become common names, if not local players, in many parts of the world. This trend is expected to intensify because the share of FDI in services constitutes about 50 percent of the world's total stock of FDI (Sauvant and Mallampally, 1996).

THE GLOBAL FIRM: A DEFINITION

The literature on the evolution of firms operating in the world economy is intriguing, yet it is full of contradictory and confusing terminology. This applies to both traditional and contemporary research on the determinants, motives, and consequences of the activities of these firms. In this section, an attempt is made to advance a working definition of global corporations. A brief illustration of prevailing perspectives among practitioners and scholars is presented in the following sections.

TABLE 6.2. Number of Parent Corporations and Foreign Affiliates by Area and Country

Area/economy	Parent corporations based in country	Foreign affiliates
Developed countries	**43,442**	**96,620**
Western Europe	**33,302**	**63,789**
European Union	**27,846**	**54,875**
Austria	897	2,362
Belgium	1,110	2,000
Denmark	5,000	2,012
Finland	1,200	1,200
France	2,078	9,351
Germany	7,569	11,445
Greece	—	798
Ireland	39	1,040
Italy	966	1,630
Netherlands	1,608	2,259
Portugal	1,350	5,809
Spain	822	6,809
Sweden	4,148	5,551
United Kingdom	1,059	2,609
Other Western Europe	**5,456**	**8,914**
Iceland	50	40
Norway	900	3,100
Switzerland	4,506	5,774
Japan	**4,231**	**3,014**
United States	**3,379**	**18,901**
Other developed	**2,530**	**10,915**
Australia	485	371
Canada	1,695	4,541
New Zealand	232	1,949
South Africa	118	2,055
Developing countries	**9,323**	**230,696**
Africa	**32**	**330**
Ethiopia	—	21
Swaziland	30	134
Zambia	2	175
Latin America and the Caribbean	**1,109**	**21,174**
Bolivia	—	257
Brazil	797	9,322
Chile	—	2,028
Colombia	302	2,220
El Salvador	—	225
Guatemala	—	287
Mexico	—	8,420
Paraguay	—	109

Area/economy	Parent corporations based in country	Foreign affiliates
Latin America and the Caribbean	**1,109**	**21,174**
Peru	10	1,183
Uruguay	—	123
Developing Europe	**1,482**	**6,045**
Croatia	70	353
Slovenia	1,300	1,792
Former Yugoslavia	112	3,900
South, East, and Southeast Asia	**6,242**	**199,469**
China	379	145,000
Hong Kong, China	500	5,067
India	187	1,416
Indonesia	313	3,472
Korea, Republic of	4,806	3,878
Pakistan	57	758
Philippines	—	14,802
Singapore	—	18,154
Sri Lanka	—	139
Taiwan, Province of China	—	5,733
Thailand	—	1,050
West Asia	**449**	**2,486**
Bahrain	—	538
Oman	92	351
Saudi Arabia	—	1,461
Turkey	357	136
Central Asia	**9**	**1,041**
Kyrgyzstan	9	1,401
The Pacific	**—**	**151**
Fiji	—	151
Central and Eastern Europe	**842**	**121,601**
Albania	—	1,280
Belarus	—	393
Bulgaria	26	918
Czech Republic	660	44,062
Czech and Slovak Federal Republic	26	—
Estonia	—	3,170
Hungary	66	15,205
Lithuania	12	1,624
Poland	58	32,889
Romania	20	6,193
Russian Federation	—	7,793
Slovakia	—	5,560
Ukraine	—	2,514
World	**53,607**	**448,917**

Source: UNCTAD, 1998b.

TABLE 6.3. The World's Fifty Largest Public Companies (Ranked by Market Value As of June 30, 1998, in Millions of U.S. Dollars)

Company (country)	Market value	Fiscal 1997 sales	Foreign 1997 sales	Employment 1997 foreign	Employment 1997 total	Total 1997 profit
General Electric (United States)	296,073	90,840	28,160	111,000	276,000	8,203
Microsoft (United States)	267,044	14,484	4,780	8,953	28,028	4,490
Coca-Cola (United States)	211,129	18,868	12,425	19,500	29,500	4,129
Royal Dutch/Shell (Netherlands/ UK)	187,763	128,690	69,456	65,000a	105,000	7,791
Exxon (United States)	174,640	120,279	107,101	50,000[e]	80,000	8,460
Merck (United States)	159,866	23,637	5,874[b]	20,000	53,800	4,614
Pfizer (United States)	141,906	12,504	5,637	28,500	49,200	2,213
Wal-Mart Stores (United States)	136,069	117,958	7,517	105,000	825,000	3,526
Nippon Telegraph & Telephone (Japan)	131,863	72,381	—[c]	52,000	230,000	2,031
Intel (United States)	125,716	25,070	18,930	31,277	63,700	6,945
Procter & Gamble (United States)	122,114	37,154	17,928[f]	100,000	106,000	3,415
Bristol-Myers Squibb (United States)	114,397	16,701	7,875	26,000	53,600	3,205
Lucent Technologies (United States)	109,140	26,360	4,553	29,878	134,000	541
Berkshire Hathaway (United States)	108,664	10,430	—[c]	—[c]	38,000	1,901
IBM (United States)	108,257	78,508	45,845	126,000	269,465	6,093
Glaxo Wellcome (UK)	107,944	13,194	13,000[e]	40,209[e]	53,068	3,055
Novartis (Switzerland)	102,698	21,315	13,437	45,776	87,239	3,565
American International Group (United States)	102,147	30,602	16,461	33,000	40,000	3,332
Johnson & Johnson (United States)	99,505	22,629	10,872	47,000	90,500	3,303
Toyota Motor (Japan)	98,730	98,741	46,731	43,611	150,736	3,112
Philip Morris (United States)	95,656	72,055	32,142	94,659[j]	152,000	6,310
Cisco Systems (United States)	95,427	6,440	864	2,000	11,000	1,049
AT&T (United States)	92,782	51,319	712	6,000	128,000	4,638
Unilever Group (Netherlands/UK)	85,502	48,721	27,206[a]	196,000	270,000	5,568
British Petroleum (UK)	84,896	71,858	44,038	37,600	55,650	4,080
DuPont (United States)	84,286	45,079	21,888	49,000	98,000	2,405
Nestlé (Switzerland)	84,074	47,851	47,551	219,442	225,808	2,762
Allianz (Germany)	80,191	51,032	24,841	36,377	73,290	1,608
UBS (Switzerland)	79,452	9,044	3,572	8,300	27,611	(89)

Company (country)	Market value	Fiscal 1997 sales	Foreign 1997 sales	Employment 1997 foreign	total	Total 1997 profit
British Telecommunications (UK)	79,172	25,860	2,967	4,200	127,500	3,405
Lloyds TSB Group (UK)	75,931	22,409	874	12,130[d]	92,655	3,841
Deutsche Telekom (Germany)	75,270	37,545	2,540	27,055	76,141	1,837
SBC Communications (United States)	73,554	24,856	—[c]	—[c]	118,340	1,474
NationsBank (United States)	73,458	21,734	826	6,882	90,500	3,077
Eli Lilly (United States)	73,367	8,518	3,106	15,100	31,100	(385)
Walt Disney (United States)	71,625	22,473	4,605	—[c]	108,000	1,966
Ford Motor (United States)	71,566	153,627	48,046	174,105	363,892	6,920
Bell Atlantic (United States)	70,827	30,194	1,764	10,600	141,089	2,455
Travelers Group (United States)	69,722	37,609	4,876	20,607	68,900	3,104
France Telecom (France)	68,800	26,057	2,353	7,944	169,873	2,469
Roche Holding (Switzerland)	68,757	12,829	12,619	41,832	73,348	2,926
SmithKline Beecham (UK)	67,964	12,889	11,789	47,000	55,400	1,862
American Home Products (United States)	67,927	14,196	5,917	29,290	60,523	2,043
Citicorp (United States)	67,389	21,616	11,814	54,800	93,700	3,591
Schering-Plough (United States)	67,222	6,778	2,627	12,300	22,700	1,444
SAP (Germany)	66,466	3,345	2,707	5,547[a]	12,856	513
BellSouth (United States)	66,460	20,561	1,350	43,734	81,000	3,261
HSBC Holdings (UK)	66,132	37,635	25,592	83,690[a,f]	132,969	5,520
Gillette (United States)	63,894	10,062	6,380	33,000	44,000	1,427
Chase Manhattan (United States)	63,742	30,381	6,988	10,453	69,033	3,708
TOTAL	$5,157,176	$1,964,918	$799,136	2,272,351	5,837,714	$168,713

Sources: The Wall Street Journal, September 28, 1998, R27; companies' 1997 annual reports; UNCTAD 1998b; and news releases.

[a] Not including European nationalities
[b] Sales outside North America
[c] Data on foreign sales or foreign employment are either suppressed to avoid disclosure or they are not available
[d] Foreign employment as of July 1997
[e] 1996 figures
[f] 1998 figures

TABLE 6.4. Value of the Gross Product of Foreign Affiliates and Their Share in GDP, by Region, 1982, 1990, and 1994 (Billions of Dollars and Percentage of GDP)

Region	Gross product of foreign affiliates			Gross product of foreign affiliates as percentage of GDP		
	1982	1990	1994	1982	1990	1994
Developed countries	**403**	**1098**	**1099**	**5.1**	**6.7**	**5.4**
Western Europe	179	607	610	6.0	8.7	7.9
European Union	164	570	568	5.7	8.6	7.7
Other Western Europe	15	37	43	9.9	10.7	11.0
North America	177	407	392	5.1	6.7	5.2
Other developed countries	47	84	97	3.4	2.4	1.9
Developing countries	**150**	**283**	**445**	**6.0**	**7.0**	**9.1**
Africa	15	28	32	4.4	7.4	8.8
Latin America and the Caribbean	59	101	162	7.6	9.3	10.3
Asia	74	151	248	5.6	5.9	8.6
West Asia	30	39	36	6.7	4.0	6.7
South, East, and Southeast Asia	44	112	211	5.0	7.0	9.0
Oceania	1.1	1.7	1.9	27.5	32.3	24.9
Central and Eastern Europe	**0.1**	**2.3**	**12.6**	**0.1**	**1.1**	**2.3**
World	**553**	**1383**	**1557**	**5.2**	**6.7**	**6.0**

Source: UNCTAD, 1997b.

TABLE 6.5. Value of Exports of Foreign Affiliates, Their Share in Total Sales, and Exports to Affiliated Firms, by Region, 1982 and 1994 (Billions of Dollars and Percentage)

Region	Exports of foreign affiliates		Exports of foreign affiliates as percentage of total sales of foreign affiliates		Exports to affiliated firms as percentage of total exports of foreign affiliates	
	1982	1994	1982	1994	1982	1994
Developed countries	**491**	**1255**	**27.7**	**25.1**	**44.2**	**55.1**
Western Europe	325	896	41.4	31.6	45.8	55.6
European Union	266	793	37.1	29.7	50.3	50.2
Other Western Europe	59	103	86.5	64.1	25.0	97.0
North America	140	288	18.1	16.5	42.7	55.7
Other developed countries	26	71	12.3	17.0	33.8	45.9
Developing countries	**242**	**585**	**38.1**	**35.6**	**49.5**	**55.8**
Africa	23	15	21.5	9.4	73.3	68.0
Latin America and the Caribbean	109	139	42.6	24.3	47.8	59.6
Asia	110	431	41.3	47.9	46.2	54.2
West Asia	15	23	20.4	20.5	84.7	47.1
South, East, and Southeast Asia	95	408	49.3	2.0	40.2	47.1
Oceania	—	—	—	—	—	—
Central and Eastern Europe	—	—	—	—	—	—
World	**732**	**1850**	**30.5**	**27.7**	**46.0**	**55.3**

Source: UNCTAD, 1997b.

Practitioner's Perspective

David Whitman (1994, p. 136), chairman of Whirlpool, has pointed out that "in fact, most international manufacturers aren't truly global," underscoring the fact that in the business world an adequate conceptualization of a global firm is not readily available. Similarly, even though many trade and academic publications consider Unilever a leading global firm, it introduces itself as " 'international,' not 'global' " (Unilever, 1996b, p. 2). P&G and Honda, on the other hand, provide examples of global firms that are more advanced in their thinking about globalization than the concept originally introduced by Levitt (1983). Both firms regard "globalization" as a term that denotes, among other things, an ability to introduce products that match the needs of each market. This is in contrast to Levitt's and other management scholars' prevailing definition of globalization as marketing "the same things in the same way everywhere."

In practice, there are considerable variations in the way that firms perceive themselves. A review of the popular business literature and annual reports of major companies produces the classifications described in the following sections.

National Firm

Companies in this category regard themselves as national companies that operate internationally to serve their global clients (e.g., Lloyds, NationsBank). For example, in a letter to the author (August 13, 1997), the Director of Corporate Affairs of NationsBank stated, "our aim is *not* to become a 'global money center bank' but, rather, a national U.S. bank with *global capabilities.*"

International Firm

Several companies, such as Microsoft and Unilever, view themselves as international rather than global organizations. Unilever, however, differentiates between an international and a global firm in terms of strategy. Tokyo Electric Power Co. regards itself as an international company with a global perspective.

Firms That Are Becoming Global

Firms in this category make a conscious effort to be globally integrated. Companies such as GM, Whirlpool, and Boeing seem to be sensitive to their economic and societal roles and appear to know what it takes to be a global firm. Despite their deep and extensive international experience, these firms believe that globalization is a major challenge. They have initiated profound changes and are in the process of becoming global firms.

Transition to a Global Firm

Firms such as Northern Telecom view themselves as MNCs that have made the transition to global corporation. ING, for example, acknowledges that it is an MNC with Dutch roots. The transition to global organization is a possibility in the near future.

Local Player

Firms in this category (e.g., British Telecommunications and HSBC Holdings) emphasize their commitment to the local markets where they operate. They use the terms "international" and "global" interchangeably. These organizations, in their operations and design, seem to fit the concept of the transnational corporation as it is advanced in the scholarly literature.

Global Firm

Several companies (e.g., ABB, Honda, Nestlé, Novartis, P&G, Roche, Siemens) perceive themselves as global corporations in both their practices and orientations. Their commitment to global economic integration and to the welfare of their communities—wherever they operate—is highlighted in their literature. Most of the academic literature refers to ABB, Gillette, and Nestlé as leading global corporations. There is a need, however, to study other companies such as Caterpillar, DaimlerChrysler, Danfoss, and P&G. The top managers of these companies appear to have internalized the principles of globalization. While most of the academic literature still advocates "think globally and act locally," DaimlerChrysler and Danfoss, instead, espouse "think and act globally."

Scholar's Perspective

Scholarly literature pertaining to the classification of firms operating across borders has its own contradictions, too. Some experts have a tendency to refer to MNCs as global corporations (e.g., Simon, 1997; Pearce and Robinson, 1997). Others use MNCs to mean transnational corporations (Amin, 1997; Dunning, 1996; Jones, 1996; McGrew, 1992). Dunning, for example, defines TNCs as "enterprises which own or control value-added activities in two or more countries." Nevertheless, Dunning, through his work with UNCTAD's Division on Transnational Corporations and Investment, has publicized the term TNC, and it has since been adopted by the UN and many scholars (e.g., Buckley; Lecraw; Vernon, etc.).

Perhaps this adaptation induces many in academic circles, specifically those in areas other than international business, to use the term loosely to mean simply a corporation that combines the benefits of local responsiveness with global efficiency in its conduct. Others, however, utilize the term TNC to imply stateless firms. Teeple (1995, p. 64), for example, defines TNCs as corporations that are "expanding internationalization of their production and decline of a meaningful home base or domestic market."

Generally, scholarly literature on the organizational forms of corporations operating on a global scale can be classified in terms of orientation, strategy, structure, and networking and alliances.

Orientation

Perlmutter (1992) contrasts provincial companies with MNCs. He argues that executives perceive that the degree of a firm's multinationality is positively related to the firm's long-term viability. He classifies firms according to their executives' attitudes toward building an MNC: ethnocentric (home-country attitude), polycentric (host-country orientation), and geocentric (world orientation).

Bartlett and Ghoshal (1992) perceive companies according to their prevailing strategic mentalities. Their typology is widely adopted in the literature. Companies are identified in the following ways:

1. *International.* Managers think of their company's overseas operations as primarily to support the domestic parent company by increasing sales or supplying materials.
2. *Multinational.* Managers of such companies recognize and emphasize the differences among national markets and operating environments. Therefore, these companies design their products and strategies to meet demands in each national market.
3. *Global.* Managers of global firms view the world as their unit of analysis. They assume that national tastes and preferences are more similar than different across nations. Thus, a global company produces and markets standardized products for the world market.
4. *Transnational.* Companies are responsive to local needs and simultaneously retain global efficiency.

Strategy

Some scholars view organizations in terms of their strategies. Hout, Porter, and Rudden (1992) classify companies operating in international markets as either multidomestic (a company that allows its subsidiaries to compete independently in different domestic markets) or global (a firm that utilizes its entire worldwide system of production and market position against the competition).

Structure

Bartlett and Ghoshal (1992) attribute differences in companies operating abroad to their administrative heritage, defined as a firm's history and its embedded management culture. They have introduced three forms:

- *Decentralized federation.* Companies adopt decentralized strategic decisions. European-based companies have utilized this organizational configuration. Subsidiaries are given considerable autonomy and each focuses primarily on its local market. This is similar to the multinational strategic mentality.
- *Coordinated federation.* Headquarters retain formal systems of control while delegating responsibility to subsidiaries. U.S.-

based firms have traditionally utilized this form of organization, which is associated with an international strategy.
- *Centralized hub.* The headquarters makes key strategic decisions. This form of organization is no longer common among Japanese-based firms and is instead associated with global strategy.

Bartlett and Ghoshal acknowledge that since the 1980s there has been a transformation from traditional multinational, international, and global forms toward a transnational organization. That is, companies seek to achieve efficiency, responsiveness, and learning capabilities simultaneously.

Networking and Alliances

Waters (1995) claims that TNCs represent regional rather than global organizations and there is an emerging form of an organization that is an "alliance"—an arrangement between firms that may involve equity swaps, technology transfer, production licensing, market sharing, etc. Dicken (1994) describes an emerging organizational form—complex global corporation, which is characterized by integrated network configurations and a capacity to develop flexible coordinating processes. Mair (1997) and Ohmae (1990) suggest that a global organization operates in a "borderless world" that does not focus primarily on its home country. It develops strong international links to such a degree that it does not display a national identity in its relationships and conduct.

WHAT IS A GLOBAL COMPANY?

Global organizations play a crucial role in internalizing the challenge of globalization. Truly global organizations have specific attributes and orientations that are reflected in specific practices. Some executives, however, still have vague ideas about globalization. For example, Unilever considers itself an international rather than a global corporation (Unilever, 1996b). Unilever views the global organization in terms of marketing strategy—selling the same product all over the world. British Steel, Walt Disney, General Dynamic, Peugeot, Merck, Boeing, and DuPont are among the many firms that are identified as global organizations by *Fortune* magazine (Kahn, 1998). All have international involvement, but such does not constitute "global" reach when the overriding goal is only to further profit. In addition, many of the firms *Fortune* lists still think of themselves as American, Japanese, British, or German. For instance, Gillette was recognized in *Fortune* as a shining example of a successful global organization. However, its CEO, Al Zeieh, appeared to indicate indirectly that having a high share of non-U.S. citizens in the management of Gillette is a matter of convenience rather than conviction. Recently, he stated that "We have to get the U.S. passport population up among our managers. Now I get a note every time we hire an American" (Zeieh, 1996). It is this orientation and a specific national identity that make it difficult to consider firms as global based only on their sales volume and/or geographic growth. Certainly, a passionate attachment to a nation-state makes the idea of being global only an illusion. To be global, a company must be a world citizen. That is, it must have a culture that is not a reflection of any particular country's culture. Its allegiances and orientations center on customers wherever they are. Likewise, it must remain close to the local market where it operates. A global organization pursues "thinking and acting" globally with exceptional flexibility and sensitivity to the peculiarity of each market and is willing to cope with the challenge of internalizing similarities while accommodating differences. Furthermore, a global firm considers improving the quality of life for its constituencies as a source of competitive advantage. Specifically, global corporations have three major characteristics—inner security, inner direction, and inner coherence:

- *Inner security.* Confidence in the ability to compete and shape the future allows global corporations to expand, recruit personnel from all over the world, and engage in various experimentations that further innovation and strengthen revitalization (e.g., DaimlerChrysler, Ford, P&G).
- *Inner direction.* Clarity of mission, vision, and foresight permit global corporations to pursue networking on a global

scale, and to engage in mergers, acquisitions, and other types of alliances (e.g., ABB, Honda).

- *Inner coherence.* Strength of culture, commitment to clearly defined purposes, and a strong sense of self allow global corporations to expand worldwide and strengthen their role as local players wherever they operate (e.g., Nestlé, ABB).

Companies that exhibit these characteristics usually have the following:

- Senior managers with extensive international experience and/or different national backgrounds. For example, ABB top executives are Swiss, Swedish, and German.
- A mission that clearly asserts global necessity and global integration. P&G's slogan and mission convey the message of a truly global corporation. Its slogan "We're at home around the world" deemphasizes national identity and culture. In addition, its mission, "We will provide products of superior quality and value that improve the lives of the world's consumers," reinforces its slogan and global involvement.
- Networks and alliances that encompass entities across several boundaries. In 1997, Siemens had more than 400 manufacturing sites located in 190 countries. It recognizes that the need for innovative solutions for its customers requires synergy to marshall resources and form strategic alliances with companies around the globe (e.g., with IBM, Toshiba, and Motorola). In fact, Siemens does not focus on national boundaries, but sets its sights on dynamic regional markets around the world.
- Subsidiaries that have ultimate authority in deciding how to run their operations. These subsidiaries are managed with the utmost concern for the interest and benefit of the local market and the whole organization. Honda and BT are examples of corporations that adopt this outlook.
- Managers who are skilled in balancing their behavior between localization and globalization. The mix of these managers must reflect the global aspirations of the firm's operations (e.g., Nestlé, ABB, Caterpillar).

- Strategies that enhance the firm's involvement globally while strengthening world economic integration (e.g., to have R&D and production sites worldwide).
- Strong commitment to being a local player. Worldcom is looking to be a local player in all markets, close to customers, and sensitive to cultural nuances to enhance the quality of people's lives.
- A commitment to seeking and utilizing opportunities anywhere in the world. In addition, a global corporation views the whole globe as a source of new ideas and technological breakthroughs.

This discussion highlights several dimensions for measuring whether or not a company is global. In this section, two dimensions are utilized: responsiveness to local markets and commitment to the world economy (treating the globe as the market while downplaying any national identity). Most of the scholars in international management and organization focus on "foreign product diversity" and "foreign sales as percentage of total sales" (Stopford and Wells, 1972), or "pressure for global integration" and "pressures for local responsiveness" (Prahalad and Doz, 1987) in classifying firms. These classifications are academically useful but do not reflect the reality of firms' involvement and commitment to globalization. Firms do not necessarily acquire global identities by going through specific stages. Likewise, globalization identity is not a result of outside pressures. It is an orientation that corporations translate into actions on a global scale: commitment and loyalty to customers and to a global marketplace. In this book, the two adopted dimensions represent what corporations actually pursue in their operations worldwide and capture the essence and meaning of globalization at the firm level (see Chapter 1). Figure 6.1 illustrates a profile of firms along the two dimensions. Below is a brief description of each:

1. *Domestic firm.* A firm that is operating only in a local market. It does not wish to be a player on the global scene. It is important to mention that in today's global environment, there is no company that is not affected, directly or indirectly, by events in the world economy. In almost all the grocery stores in the United States, for example, the price of olive oil skyrocketed during the 1995-1997 period due to bad seasons in Italy and Spain, the principal exporters of olive oil.

2. *Domestic company with some international involvement.* A company, on occasion, gets involved in some international interactions (e.g., filling an international order, importing, etc.). This type of company, while not interested in being a global player, handles each international order with some sensitivity to satisfying the client's needs. NationsBank in the United States is an example of such a firm. NationsBank describes its primary goal in its international activities as an attempt "to serve the financial needs of our domestic clients who are engaged in international business activities. We accomplish this goal by providing clients a broad range of corporate finance, capital markets, and transaction-oriented products and services from a network of offices around the world" (NationsBank, 1997, p. 1).
3. *MNC.* The company views itself as a collection of relatively autonomous subsidiaries operating in two or more countries. Each subsidiary is managed relatively independently to maximize involvement in the local market. There is no attempt, however, by the headquarters (HQ) to play a significant role in advocating issues that enhance market integration on a global scale. ITT is an example of a corporation that operates in more than 130 countries, but that gives its subsidiaries substantial autonomy.
4. *International firm.* This type of company has experience in the international market and values its international operations to a degree. The HQ, however, manages most of the international operations and relations. The company, because of its senior managers' orientation, type of business, or the extent of its operations, does not show any sensitivity to variations in international markets. Toys "R" Us and Tokyo Electric Power are examples of such companies.
5. *Becoming global.* Companies at this stage understand the globalization imperative and seek to maximize their commitment to the global market and to the need to be responsive to local market variations. David Whitman (1994, p. 142), chairman of Whirlpool, asserts that "We've made a lot of progress, [but] we are not yet a truly global organization. It will take more time to become one." Similarly, Jack Smith (1997), chairman of General Motors, states "to succeed in the growing markets of tomorrow, GM needs to be a truly global organization."

6. *TNC.* Transnational corporations seek to capitalize on meeting local demands while achieving economies of scale and efficiency. A typical TNC displays the highest possible flexibility in acting in each national market but has only a moderate commitment to standardize its operations. 3M manages to be responsive to local markets while attempting to maintain a global outlook.
7. *Worldwide company.* This is a company that has, for the most part, largely standardized its products and operations all over the world. It highlights similarities among countries in terms of tastes and demands, and minimizes differences. Efficient operations are given the highest priority in its conduct. Bayer is an example of a company that is highly integrated worldwide and seeks to continuously improve its operations.
8. *In transition to a global firm.* A firm in this category is setting the stage for being sensitive to the peculiarities of local markets and seeking an active involvement in the global economy. The company, however, has a long way to go to become a global corporation. Northern Telecom (1997, p. 5) has declared that it made "the transition to a global corporation offering a broad portfolio of network solutions to a growing and diverse group of customers."
9. *Global firm.* Global corporations are those that internalize globalization's challenges. These corporations have a culture that reconciles, in their mission and orientations, contradictions that are common among TNCs and MNCs. These companies de-emphasize boundaries in their conduct and view the world, rather than any country, as their market. Therefore, in their orientations and conduct, they do not exhibit an obsession with a national culture or politics. More important, commitment to the quality of the lives of their customers in every part of the world is considered a source of competitive advantage. Global corporations seek to translate "thinking and acting globally" into a reality.

MAKING GLOBALIZATION WORK

Global firms, such as P&G, develop key ingredients for operating globally. CEO Edwin Artzt asserts that P&G is a truly global

FIGURE 6.1. Global Firm Matrix

company, as more than half of its business comes from overseas and it serves more than 140 countries with over 300 brands. More important, the company has more than 100 plants and headquarters operations in nearly sixty countries. Its ingredients for winning globally are (see Pepper, 1991):

1. *Understanding consumer needs.* P&G delicately develops an understanding of consumer habits, practices, demographics, and preferences. Some basic consumer needs (e.g., desire for attractive complexion, cavity-free teeth) do not vary. Other needs do vary across countries or regions. For example, in the Middle East there is a particular need for diapers that are not too bulky or too tight fitting and for promotional materials that are designed specifically for that region.
2. *Fast flow of superior quality products and superior advertising to communicate product benefits.* P&G designs its product testing and development plans to expand what works worldwide faster than ever. It uses superior technology to produce the highest quality products and communicates performance advantages through effective promotion programs.

3. *Developing sound strategies.* P&G takes the right amount of time and involves the right people to develop sound strategies, which is critical to its global success.
4. *Having the right structures and systems.* Over the past fifteen years, P&G has adopted a flexible structure to facilitate the decision-making process at three levels:

   - Local markets. A general manager heads each country.
   - Regional. A president heads each region (e.g., Europe, Far East, North America, and Latin America).
   - Global. Develops and reviews goals, plans, and strategies, at all three levels, with feedback and communication among the three.

5. *Having clear values and superior personnel.* Senior managers at P&G believe that competing effectively in today's global environment requires stronger personal leadership, combined with openness to the ideas of others; deep and fast communication from top to bottom; and high standards of professionalism and leadership. Its values and principles are communicated to its employees and other stockholders, and these values and principles are constantly reinforced in practice. Most important, the structure of its top management team reflects broad international experience.

BENEFITS OF BEING GLOBAL

Global corporations think of everything they do in terms of the entire world. They are not limited in their thinking and scope of operations to any single market irrespective of its size. Certain benefits can be realized; some are immediate and others result from broader involvement, creative cultures, and innovative approaches. P&G (see Pepper, 1991) achieves three benefits:

1. *Capitalizes on ideas everywhere.* P&G manages to bring better products and concepts to consumers by tapping into the best ideas of its human resources in each part of the world and transferring these ideas, on time, to other markets.

2. *Produces stronger world-class technology.* P&G capitalizes on its size and world competition to invest a large portion of its sales in R&D. This allows it to develop innovative products that meet consumer needs in a creative way.
3. *Accesses the most qualified people.* P&G has more than twenty technical centers around the world and plants in more than sixty countries. It hires and attracts people from all parts of the world. Therefore, it has been able to draw on its stock of world-class talents to nurture, develop, and design competitive ideas and products.

Additional benefits that other global corporations appear to gain by globalization are:

4. *Networking.* Global firms, more than other types of firms, are able to cultivate a complex network of relationships and alliances. A global network allows ABB, Nestlé, Honda, and Toyota to effectively conduct their worldwide operations.
5. *Revitalization and growth.* Globalization offers ample opportunities for global firms to revitalize and continue growing. Worldwide competition and demand for quality and efficiency induce firms to be innovative and creative (e.g., Bertelsmann and Siemens).
6. *World citizen image.* A public image has become a crucial factor for success in the global marketplace. Global firms, with their intensive involvement in noneconomic issues and world development, get positive publicity and exposure. Instant dissemination of information and actual contact with corporations allow people all over the world to differentiate between firms that are world citizens and those that are "exploitive."

It is essential to note that global firms are not yet a widespread phenomenon. Profound transformations in practice and outlook are needed before firms can realistically call themselves global. Many managers have found it to their advantage to initiate steps to move in the global direction. Economic and political nationalism and strong attachment to company tradition and culture, however, create serious obstacles for many firms to seize global opportunities. The desire to achieve sound global practice on the part of many executives and the reality of many firms' nationalistic outlooks and identities often perpetuate the illusion of being global. Therefore, the outcome of this tension is far from clear.

Chapter 7

Structuring Global Organizations

There is a big difference between selling products in 140 countries around the world and truly planning and managing lines of business on a global basis. We believe this difference can be measured, over time, in billions of dollars in sales . . . and we're organizing ourselves to take better advantage of this opportunity.

John Pepper
Chairman and CEO, P&G, 1998

Each of the major markets around the world . . . has become more distinct. This change requires a global company to introduce products that match the needs of each unique market. . . . Honda continues to focus on meeting global business challenges while implementing autonomy for the four major regional operating areas.

Honda, *1997 Factbook*

Attali (1997) argues that for all the talk of free markets and equality among individuals, companies and bureaucracies are organized on the basis of fixed plans and strict hierarchies. He asserts that there is a need to find a compromise between democratic and authoritarian decision-making mechanisms, rather than indulging in "triumphalist rhetoric about the globalization of values" (p. 61). Attali's arguments stem from a concern for a broader role for relationships in and between societies and firms. The point he raises challenges prevailing societal and organizational arrangements. In organizational life, globalization induces unprecedented change. Alliances and networking among companies, at home and abroad, and the application of information technology give rise to boundaryless firms and contribute to the blurring of boundaries among firms. In addition, instant access to information, the changing nature of work, and the ascendancy of intellectual capital in the firm's competitiveness render strict adherence to hierarchical arrangements obsolete. Reinicke (1997) indicates that globalization represents the integration of a cross-national dimension into the very nature of the organizational structure and strategic behavior of individual companies. Likewise, globalization accelerates the regrouping and rearrangement of tasks and responsibilities within a firm in a way that facilitates flexibility, responsiveness, and agility. This chapter, therefore, deals with the organizational frameworks that the global organization utilizes to strengthen the firm's market involvement and commitment.

WHAT IS ORGANIZATIONAL STRUCTURE?

The organizational structure (generally represented by a chart) is the framework that depicts job arrangements, lines of influence, and coordination mechanisms. Simply stated, structure is the hierarchical arrangement of positions that aims at facilitating the performance of organizational activities. Since firms pursue a variety of goals and are involved in numerous activities, structure varies among organizations. Structure has four dimensions:

- *Clustering of jobs (division of labor).* This dimension revolves around job specialization, departmentalization, and line-staff relationships.
- *Influence.* This dimension reflects and depicts the lines of authority, responsibility, and control. A glance at the organizational chart easily identifies the formal authority. Nevertheless, informal authority exists but is impossible to recognize by merely looking at the organization chart.
- *Coordination.* This is a process that must be undertaken to ensure smooth operations and functions within an organization.
- *Integration.* This dimension goes beyond the function of coordination. It focuses on ensuring the plasticity and adaptability

of an organization to dynamic changes and to complex global networking and alliances.

The literature on the structuring of organizations suffers from three weaknesses. First, it generally addresses the organizational structures of firms that operate solely in a domestic market. Second, the literature that examines structure mechanisms in an international environment appears to focus on the evolution of a firm's involvement in international operations. Therefore, it limits its coverage to issues that are peculiar to each stage in the evolutionary process. Third, most of the literature overlooks the fact that firms within the same industry may have different structures and designs. Large firms, for example, may utilize various structures that better serve the needs of each of its divisions or subsidiaries. Firms often do not have a predetermined or fixed structure. Furthermore, globalization, as shown in the preceding chapters, renders many conceptualizations and models of organizations obsolete.

APPROACHES TO ORGANIZATIONAL STRUCTURE

In academia there are various approaches for structuring organizations. Though scholars generally agree that structure is influenced by organizational strategy, technology, history, size, environment, and cultural outlook, three general approaches to structuring organizations may be identified:

Configuration Approach

Mintzberg (1983) proposes that there are certain forces that help to explain why organizations adopt a particular structure. Those forces require specific coordination mechanisms. Therefore, he suggests five structural forms:

- *Simple structure*. This is a centralized structure based on direct supervision. Strategic apex is the key part in designing the organization.
- *Machine bureaucracy.* This structure is based on standardization of work processes, in which the technostructure is the key element.

- *Professional bureaucracy.* Standardization of skill is the driving force; therefore, the operating core is the key element.
- *Divisional form.* This structure is based on standardization of outputs, in which the middle line plays a key role.
- *Adhocracy.* This is an organic structure with little formalization of behavior, relying on liaison devices that encourage mutual adjustment.

Mintzberg focuses primarily on size, nature of industry, environment, power, and on the corresponding coordination mechanisms. Therefore, he is not concerned with the scope and depth of the organization's involvement in the global economy. In essence, Mintzberg's model does not remotely capture the meaning, complexity, and imperative of globalization in an organization's activities.

Administrative Heritage

Bartlett and Ghoshal (1992) argue that each company is influenced by its history and management culture. They suggest three configurations:

- *Decentralized federation (multinational).* This is common among European-based firms. Companies develop an internal culture that highlights personal relationships rather than formal structures and financial controls more than coordination of technical or operational detail. Subsidiaries are given autonomy in conducting their affairs.
- *Coordinated federation (international).* U.S.-based firms are said to adopt this model. Central management retains overall control through sophisticated management systems and special corporate staff. Subsidiaries are given freedom to adopt strategies that reflect market differences. Nevertheless, they depend on the parent company for new products, processes, and ideas.
- *Centralized hub (global).* Japan-based firms have traditionally adopted this configuration. Primary decisions and control are made at the center. Subsidiaries are assumed to implement the parent company's strategy.

Bartlett and Ghoshal indicate that these models are inadequate for meeting globalization's challenge. They propose a configuration that facilitates the achievement of efficiency, responsiveness, and learning capabilities simultaneously. They claim that the transnational form will capture the reality of a company's global involvement (dispersed, interdependent, and specialized capabilities).

Previously, Hofstede (1983) noted that even in Europe, the national environment exercises tremendous influence on the structuring of firms. He provides four possible models of organization:

- *Pyramid organization.* Found mostly in France, it is characterized by being both centralized and formal.
- *Well-oiled machine.* This type of organization is common in Germany. It is formalized but not centralized.
- *Village market.* It is neither formalized nor centralized and is found in Britain.
- *Family organization.* The firm is centralized but not formalized in this model, which prevails in India and some other countries.

Stages Model (Evolution)

The stages model was originally advanced by Stopford and Wells (1972). The authors identified "foreign product diversity" and "foreign sales as a percentage of total sales" as the two most important factors, reflecting the strategy and structural components of firms operating abroad. Phatak (1995), among others, utilized Stopford and Louis' conceptualization and suggested three forms of structure:

- *Pre-international division phase.* At this stage, a firm engaged in exporting activities utilizes different structural arrangements depending on the importance of exports in its total sales. Initially, an export manager position is established that reports to the marketing department. As the firm's exports increase and its products mature, there is a tendency to elevate the export manager position to a level equal to that of other managers. The export manager, therefore, reports to the CEO. When a firm recognizes that it could serve an international market better through production abroad, it establishes foreign subsidiaries. These subsidiaries report directly to the CEO.

- *International division structure.* A company merges all international activities into one division. The international division reports to the CEO. The head of the division supervises all subsidiaries abroad as well as related international engagements. These in turn are organized either by geography (e.g., country or region) or by product. Advocates of the stages model argue that companies that are still at the developmental stage of international business, or have limited product/geographic diversity, and small international sales, would benefit from utilizing this structure. However, this is not the case in practice. Enron, for example, has extensive international experience, broad global operations, and generates a substantial portion of its revenue from overseas operations. Nevertheless, Enron groups all its international activities into one unit, Enron International. Similarly, British Telecommunications has extensive experience abroad. However, it houses its international operations in one division, Global Communications.
- *Global structure.* At this stage, the firm has extensive international experience and a strong commitment to operating abroad. Therefore, the company is inclined to move away from a domestic-international configuration to form an integrated corporate structure. Resources and priorities are set according to worldwide opportunities and challenges. Companies at this stage are designed according to product, area, function, or a combination of these (multidimensional).

The administrative heritage and evolutionary stages models help in understanding why organizations have opted to select a particular structure over others. In addition, both approaches have been useful for focusing managers' attention on issues that are vital for achieving a firm's goals. Nevertheless, these approaches appear to offer a predictable or predetermined structure for each situation or stage. In reality, this is not the case because other factors, such as internal power structures, top management orientations, environment, and technology, among others, play significant roles in shaping decisions that lead to establishing a structure. Likewise, both approaches minimize the fact that firms in a global environment seek to optimize operations and involvement on a global scale. As a result, the firm always searches for a structure that makes it possible to realize this goal. Furthermore, in terms of global organizations, thinking and acting globally influence the selection of the means, including structure, that are deemed vital for enhancing global integration mechanisms. This point is articulated by John Pepper (1998): "The key to operating globally is to be global and local at the same time." In addition, as explained in Chapter 5, the global organization is defined as the organizational form that recognizes and internalizes the necessity and essence of being a global actor. Size and stages of involvement in a firm's international operations, therefore, are not limiting factors. Neither the size nor the scope of international operations is a sufficient measure of its being global. Small, medium, and large organizations can all be global. Therefore, the framework that was developed in Chapter 5 is quite adequate, relative to the above approaches, for representing an organization's reality. Firms are classified based on the degree of their commitment to the global market and their responsiveness to local markets. Therefore, structure will be treated in terms of the framework developed in Chapter 5.

STRUCTURE IN PRACTICE

In structuring organizations in the globalization era, companies have a wide range of organizational frameworks to choose from. Factors such as technology, size, environment, and power considerations still have a tremendous influence. Globalization, however, highlights new factors that have not only widened the existing range of alternative designs but also strengthened the flexibility, plasticity, and alterability of the structure. These factors are:

- *Centrality of customer desires in corporate priorities.* In 1998, Procter & Gamble restructured itself, moving from geographic to product lines. Its chairman, John Pepper, argues that this action enhanced P&G's ability to effectively meet market changes: "We will be able to deliver bigger innovations to consumers faster, better serve our global and local customers, and build stronger market partnerships" (Pepper, 1998). Similarly, when General Motors restructured itself in 1992, the underlying motivation was to serve customers better. As a company document describes it, "The key to GM's success was understanding the customer. GM's real competitive advantage was its ability to anticipate what customers wanted, develop it, and get it to the market fast" (see GM, n.d., p. 3).

- *Diminishing time and geographic utility as a limiting factor in corporate endeavors.* The proliferation of information technology—digital TV, the Internet—offers speedy access to cyberspace. In increasing numbers companies are utilizing cyberspace infrastructure to minimize the effect of distance in time and place, thereby improving their flexibility and speed while enhancing their integrative capacity.
- *Growing importance of alliances and networking.* This development induces firms to surrender some of their individual sovereignty while enhancing their opportunity to become more heteroarchical in their organizational structure (Dunning, 1997).
- *Global self-awareness.* The globalization process and the intensity of worldwide interactions induce firms to be sensitive to their roles beyond pure business concerns. This broader role gives firms a requisite kind of flexibility, strengthens their sense of self, and normalizes the evolution of structural overhaul. Nobuhiko Kawamoto (1997, p. 3), president and CEO of Honda, has expressed the idea succinctly: "While striving to please our individual customers, we, at Honda, also recognize the vital importance of working for society on a broader scale." These expanded roles allow global corporations to adopt different forms of structure that facilitate a maximum degree of flexibility in coping with complex demands and ever-changing environments.

Various forms of organization were discussed in Chapter 5. In this section, certain structures that are utilized by firms are introduced. It is important, however, to note that in practice three inescapable facts exist. First, a structure reflects the preference of the firm in particular circumstances. That is, structures are not exclusive designs but represent the reality of organization at a given point in time. Second, other forms of structure may emerge as organizations realize that existing structures are not serving their objectives adequately. Third, various forms of structure may be used simultaneously, especially by multidivisional organizations.

Domestic Firm

Even though the purely domestic firm is difficult to maintain, some firms do not wish to be players on the international scene or do not want to acknowledge the reality of global business. The manager or owner of such a firm is not motivated by opportunities outside the local market. The overriding purpose is control. Therefore, the structure is more likely to be a simple one. Figure 7.1 depicts the structure of a "typically" domestic firm.

Domestic Firm with Some International Involvement

This type of company does not purposely pursue globalization or even internationalization. It does, however, handle international orders to satisfy its clients' needs. NationsBank, before its merger with Bank of America, operated internationally just to serve the financial needs of its domestic customers "who are engaged in international business activities." These clients included major corporations and federal government agencies who rely on global transactions. Figure 7.2 illustrates the structure of NationsBank in 1996, which was organized according to major activities (product structure). Overseas activities were housed in the global finance division. This division provided financing and advice on corporate finance, structured and project financing, interest rate and currency risk management, and other related activities.

FIGURE 7.1. Typical Domestic Firm Structure

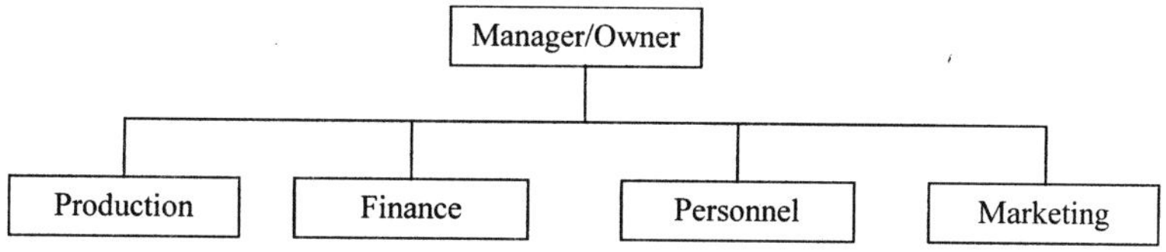

FIGURE 7.2. Domestic Company with Some International Involvement

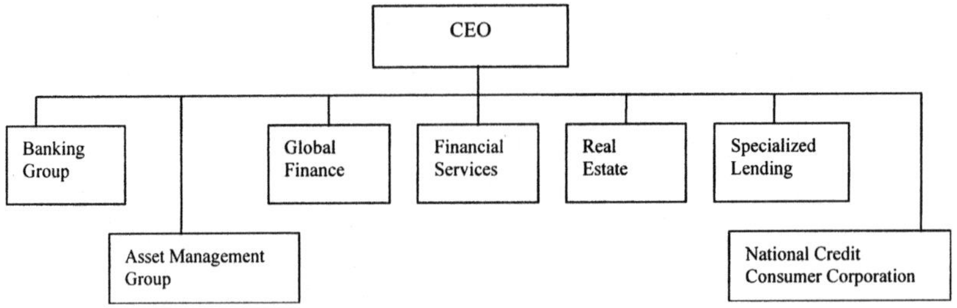

MNCs

Under this arrangement, a company is structured in such a way as to give its units and subsidiaries maximum possible autonomy in their respective markets. The HQ, however, retains control over major resource allocation and strategic decisions. Allianz, an insurance company, has grown into a "multilocal insurance group." Its 1997 corporate profile (Allianz, 1997) indicated that "Growth has been achieved in part by bringing into the Group companies that are well-positioned in their own individual markets" (p. 4). Figure 7.3 depicts the organizational structure of Allianz, which revolves around five business divisions that are arranged geographically with a major emphasis on the company's home market (Germany). The German market has two divisions: property/casualty insurance and life/health insurance. The HQ is responsible for the financial, as well as the controlling, accounting, and tax divisions.

International Firm

This is a company that is structured to facilitate its growing or potential business abroad. The HQ manages most of the overseas operations and relations. Tokyo Electric Power (TEPCO) is an example of a firm that fits this category. Figure 7.4 represents the company's structure with an international division. The international division's primary concern is the markets of China, Indonesia, and other East Asian countries. The purpose of this division is to utilize TEPCO's technology and management expertise, and to ensure profitability in international energy markets.

FIGURE 7.3. Allianz Management Structure

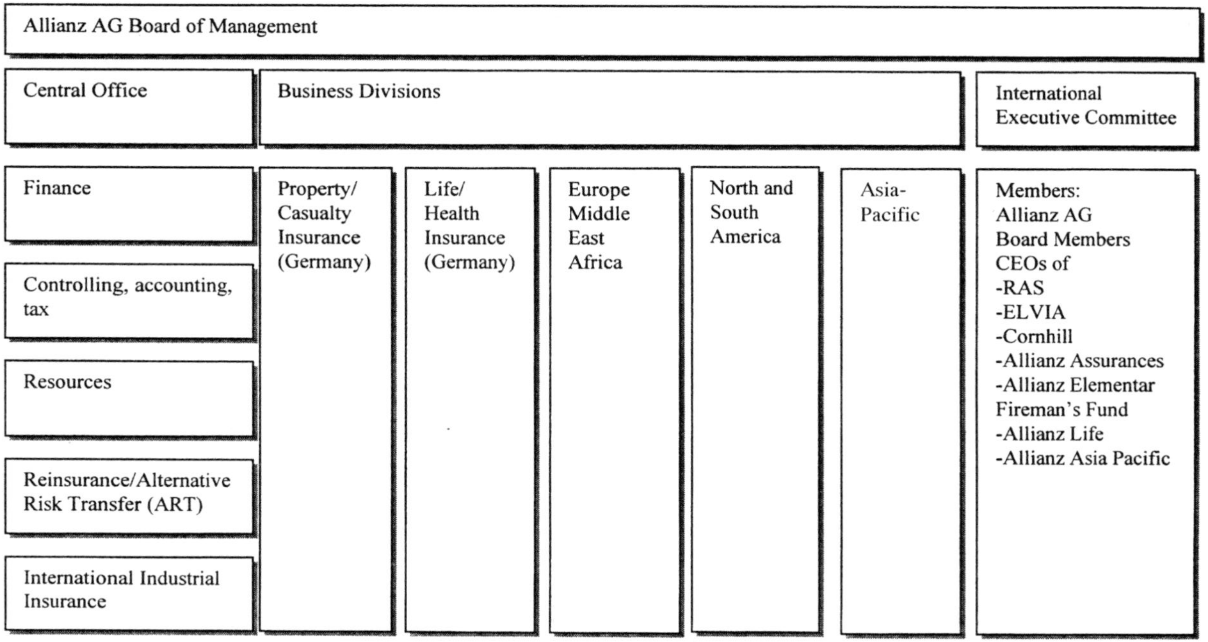

Source: Allianz, 1998.

FIGURE 7.4. TEPCO Structure 1997

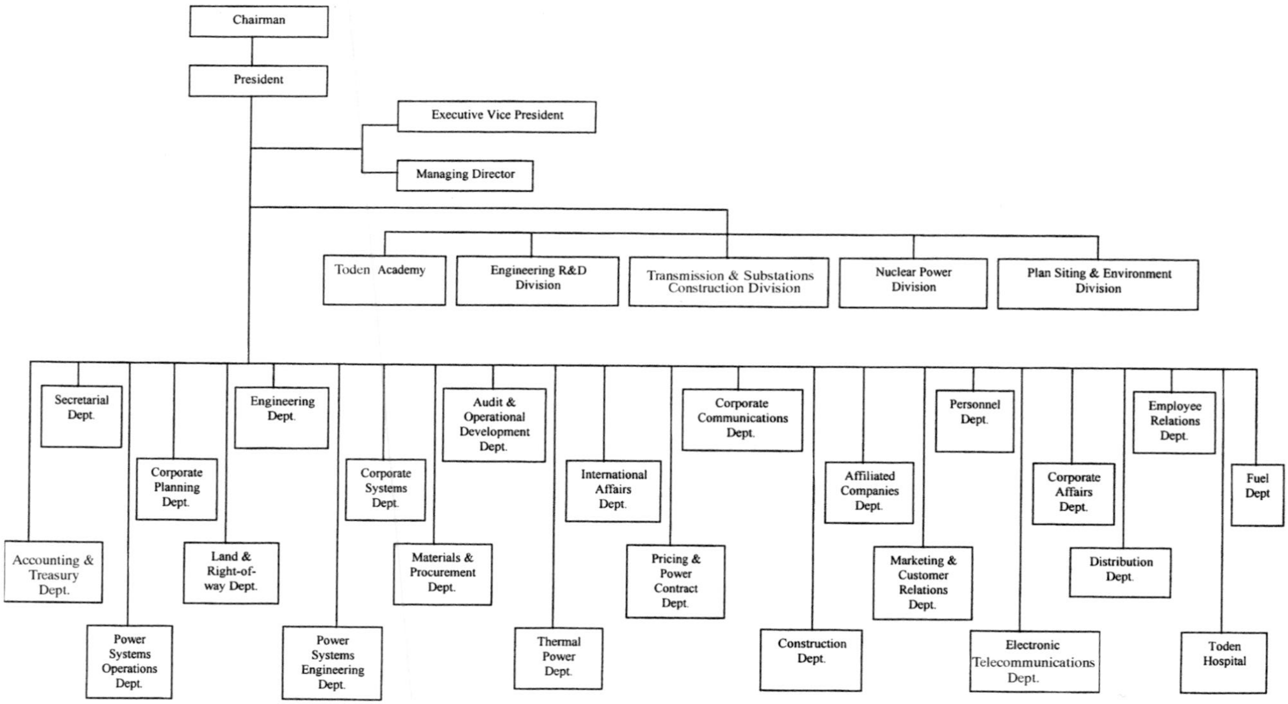

Becoming Global

Corporations in this category aim at strengthening the global market commitment while being responsive to local market variations. GM is a typical company that reorganized itself around global rather than regional platforms and processes. The decision to restructure GM in 1992 was based on achieving four business objectives: to improve common business processes and systems, to think lean and act fast, to compete on a global basis, and to grow the business in all sectors. The restructuring sought to leverage on its unrivaled global size and scope as a strategic advantage, with the automotive sectors divided into North American Operations and International Operations. The primary focus is on having common processes and systems across geographic regions and business units. GM hopes that the new structure will serve its goal of having a global reach while meeting its customers' various desires and needs. The 1992 restructuring is presented in Figure 7.5. Xerox is another corporation that realigned its structure to meet global challenges. On March 18, 1997, Xerox was restructured to pursue growth opportunities in document services, supplies, and emerging markets. In 1997, Xerox recognized market opportunities and determined to be a global corporation. Under the new structure (see Figure 7.6) Xerox has five business groups (production systems, office products, document services, channels, and

FIGURE 7.5. GM Organizational Structure

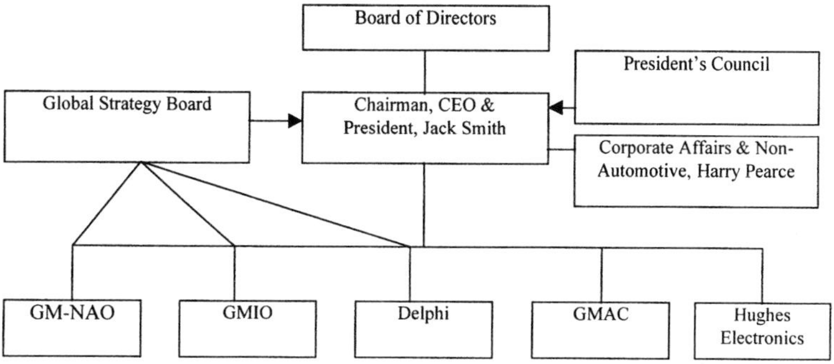

Source: GM, n.d.

FIGURE 7.6. Xerox Organizational Structure 1999

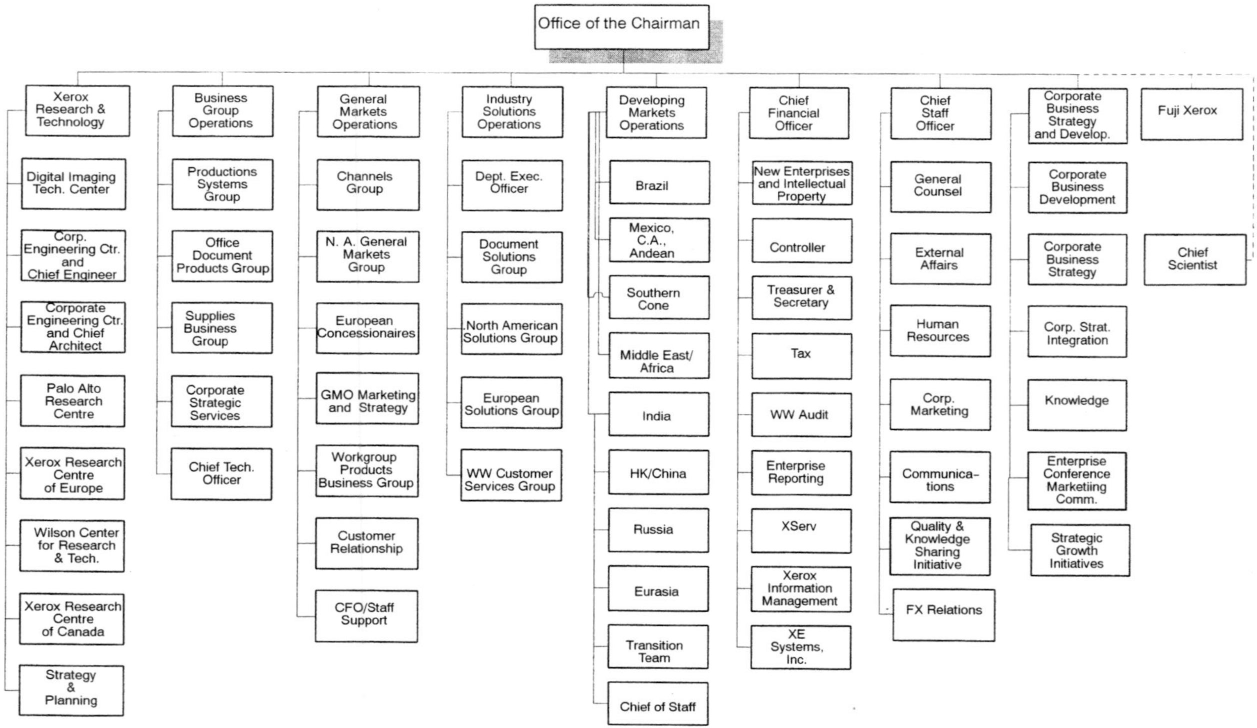

supplies). The new structure is designed simultaneously around areas, groups, and function.

Transnational

The objective of having a transnational structure is to achieve maximum flexibility in responding to each national market while maintaining commitment to the global market. 3M has organized itself to achieve this objective with three major business units—health care markets, industrial and consumer markets, and transportation, safety and specialty material markets along with international operations, corporate services and supply chair management, legal affairs, marketing, and research and development. The structure combines both functional and product structure. About forty-one companies operate abroad. All report to international operations divisions. These companies are given autonomy to conduct their business. 3M's structure is shown in Figure 7.7. Unilever is another example of a company that is structured to give autonomy to its business units and companies and to simultaneously maintain a global outlook. Unilever moved from a regional to a divisional structure (business group). The building blocks in the new structure are the individual companies, which are organized into fourteen business groups, each with a president who is accountable for the companies within his group. Each president is responsible for developing and implementing regional strategies and resource allocation. The business group presidents report to the executive committee (corporate strategic leadership). This committee, which is chaired by the Unilever cochairman, is responsible for setting priorities and goals, allocating resources, monitoring and identifying opportunities, and managing relations with the external world. Figure 7.8 presents Unilever's top management structure.

Worldwide Company

This type of firm is structured to achieve maximum operational efficiency by standardizing activities on a worldwide scale. Various companies, especially in insurance, financial services, and technology, have adopted this approach to penetrate and seize global market opportunities. The Deutsche Bank, for example, is committed to

FIGURE 7.7. 3M Organizational Structure

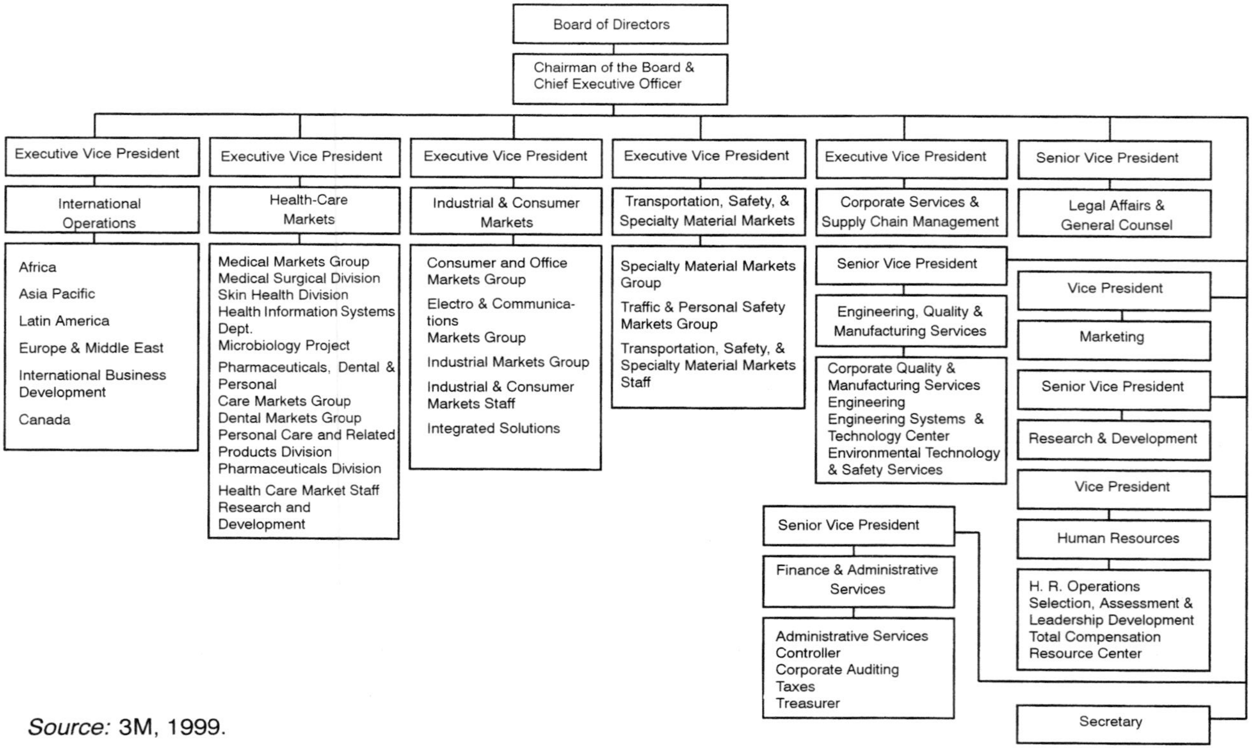

Source: 3M, 1999.

FIGURE 7.8. Unilever Top Management Structure

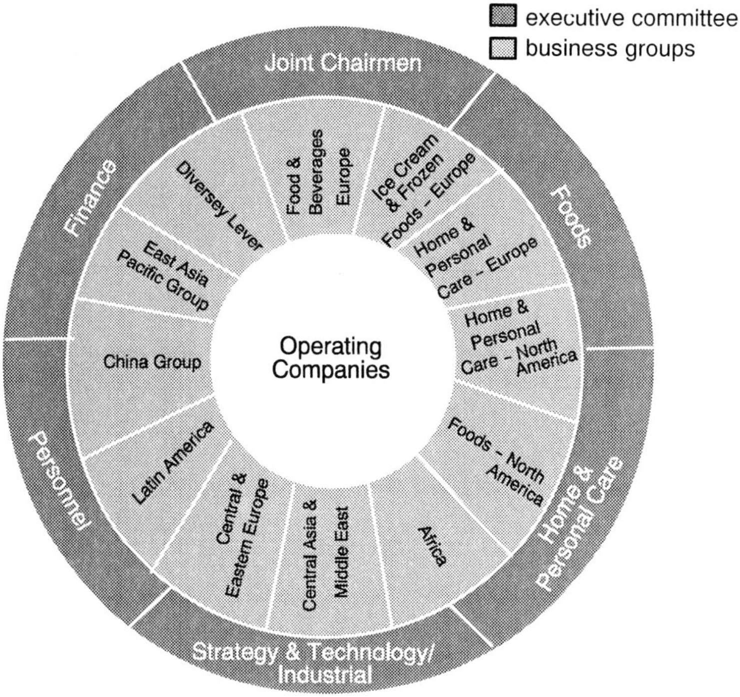

Source: Unilever, 1996c.

global operations but does not vary its services and operations. Standardization of quality of services and approaches is revered by the Deutsche Bank. Figure 7.9 shows that the bank's structure is primarily divisional (product), with the majority of international operatives reporting to the CEO of each overseas region.

British Telecommunications is a worldwide corporation that understands that the global telecom market is growing at an extraordinary pace. The company realizes that no single firm can capture all existing opportunities. Therefore, BT establishes alliances and partnerships with other companies in most regions. More important, BT gives priority to providing seamless services anywhere in the world. Figure 7.10 presents the structure of BT in 1997. BT simultaneously

FIGURE 7.9. Activities and Structure of the Deutsche Bank Group

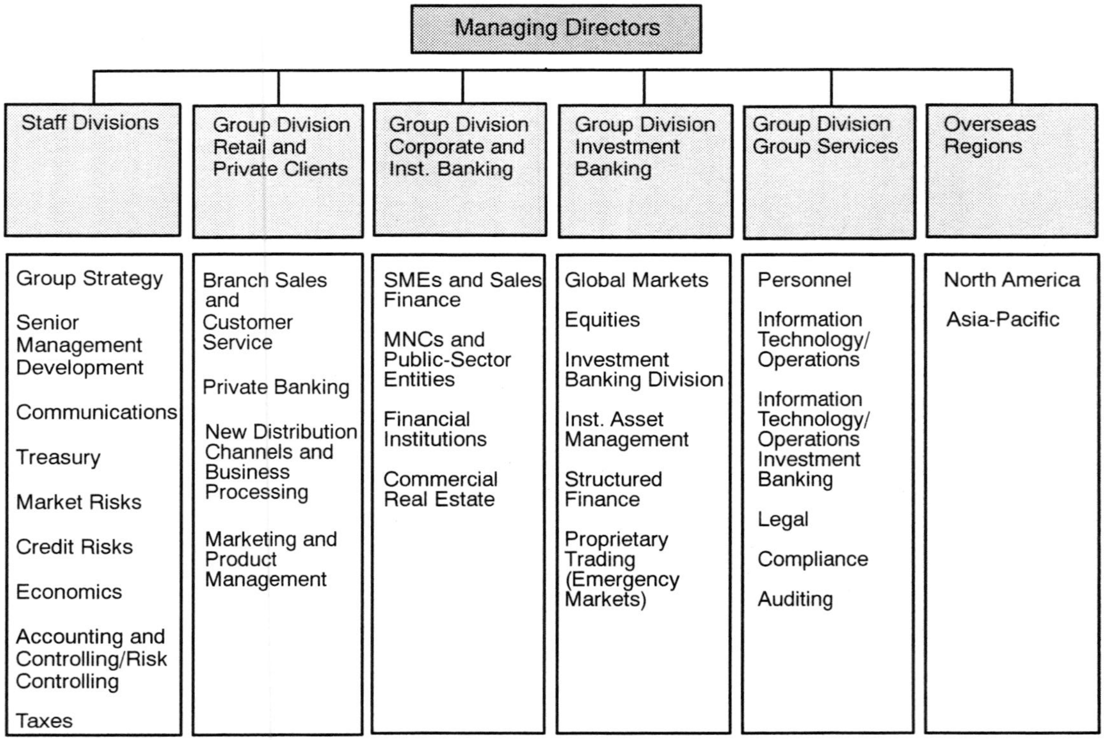
Managing Directors
Staff Divisions
Group Division Retail and Private Clients
Group Division Corporate and Inst. Banking
Group Division Investment Banking
Group Division Group Services
Overseas Regions
Group Strategy
Senior Management Development
Communications
Treasury
Market Risks
Credit Risks
Economics
Accounting and Controlling/Risk Controlling
Taxes
Branch Sales and Customer Service
Private Banking
New Distribution Channels and Business Processing
Marketing and Product Management
SMEs and Sales Finance
MNCs and Public-Sector Entities
Financial Institutions
Commercial Real Estate
Global Markets
Equities
Investment Banking Division
Inst. Asset Management
Structured Finance
Proprietary Trading (Emergency Markets)
Personnel
Information Technology/ Operations
Information Technology/ Operations Investment Banking
Legal
Compliance
Auditing
North America
Asia-Pacific

Source: Deutsche Bank, n.d.

FIGURE 7.10. BT Organization Structure

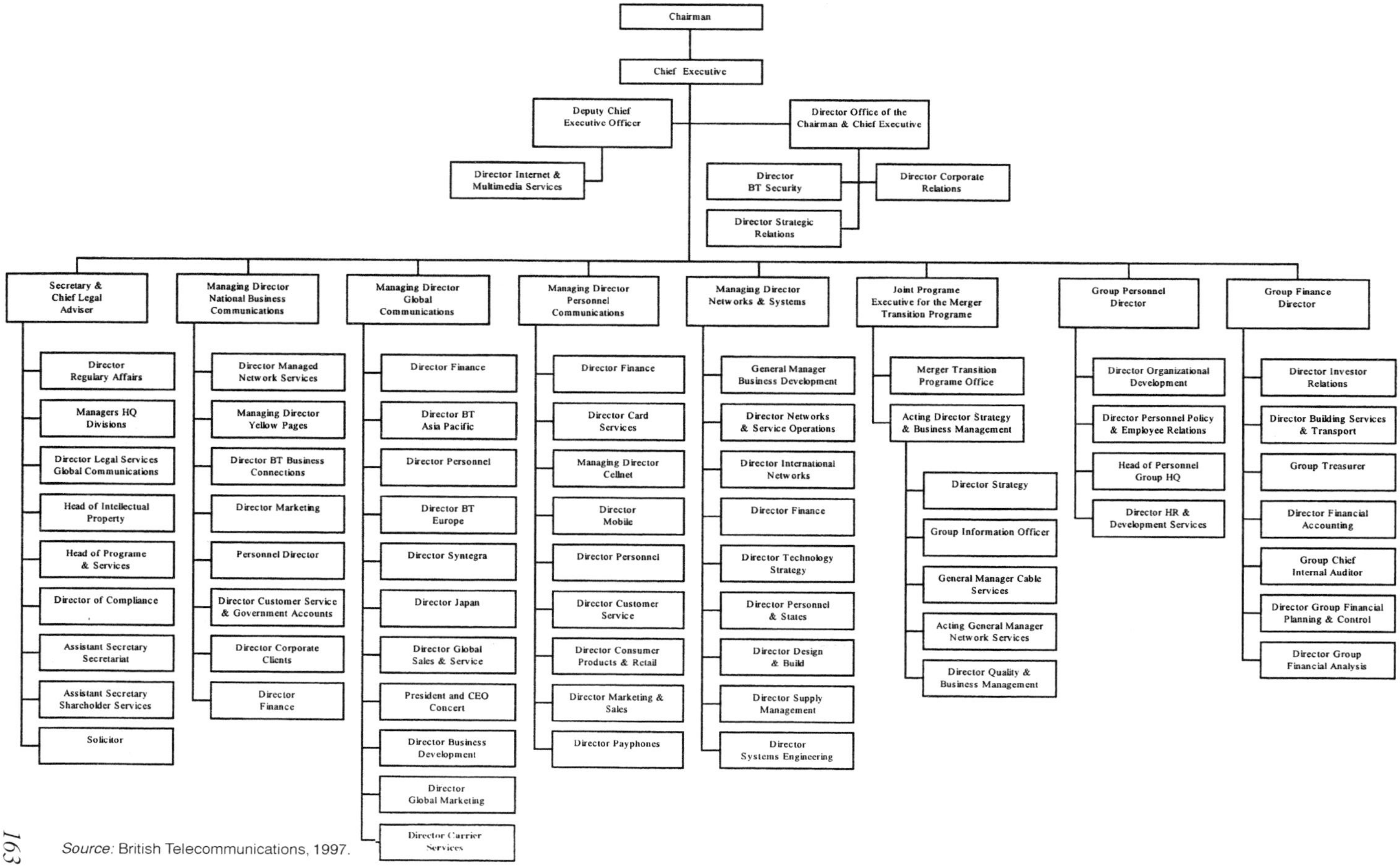

Source: British Telecommunications, 1997.

utilizes product, functional, and area structures. The core business is divided into Global Communications and National Business Communication.

In Transition to a Global Firm

This type of company has an active involvement globally and is sensitive to variations in its markets. In their strategies and orientations, ING, Northern Telecom, and Whirlpool conform to this type. ING, a Dutch-based company with wide experience in financial services, is active on a global scale, offering its customers a full range of financial products and services through multiple channels of distribution. Figure 7.11 depicts ING's organizational structure in 1996. ING's structure represents both area and product divisions. ING Financial Services International Division, for example, is responsible for all the insurance activities outside the Netherlands in conjunction with banking activities for private customers and small- and medium-sized firms. International banking activities for corporate clients are housed in the ING Corporate and Investment Banking Division.

Global Organization

Global firms treat the whole world as their market. National boundaries are not a binding factor in their decisions. In structuring their operations, these firms favor the simultaneous integration of ctivities and resources across functions, products, and areas. ABB, Nestlé, and P&G are examples of global firms with a compatible structure that permits them to achieve effective organization of resources and maximum adaptability and adjustability in operations. ABB, for example, is organized into three regions, four business groups, and one functional area (financial). Recently, P&G restructured itself into seven global business units based on product lines. The primary reason for such a change was to achieve greater innovation and speed by centering strategy and profit responsibility globally on brands, rather than on market geographies. Nestlé recognizes that globalization allows production sites to be set up far from where its products are consumed.

FIGURE 7.11. ING Structure

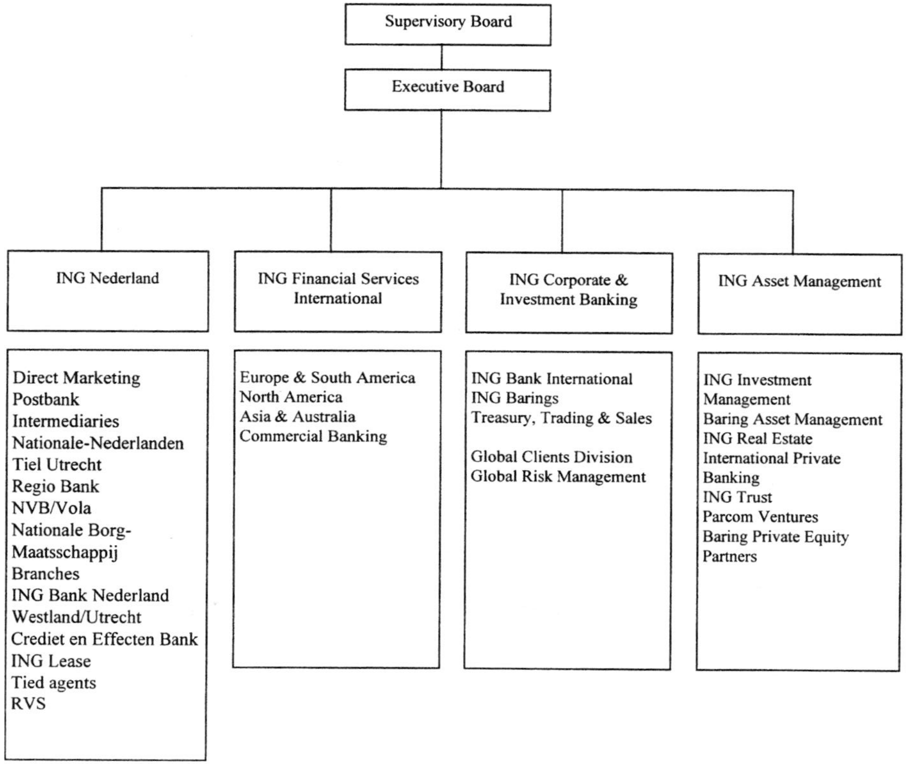

Source: ING, 1996.

In addition, the globalization of consumption habits creates single global segments (e.g., Levi's jeans, McDonald's, Nescafé, etc.). At the same time, regional and national habits of consumption, especially in the food branch, are not changing. Therefore, Nestlé, in an attempt to serve customers in every part of the world, restructured itself. Nestlé's structuring gives priority to the decentralization of operations, global connections, and coordination. Figure 7.12 shows Nestlé's structure as of July 1997. Nestlé uses strategic business units (product line), areas, and functional arrangements simultaneously.

Most of the actual frameworks of organizations discussed here represent multidimensional configurations. In the globalization era, firms become increasingly dependent on the flow of information to integrate their resources and activities. In fact, it is the availability and speed of information in organizational life that accelerates the search for a corporation without boundaries. The use of committees across units and functions, flexible tasks, and changing arrangements are steps in this direction. This means that structure is more likely to become a reflection of management's orientations and priorities. It is the management and members of the organization who give meaning to the structure. Structure, therefore, is, among other things, a question of "shared meaning" (Alvesson, 1990).

Globalization profoundly changes the priorities and orientations of organizations. Consequently, new and diverse strategic approaches have been adopted to effectively compete in the global marketplace. Organizations, therefore, have become more innovative in developing structural forms that ease transformation and adaptation to market demands and realities. This development raises two concerns: the relevance of the corporate center or HQ in today's environment and what makes one structure more appropriate than another. Ohmae (1989) argues that in the era of globalization there is a tendency among global organizations to decompose the corporate center into several regional HQs. These companies have decentralized responsibility for strategy and operations in each of their major markets. Having multiple HQs is considered essential for nurturing a global identity. Honda, Toyota, and Daewoo Group give regional HQs considerable authority to make decisions that were once made at the

FIGURE 7.12. Nestlé Organizational Structure

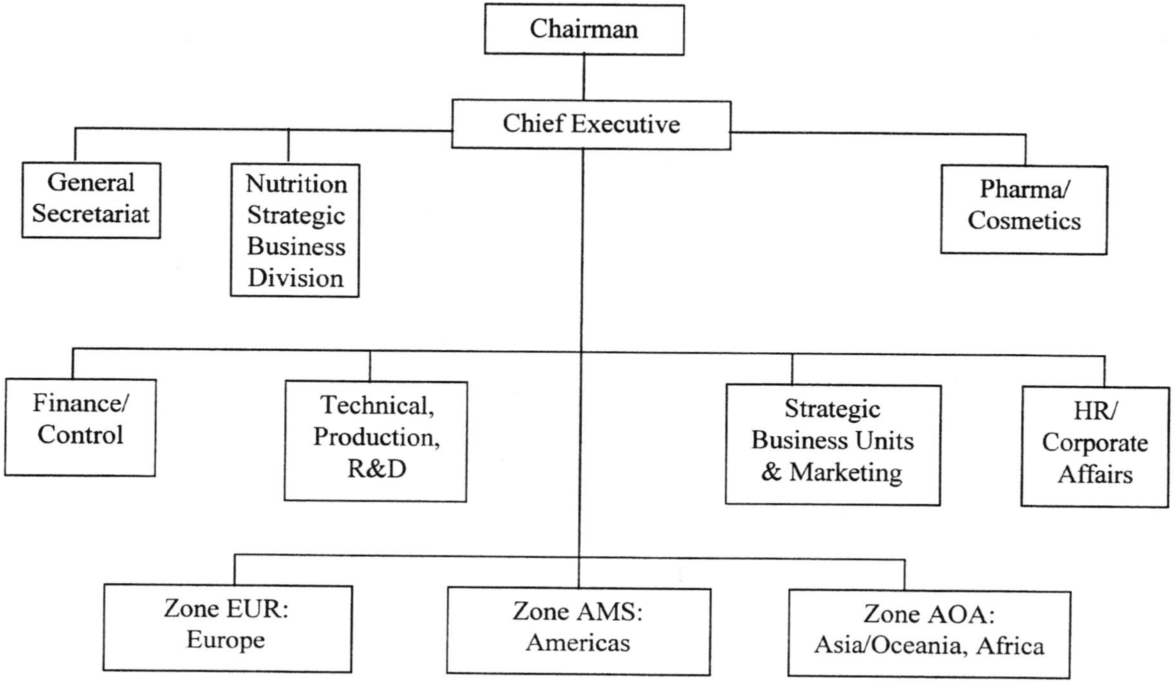

Source: Nestlé, 1997.

central HQs. At Daewoo, regional HQs are responsible for managing local design, production, sales, service, finance, and personnel programs. Sassen (1993) asserts that many specialized functions (e.g., accounting, advertising, legal, public relations) that used to be performed by the HQs are increasingly undertaken by specialized firms. That is, corporations have discovered that it is more efficient and less costly to buy these services from other specialized firms than to produce them in-house. Thus, the central HQs perform only the few necessary functions concerned with planning, coordination, and integration. Centers are needed, therefore, to induce and monitor innovation, articulate a sense of the firm's identity and future direction, disseminate information, nurture and develop a set of beliefs and social and business networks to enhance organizational continuity, and to integrate ideas and activities across diverse functions, places, and products. Jack Welch (1993), chairman and CEO of GE, outlines three jobs for the HQ: allocate resources, both dollars and people; set corporate initiatives and programs; and transfer ideas from outside into the company and across businesses.

In the context of structure selection and adoption, there is an increasing understanding among managers that structure is an instrument for implementing strategies and achieving goals. The meaning of structure, therefore, stems from specific attributions that are given to it by the corporate community, managers, and employees. Consequently, corporations are inclined to select those structures that facilitate their operations globally. A single structure or simultaneous utilization of multiple structures is common practice. For example, in a letter to shareholders in 1996, David Coulter, chairman and CEO of BankAmerica, mandated that because of market globalization, the bank had to streamline its operations around the world by centralizing the management of branch back-office activities and some of its processing activities of foreign exchange, options, derivatives, and other transactions. In contrast, ING attempted to meet the globalization challenge by transforming itself into an integrated provider of financial services and by emphasizing teamwork. ING has a structure designed to reap the maximum benefit from globalization. It has four management centers: ING Netherlands, ING International, ING Corporate & Investment Banking, and

ING Asset Management. That is, both firms, despite similarities in their services, have adopted very different structures.

Virtual organizations have evolved to cope with emerging globalization challenges. In Italy, for example, Italian-based firms, especially in the central northeast, have adopted a flexible organizational model, which depicts a system that is made up of several independent firms (see Inzerilli, 1990). In this system, there is a deverticalization and decentralization of all the major functions of the organization. Each of these functions (purchasing, production, and marketing) is assigned to an independent firm. One of these firms usually performs some degree of planning and coordination. The system does not have a formal, hierarchical authority or a strong central firm. The prevailing social structure and norms reinforce the integration mechanisms. The system allows the small firms to achieve economic efficiency and growth in today's global economy.

Alvesson (1990) provides another example of a corporation that is specifically structured to reduce formality and boundaries. Alvesson describes a flat structure that was adopted by a medium-sized Swedish-based computing firm. With about twenty subsidiaries, the company is characterized by a somewhat mixed picture of differing companies and organizational forms, as operations have developed very rapidly and corporate strategies are centered on seizing emerging opportunities. Therefore, the corporation is designed to respond with extreme flexibility.

Mitsubishi Electric pursues a development of virtual organization in order to act quickly, flexibly, and efficiently in the global marketplace. Takashi Kitaoka (1997), president and CEO of Mitsubishi, outlines the steps his company took to create a corporation without boundaries:

- Engage in global engineering, manufacturing, and purchasing activities and link them in a seamless global network
- Break company boundaries through alliances, outsourcing, and dispersal of authority
- Break business boundaries by making global decisions and looking beyond the company for new ideas

In summary, organizations adopt different structures to enable them to compete in the global economy. Multidimensional structures, along with simple configurations that ensure rapid adjustability and change in structural arrangements, are the major aspects of today's restructuring of corporations. Virtual organizational structures, where speed and adaptability take priority, are expected to be common in the twenty-first century. Boundaries between and within organizations gradually lose their distinctness.

Chapter 8

Global Strategies

Consumers aren't some great amorphous aggregate. They are individuals who live in 150 different countries.

Niall FitzGerald,
Chairman, Unilever, 1999

If we don't want to fall behind, we must develop an individual internationalization strategy for each of our core businesses.

Ulrich Hartman
Chairman and CEO, VEBA, 1997

Traditionally, we developed platforms for specific regions or models rather than with an eye to global applications. Now, we have begun rationalizing platforms for global application.

GM, *A Look at General Motors Today,* n.d.

Globalization induces fundamental changes in strategic postures, intentions, and approaches of nations and firms alike. At the state level, nations in general have witnessed a significant change in their orientations and conduct. The era of self-sufficiency and hostility toward FDI is over. Governments are competing to attract FDI and are pursuing "export promotion" rather than "import substitution" strategies. At the firm level, companies have developed a wide range of strategies to enhance their competitive advantage. Having access to customers has become the focus of competition. In this chapter, the primary emphasis is on firms' strategies and policies.

Strategy is a subject that provokes curiosity, interest, and fear among policy and decision makers and common individuals alike.

This is because strategy always conveys an action or an intent to act. The word derives from the Greek *stratego* (a general in command of an army). *Stratos* means "army," and *ag* means "to lead." Initially, strategy was the art of the general and evolved in the ancient Greek civilization to indicate the skill of utilizing resources to overcome opposition and to create a unified system for governing. In recent years, strategy has been used by a wide range of organizations and specialists to convey a meaning particular to their areas of concern that is generally focused on achieving goals. In the business world, strategy assumes a pivotal role in corporate life and in executives' priorities. A firm's survival, growth, and potential hinge on developing and executing relevant, practical, and sound strategies. Competitive firms are always recognized as those that are blessed with an excellent strategy that gives meaning and direction to their actions and behaviors in the marketplace.

In the era of globalization, strategy becomes more complex and more important than ever. Its complexity reflects the multiplicity of forces that shape and impact strategy (e.g., governments, competitors, partners, etc.) and the nature and scope of these forces. The importance of a firm's business strategy arises from the fact that in a dynamic global market, trial and error or other unsound practices are not tolerated and may lead to the rapid demise of a firm. Strategy in the age of globalization is more than a road map for achieving certain goals. It is a process of continuous revitalization of a firm's activities that aims at solidifying its present and future competitive position. Traditionally, firms navigated familiar terrains. In today's environment, the emphasis is on navigating unfamiliar terrain (e.g., new markets, new industries, partnerships, etc.). Ford, Honda, Merck, Nestlé, Roche, Siemens, and 3M, among others, are pioneers in adopting new strategic outlooks characterized by alertness and foresight.

STRATEGY PERSPECTIVES

Hamel and Prahalad (1994) argue that being competitive in the future will mean creating and dominating emerging opportunities. That is, the focal point of a strategy is to imagine and create the future. A company, therefore, has to shape the structure of future industries and, ultimately, preempt competitors in major global markets. The latter mandate resembles the meaning of strategy in the original Greek: deploying forces to overcome opposition. Indeed, envisioning market needs and thwarting competitors are integral parts of strategic aims. Unfortunately, most of the literature on global strategy is heavily influenced by Levitt's (1983) conceptualization of strategy—the delivery of products that are globally identical with respect to design, function, and even fashion. Many business scholars have subscribed to this conceptualization (e.g., Griffin and Pustay, 1996; Johansson, 1997; Mair, 1997; Pearce and Robinson, 1997; Yip, 1995). This conceptualization is not, however, a global strategy; rather, it is a worldwide approach to lower unit production costs by the utilization of economies of scale in production and marketing. Lussier, Baeder, and Corman (1994) indicate that global corporations must set all their resources against competitors in a highly integrated way. The strategy, they argue, must be centralized with various aspects of operations decentralized according to what economics and effectiveness dictate. The authors further suggest that decentralization in strategic decisions should revolve around only the operational aspects of strategy, and they reaffirm the pivotal role that a centralized strategy plays, similar to Levitt's and others' conceptualization of global strategy. Mair (1997) differentiates between a global strategy (the same product is produced for sale in all world markets) and a "global local" strategy (a strategy that is designed to benefit simultaneously from global economies of scale and the capacity to meet local requirements). This strategy, as indicated in Chapters 6 and 7, is utilized by TNCs. In line with the view of a global corporation that was advanced in Chapter 6, a global strategy is defined as an integrated, comprehensive plan of major activities that permit a firm to effectively and coherently achieve goals on a global scale without obstructing its abilities to meet national or regional challenges. A global strategy translates a corporation's capabilities and commitment into general directions and actions necessary to enhance responsiveness, speed, and flexibility in dealing with ever-changing consumer needs.

In the business world, the development and execution of a global strategy are recognized as the most important factors in facing competitive pressure and sustaining competitiveness. For example,

Edwin Artzt (1990), chairman and CEO of P&G, asserts that at P&G "We have tremendous growth potential in the businesses and countries that we are now in, and that's going to be the primary thrust of our efforts for the foreseeable future." Artzt identifies six strategies that are basic to P&G's long-term success:

- Globalization of the company
- Focusing on technology-driven product initiations for core businesses, with particular priority on product technology that can be reapplied worldwide
- Judicious strategic use of acquisitions and alliances to achieve category and globalization goals
- Relentless pursuit of worldwide systems change to improve quality and to increase profit margins through greater systems efficiency
- Proactive environmental programs to assure leadership in meeting the need for more environmentally friendly packaging, products, and raw materials
- Organizational restructuring and programs designed to push responsibility closer to consumers and customers

Jack Welch, chairman and CEO of GE, asserts that if the strategy is right, "it's the future of the next century for this company." He views GE's strategy as one of pursuing growth wherever "the growth is." This orientation places GE apart from other companies. That is, GE searches for fresh markets rather than cheap labor (Smart, 1993). Penetrating fresh markets implies that GE focuses on outmaneuvering its competitors. The objective is to be ahead of competitors. To realize this objective, GE's senior executives answer five questions before formulating their growth strategy (see Day and LaBarre, 1994):

- What does our global competitive environment look like?
- In the last three years, what have our competitors done?
- In the same period, what have we done to them?
- How might they attack us in the future?
- What are our plans to leapfrog them?

Answering these questions allows GE to identify the range of available options. One of GE's preferred options is joint ventures/

acquisitions, which it advances to outmaneuver competitors and to strengthen its global presence.

Daimler-Benz, too, embraced a strategy for growth through mergers and acquisitions that lessened its dependence on luxury cars. Long before its merger with Chrysler, the chairman of the board, Jurgen Schrempp (1998), identified three elements of this growth strategy:

- *Value-based management.* This means that the firm's primary goal is to create value to customers, employees, and shareholders.
- *Innovation.* The firm seeks to establish a corporate environment where everyone is thinking creatively, challenging the way things are done, and connecting with people across organizational boundaries.
- *Globalization through regionalization.* A key to further growth is to tap new markets. Globalization is viewed as regional development. In each location, the company has a far-reaching program to demonstrate and communicate its social and environmental responsibilities to these communities.

By giving priority to a growth strategy and global integration, many companies are able to reconfigure their competitive advantage. In fact, in recent years, companies have experienced major shifts in their strategic focuses and approaches.

Strategic Focus

Focus differs across firms and industries. Nevertheless, the focus of global corporations stems almost exclusively from customers. The customer is the ultimate concern. As Siemens notes in its 1996 annual report, "In tomorrow's competitive global marketplace, cutting edge technology alone won't be enough. We will also need to nurture especially close and long-term partnerships with customers" (Siemens, 1996, p. 6.) Charles Knight (1996), chairman and CEO of Emerson, attributes his company's outstanding performance to the company's effort to increase its focus on top-line sales growth. This focus is built on several initiatives, including the following:

- *Repositioning for growth.* Emerson narrowed its focus to seven businesses (electronics and computer support products, HVAC

components, industrial motors and drives, motors and appliance components, process control, tools, and industrial components and equipment) to reposition the company for improved growth.
- *Technology leadership and new products.* The firm made a commitment to new products and technology development as a basis for leading industry and market change.
- *Global expansion.* Emerson has made substantial investment in strengthening its global presence in each of its seven businesses. In 1998, Emerson doubled sales and marketing personnel in Asia, increased the number of joint ventures from fourteen to twenty-nine, and added fifteen new manufacturing plants. In Latin America, Eastern Europe, and the Middle East, Emerson has made remarkable annual business growth since 1993 (over 20 percent).
- *Strategic partnerships.* Emerson set out to create value through acquisitions and joint venture relationships to gain critical mass, access technology, and expand distribution channels.
- *Best cost producer.* This strategy is aimed at improving operating margins, quality, customer service, and asset utilization.

Companies such as Honda, 3M, and Enron have also refocused their strategies to achieve competitive advantages. In terms of geographic scope, the following focuses are common:

Worldwide Focus

Companies such as Gillette and Deutsche Bank provide a wide range of products and services worldwide. The objective is to capitalize on the economies of scale and brand recognition in repositioning themselves in the global marketplace.

Regional Focus

Integrating operations by region has become a strategic choice for firms in various industries. DuPont, Honda, Siemens, Toyota, and Unilever are pioneers in the practice of shifting strategic choice away from global or domestic toward regional emphasis. Siemens, for example, states, "Rather than focusing on national boundaries, global players need to keep their sights set on dynamic regional markets around the world. For our part, we have been building up an international network of cross-border structures and global centers of competence" (Siemens, 1998). Honda, too, focuses on regional operations: "The global organization makes more efficient use of Honda's existing resources by providing more autonomy for regional operations. Each operation is developing regionally self-reliant, yet globally integrated, capabilities" (Honda, 1997d).

National Focus

Recognizing national differences and cultural nuances is the focus of some companies operating across borders. Novartis, a Swiss-based life science company, in its 1996 annual report, recognizes that "its different sites have different HSE [Health, Safety, and Environment] needs, issues, procedures and regulations. Working in an ongoing dialogue with individual sector companies, the HSE Country organization supports the HSE management process when specific aspects of the country take precedence over Sector concern" (Novartis, 1996a, p. 8). Similarly, Toshifumi Suzuki (1997), president and CEO of Ito-Yokato Co., states, "Retailing is perhaps one of the best examples of a truly domestic industry. Consumer tastes and price levels vary widely from country to country and concepts of customer service may differ according to cultural factors" (p. 2). Therefore, the company places a premium on cultural and domestic market variations in conducting its business.

Global-Local Focus

In pursuing strategies for global growth, some companies recognize the advantage of combining common forums across the globe with sensitivity to cultural and national nuances. GM, Ford, P&G, and Mitsubishi are examples of companies that emphasize this focus. GM, for example, highlights this focus to strengthen its operation worldwide. *A Look at General Motors Today* states (GM, n.d.):

> Traditionally, we develop platforms for specific regions or models rather than with an eye to global applications. Now, we

> have begun rationalizing platforms for global application. Today, the focus is on common platforms, with the models built on each platform varying widely among markets to meet varying customer desires and needs. Our vision is to get to seven global platforms, compared to sixteen platforms we had in 1995 and the fourteen platforms we have currently. With our global reach, common vehicle platforms are a major lever for increasing our efficiency and speed-to-market.

Likewise, AT&T has achieved significant economies of scale by designing high-quality global product platforms that are easily tailored for various national and regional markets. Just before a product is marketed in a country, it has to meet three technical requirements (Fonton, Fong, and Mizrahi, 1993): type approval (mandatory standards), additional interfaces to the public networks (voluntary standards), and product review to ensure that the item has essential features which make that product a success in a certain country (familiarity with customer expectations). In fact, AT&T has achieved remarkable success in adapting its DEFINITY system to various customers and official requirements in the world market.

P&G has full-time professionals who study consumer needs around the world. These professionals, along with other P&G employees, interact yearly with more than seven million consumers to discover their particular needs. This enables P&G to meet the needs that consumers everywhere have in common as well as those which are specific to individual markets.

One of the most unique types of global-local focus which has recently emerged is one that seeks to create a customized value chain for every customer order. Li & Fung, a Hong Kong-based trading company, for example, focuses the operation of an entire division on serving one customer. Li & Fung, however, is unique in its focus on large and small orders from customers; it purposefully structures itself around customers.

Strategic Approaches

A firm's renascence represents an effective translation of a vision into a reality. In practice, this is called a strategic approach. Firms that have been innovative and adaptive in meeting the globalization challenge employ various strategic approaches (e.g., licensing, contracting, offshore operations, alliances, etc.) which ensure renewal and revival. Three major approaches are the focus of this chapter: offshore operations, alliances, and mergers and acquisitions. These approaches have not only been common in the last few decades but have also been instrumental in speeding firms' integration into the world economy. Each is briefly discussed in the following sections.

Offshore Operations

The oldest approach that companies have utilized in conducting their businesses is offshore operations. Yet, its renewal and utility are far from over. Traditionally, this approach is used to secure access to cheap labor or materials, avoid high transportation costs, meet regulations and government restrictions, and compete with other companies on their home turf. Globalization, however, highlights other important aspects such as:

- flexibility in meeting demands in various markets and regions;
- enhancing the firm's worldwide image;
- competing effectively in a dynamic global market;
- capitalizing on opportunities wherever they are found;
- enhancing a firm's freedom to choose and locate according to site attractiveness, thereby minimizing dependency, be it contractual or locational; and
- maximizing opportunities to attract talent globally.

Caterpillar, for example, has a significant manufacturing presence outside the United States. It has more than thirty plants in eighteen countries (Australia, Brazil, China, France, Hungary, India, Japan, Russia, Sweden, etc.). Similarly, Roche, in 1997, had eighty-six manufacturing plants outside its home market (Switzerland). These plants are located in countries including Argentina, Australia, Bermuda, Brazil, China, the Congo, Costa Rica, India, Japan, Nigeria, Peru, South Korea, the United States, etc. In addition, in the same year, the company had more than 179 sales sites abroad. Siemens operates about 466 manufacturing facilities around the world, and more than 220 major sales and service locations are maintained in 190 countries.

Ferdows (1997) found that, in terms of manufacturing sites, managers who do not consider manufacturing to be a source of competitive advantage are likely to establish offshore factories with a narrow strategic scope. In contrast, managers who regard manufacturing as a major source of competitive advantage are found to expect overseas factories to be highly productive and innovative, to achieve low costs, and to provide exemplary service to customers throughout the world. He identifies six strategic roles for overseas manufacturing:

1. *Offshore factory.* This type of factory is established to produce specific items at a low cost and then export them either for further processing or for sale. Little development or engineering occurs at this site.
2. *Source factory.* This factory has a mandate broader than that of the offshore factory. Its managers have greater authority relative to purchasing, production, planning, outbound logistics, and product-customization and redesign decisions.
3. *Server factory.* The mandate for this manufacturing site is to supply specific national or regional markets. Nevertheless, managers have some authority to modify products and production methods to meet local conditions.
4. *Contributor factory.* This site serves specific national or regional markets. Its responsibilities, however, extend to product and process engineering as well as to the development and choice of suppliers.
5. *Outpost factory.* The primary role for this site is to collect information relative to suppliers, competitors, research laboratories, or customers. This site assumes a secondary role as a server or an offshore factory.
6. *Lead factory.* The primary mandate of the lead factory is to create new processes, products, and technologies for the entire company. Managers at this site have autonomy to conduct their affairs and to initiate changes.

Alliances

Cooperative agreements among firms have increased markedly in recent years. Alliances take several forms (e.g., franchising, licensing, joint ventures, and cooperation), which can be either equity or nonequity investment agreements. Alliances are traditionally common among individuals, groups, and governments. Such alliances are well documented throughout history. According to time and situation, these alliances seek to: maximize necessary support; enhance one's position politically, economically, or socially; defeat a common enemy; facilitate operations and survival; and so on. In seeking alliances, businesses have similar objectives in mind. Chief among them are minimizing certain deficiencies, enhancing competitive advantage, competing effectively, and enhancing flexibility and speed in reacting to certain strategic alerts. These objectives have taken on additional value due to globalization and economic integration. Firms have become sensitive to their critical deficiencies. Alliances are seen as a means to overcome these deficiencies and to gain a competitive edge. The effectiveness of alliances is determined by several factors such as compatibility in strategic objectives, shared values, and orientations and priorities of the senior executives of the allied companies. Trust, clear vision, lack of fear, and a solid agenda are preconditions for successful alliances.

The joint venture (JV) is one form of alliance. Joint ventures represent an agreement between two or more firms to create a separate organization to achieve specific goals. GE, for example, utilizes JVs to grow globally. It has JVs in Italy, India, Japan, France, Mexico, Germany, China, Brazil, Indonesia, and many other countries. Likewise, Emerson utilizes JVs to reach critical mass, to access technology and distribution channels, and to establish the best-cost manufacturing facilities worldwide. The company has more than forty JVs of many different forms and arrangements throughout the world.

Another form of alliance that has been increasingly adopted by firms is nonequity collaboration in R&D, marketing, management service, and so on. This type of contractual or semicontractual collaboration offers firms access to market opportunities and certain advantages without the trouble of control issues, conflicts, possible compromise of technological advantage, or conceivable failures that are often associated with equity alliances. SmithKline has extensive experience in alliances in R&D and marketing. The company, for example, has engaged in drug-discovery collaboration with five international pharmaceutical companies (Merck, Synthelabo, Schering-Plough, Takeda Chemical, and Glaxo Wellcome). Likewise, the company collaborates with two leading research centers in China: the National Key Laboratory & Medical Genetics and the Shanghai Second Medical University. The collaboration focuses on developing state-of-the-art technologies for unraveling the molecular mechanisms of disease. In 1999, SmithKline joined nine other leading drug companies to create a research consortium to study how variations in human DNA affect disease development. Similarly, Dell Computer, in March 1999, signed a collaboration agreement with IBM to jointly develop new computer technology. This cooperation is said to allow Dell to boost its competitiveness in notebook PCs, storage products, and servers. In a similar move, Microsoft and BT collaborated to develop a new generation of mobile devices for accessing the World Wide Web without PCs.

Mergers and Acquisitions

Mergers and acquisitions (M&As), are the most advanced form of alliance. Many firms, for various reasons, have found that joining forces through mergers or acquisitions is the best possible course of action. M&As have become an attractive means for corporations to reconfigure their competitive advantage. The year 1998 was the biggest ever for M&As. The total value of M&As surpassed $2.4 trillion, 50 percent above 1997's total (*The Economist,* 1999d). About a quarter of M&As were cross-border mergers. The following is a list of the top ten mergers in 1998 (see *The Economist,* 1999a):

Merger	**Value $billion**
Exxon/Mobil	86.4
Travelers/Citicorp	72.6
SBC/Ameritech	72.4
Bell Atlantic/GTE	71.3
AT&T/TCI	69.9
NationsBank/Bank of America	61.6
BP/Amoco	55.0
Daimler-Benz/Chrysler	40.5
Norwest/Wells Fargo	34.4
Zeneca/Astra	31.8

In 1995, more than 27,600 companies merged, completing more mergers than in the whole decade of the 1980s (Wayne, 1998). The M&A movement appears to have accelerated in 1999, as major corporations merge or acquire other firms (e.g., Ford bought Britain's KWIK-FIT and acquired the passenger car operations of Volvo; GE acquired Gulfstream Aerospace; Securitas acquired Transamerica, etc.). Several factors account for this sharp rise in M&As besides deregulation: the size of companies in a highly competitive market is viewed by executives as a means for strategically positioning companies as global players in the world economy; companies join resources to seize worldwide opportunities to outmaneuver competitors and to better serve growing numbers of worldwide customer needs by offering a wider range of products or services (e.g., the Citicorp/Travelers merger is intended to create a financial supermarket that offers a one-stop shopping center).

EVOLUTION OF STRATEGIC OBJECTIVES AND APPROACHES

Certainly, firms' strategic objectives and focus evolve over the years. The nature, structure, and scope of competition have tremendous impact on the evolution of strategic objectives. GM's story is a practical indicator of a change in objectives for a very large organization. Between 1908 and 1920, the focus was on managing each unit within GM separately. Therefore, the objective was to expand market share through acquisition. From 1923 to 1980, the focus shifted to maintaining efficiency through coordinated control of decentralized operations. The priority centered on innovation and marketing. GM maintained manufacturing bases in key regions and at least a marketing presence in all potential growth markets. The period between 1984 and 1992 was a time to rethink GM's strategic focus. That period, however, was characterized by the failure to run a lean organization and an absence of common components, business processes, and systems. Since 1992, GM has focused on customers and pursued growth globally. Strategically, GM places emphasis on common processes, and systems across geographic regions and business units, and on integration of global operations. As of 1996, GM had more than 160 subsidiaries, JVs, and affiliates. The underlying strategic goal of global growth is to be the world leader in transportation products and related services (see GM, n.d.). In contrast, ING's strategy was to shift its focus from its home to the global market. As the Netherlands market matured and offered little opportunity for continued growth in the long term, ING expanded its operations globally through organic growth and active acquisitions and partnership programs. ING gives its units all over the world a substantial degree of autonomy, and each unit is allowed to serve its market under its own brand name so each can retain its identity.

Strategic objectives can be grouped in terms of market reach, market competition, and market sustainability (see Figure 8.1). These objectives reflect changing business priorities and evolution toward an integrated world economy. Below is a brief discussion of each.

FIGURE 8.1. Evolution of Strategic Objectives and Approaches

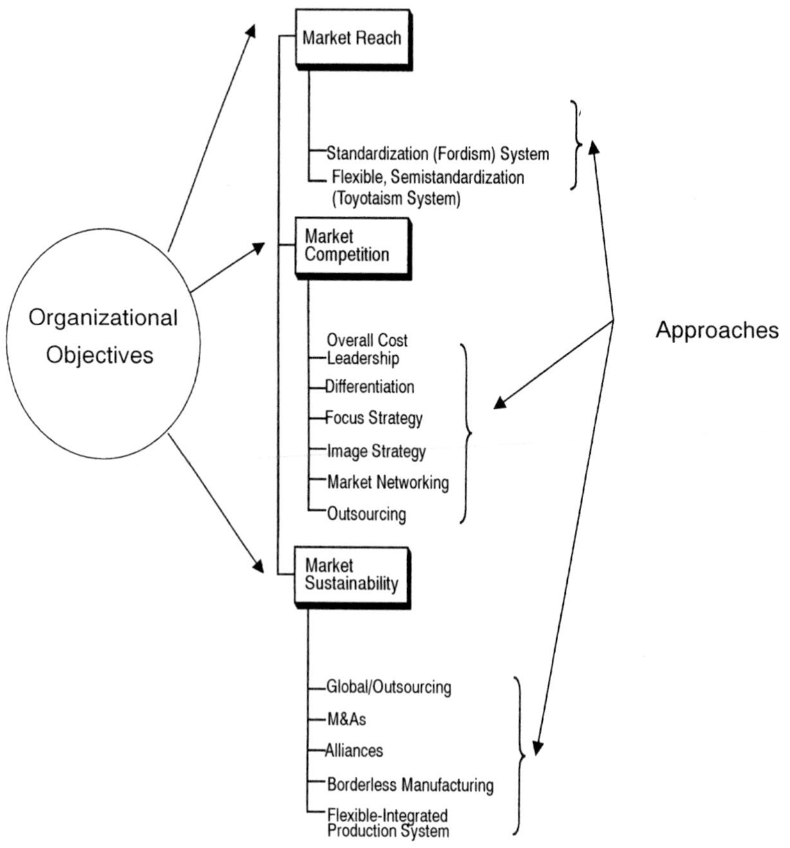

Market Reach

The aim of a company operating in this category is to reach new markets (Reacher). International expansion is the central focus of a firm and a company's top priority is to extend operations overseas and obtain a sizeable market share. American- and European-based companies, traditionally, were motivated by this strategic objective. There were no strong competitors and many new markets became accessible. Two systems have been employed by companies to achieve this goal: standardization and the semistandardization flexible system.

Standardization

Standardization is a mass production system, often called Fordism. Products are standardized and promoted through an intensive marketing program. Through mass production and marketing, companies realize economies of scale and reach distant markets. Therefore, firms search for the lowest price suppliers and attempt to locate assembly near customers or in lower-cost locations. Achieving efficiency of operation is a guiding principle.

Semistandardization Flexible System, or Toyotaism

Toyotaism is a system of production that aims at achieving flexibility and quality through flexible specialization, spatial agglomeration, and just-in-time (JIT) delivery logistics (Fujita and Hill, 1995). Instead of mass production, Toyotaism relies on producing a variety of high-quality products of relatively small value. In addition, the Toyotaism system utilizes information technology to easily process work and achieve efficient connectivity with other business units, partners, suppliers, and customers. The primary objective of both standardization and semistandardization systems is to reach the market in an efficient way.

Market Competition

The primary objective of this strategy is to position a company in a market, thereby realizing a competitive position (Competitor). As competition increased in the 1970s and Asian-based companies and others aggressively entered the global market, American- and European-based companies felt the heat. Old strategies had to be dismantled; new goals had to be formulated, and new strategies for competition had to be developed. Firms discovered that a first mover advantage in a market is not enough to fend off competitors. They have to utilize certain strategies to compete. In 1996, for example, Pepsi, after fifty years of being a leading soft drink in Venezuela (holding a 40 percent market share), lost its independent bottler to its rival Coca-Cola. Likewise, in the same year, Coca-Cola managed to take the lead in Russia, a market of huge size (150 million people) and scope (see Saporito, 1996). Porter (1985) identifies three generic strategies: cost leadership, differentiation, and focus.

Overall Cost Leadership

This strategy seeks to serve a broad range of market segments. The company provides a relatively full range of products to be the low-cost producer in the industry. Honda, Nissan, and Toyota are examples of companies that adopted this strategy for a long time, until they started to target high-scale segments by introducing luxury models around 1989. Enron directs its energies toward being a low-cost producer in the oil and gas industry. Porter indicates that cost leadership can be sustained through scale of operations, effective interrelationships among business units, adequate linkages to suppliers and distributors, realizing proprietary learning, and replicating product innovation or new production processes.

Differentiation

This strategy focuses on providing a broad range of products while seeking to be unique in some ways relative to competitors. The strategy targets either a broad group of buyers or particular market niches. P&G simultaneously offers products that appeal to a broad customer base (e.g., Pantene Pro-V hair care products, Vicks, Head & Shoulders shampoo, Folgers coffee) and to special segments (e.g., diapers that meet the Middle East market's special needs). Similarly, Coca-Cola emphasizes traditional brand names (flagship, the core product) for a large market segment globally. In India, however, it promotes a local brand—Thumbs Up. This local brand has become the company's leading soft drink in India.

Focus

A company can focus on being the low-cost producer in a particular segment or differentiate itself in that particular segment. Kia exploits the first strategy to its advantage. BMW, Audi, and Mercedes have been rather effective for many years in adopting the second approach.

Firms, however, recognize that competing in the global marketplace may demand more than cost leadership, differentiation, or focus. Therefore, firms have been innovative in engaging other strategies to strengthen their market positions. Image strategy, market networking, and outsourcing are utilized in combination with one or more of Porter's suggested strategies. Following is a brief discussion of each.

Image

Many firms find it impossible to compete in the market by relying on just one or a combination of the strategies previously discussed. A company has to cultivate a positive image of its market position. A public relations campaign that is persistent in reminding customers that the company is trustworthy and concerned for their welfare becomes a competitive weapon. Honda, Roche, and Nestlé are effective in projecting this image. Companies such as Monsanto, despite its remarkable success in the United States, have an image problem in many parts of the world, especially in India and Europe (see Kilman and Cooper, 1999). Two service companies have used their positive image to fend off competitors. Telefonos de Mexico (TELMEX) utilized its familiarity with legal systems and customer expectations in Mexico to keep its giant opponents, AT&T and MCI, in check and defended its home turf (see Friedland, 1998). Similarly, Banco de Brazil established automatic teller machines even in remote areas. Recognition of customers' needs for adequate service and the high telecommunication costs in Brazil induced the bank to implement an asynchronous transfer mode (ATM) multiservice network platform for delivering worldwide electronic business and personal and private banking services. The bank gained customers' trust and loyalty, and strategically positioned itself in a highly competitive market.

Market Networking

Formal and informal relationships among firms are increasingly used to achieve market competition. Firms may discover that none of Porter's three strategies are adequate for competing in the market. This can be attributed to either lack of resources or size, or because they are new entrants. Therefore, these firms utilize their networks with customers, suppliers, and even competitors to sharpen their competitve skills and gain needed experience in the market, thus strengthening customer loyalty and improving model and brand category images. These alliances seek, therefore, to strengthen the company in the current market. The success of Keiretsu in Japan has prompted firms in many parts of the world to establish some kind of relationship to secure their positions in the market.

Outsourcing

For more than two decades many firms have placed intense emphasis on outsourcing. Operations that are not central to the company's primary functions are subcontracted. Companies shop around to contract suppliers that best fit their overall strategy. Outsourcing, at this stage, is done to reduce the needed capital for investment and control cost, enhance market position, create networking, and allow senior managers to better deal with major priorities.

Market Sustainability

At this stage, a company looks beyond the current market and the ability to compete. The company is a sustainer and considers the globe, rather than regional or major markets, as its arena of operation. That is, it seeks not only to maintain its present domination in the market but also to sharpen its market focus, and continuously revitalize itself to restructure its industry and shape, if not invent, market events. Coca-Cola, despite its leading role in major markets, always feels pressure from PepsiCo's significant efforts globally. Coca-Cola has to spend lavishly in primary markets (Brazil, Japan, Indonesia, and Russia) to fight off a reinvigorated PepsiCo, which is aggressively attempting to regain its lost market share. In Mexico, Coca-Cola has to be innovative. The company's retailers are mostly single mothers and retirees who cannot afford health insurance. Coca-Cola created an incentive program offering access to group health insurance to shopkeepers who sell enough Cokes. This increased Coca-Cola's sales volume in Mexico in 1998 by 13 percent (Foust, Smith, and Rocks, 1999). This strategic move allowed Coca-Cola to reinvent the market and set the rules for competition. In the globalization era, however, competitors are expected either to follow suit or to invent new competition games.

To lead and shape market events, companies must be ever alert. In the automobile industry, Ford, Chrysler, Toyota, and other major corporations continuously search out ways to revitalize themselves. All have engaged in serious searches to maintain domination. The result is a "sex change" in their operation (Meredith, 1999). In recent years, these companies have spent millions of dollars to change their designs to meet customer desires for models that are masculine and sexy. So their current designs resemble "muscle cars"—the Durango, the "hard body" Pathfinder, the "chiseled" Jeeps, and the Ford Excursion. Auto experts argue that the end of the Cold War produced a sense of confidence and a "go-anywhere" mentality in customers. This created a need for a car design that was friendly, yet conveyed confidence and mastery of the road.

ING Group, too, is an example of a company that has been forced, due to globalization and changing customer expectations, to change its strategic approach to be competitive. Traditionally, the company relied on organic growth and acquisition to expand its market. Recently, it utilized alliances to sustain its competitive advantage. The company recognizes that in "the rapidly growing international money and capital markets, there will be room for only a limited number of financial institutions which will be able to continue to play a significant role on a global scale" (ING, 1996, p. 19). Operating companies, however, have substantial autonomy in serving their local markets under their own brands so that they can adequately meet customer needs.

The primary driver for change at this stage of evolution is the customer. Customers have become the focus and the source of innovative change. Indeed, consumer sovereignty intensifies competition among firms and generates profound changes in corporate priorities. Globalization opens new frontiers for customers: they have more options, more complex needs, and they can go anywhere. They value their freedom, choices, and control. Neither geography, time, nor price is a major hurdle for the majority of customers. Firms can no longer take a competitive advantage for granted, and customer loyalty is anything but certain. Therefore, firms have used various approaches, individually and collectively, to gain or maintain advantage. Each approach is briefly discussed in the following sections:

Mergers and Acquisitions

M&As represent a means for firms to take control of their destinies. As indicated in previous sections, M&As are not a new phenomenon. Early in the twentieth century, there were major M&As, especially in the auto industry. Current M&As are different, however. Many of them are cross-border enterprises, and occur among big, medium, and small corporations across industries. Most important, M&As are undertaken to enhance competitive positions rather than to maintain monopolistic control and exceptionally high profit margins. In addition, today's M&As are motivated by the desire to serve customers better, meet their needs, and creatively be ahead in anticipating and responding to the ever-changing needs of sovereign customers. This is exactly what AT&T hoped to achieve in acquiring Media One Group and cable giant Tele-Communications Inc., in 1999 and 1998 respectively. These acquisitions allowed AT&T to grab the future by transforming itself from a long-distance phone company into a provider of telephone, television, and Internet services. In fact, the mergers have given AT&T global dominance in a market that is yet to be fully exploited, offering unlimited opportunities.

Alliances

The majority of today's alliances are different from the traditional equity (e.g., JVs) and nonequity investment (e.g., research and development [R&D] or marketing alliances). JVs aim, among many other objectives, at reducing risk and achieving access to critical technologies and markets that a firm does not otherwise have. Like traditional R&D, a JV minimizes risk, reduces costs, and offers new opportunities for major technological advancement. Globalization, however, creates a need to enter alliances that enhance focus, flexibility, and speed in meeting customer demands and the opportunity to be a vital player in the global marketplace. The alliance in July 1998 between the stock exchanges of London and Frankfurt aimed at creating a pan-European trading system in line with the move to establish a single European stock market after the introduction of the Euro. The alliance offers clients and investors an efficient and accessible equity market infrastructure. Similarly, the alliance between IBM and Dell will sharpen both companies' competitive edges. The alliance between Microsoft and AT&T in early 1999 promises to provide Microsoft with an opportunity to move beyond desktop computers into a new frontier where customers use a seamless bundle of TV, phone, and Internet services.

There is, however, a growing interest among firms in a particular industrial region or across regions in formulating informal alliances. This is because production systems, in particular, and businesses, in general, are increasingly being viewed as network relationships. These alliances have various forms. Some of the networking occurs by necessity as firms share a common infrastructure (e.g., telephone services, warehouses, media and advertising, public relations agencies, etc.). Other alliances are undertaken because of prevailing professional and industrial cultural norms. In this context, manufacturers, suppliers, customers, and competitors share common expectations of how each demand should be met. That is, there are reciprocal obligations or psychological contracts (clearly understood but not written agreements) that spontaneously induce each firm to act in an expected way to smooth operations in a network that is characterized by trust, interdependency, and connectivity.

Borderless Manufacturing

This system is common in East Asia. A company has a huge network of thousands of suppliers around the globe and multiple networks of dispersed manufacturing—high-cost hubs that do the sophisticated planning for regional manufacturing. Magretta (1998) contrasts this model with the 1980s model, in which the emphasis was on supplier partnerships to improve cost and quality. The borderless model focuses on innovation, flexibility, and speed. Magretta studied Li & Fung and found that the company does the high-value-added front (design, engineering, production planning) and back-end tasks (quality control, testing, logistics) in Hong Kong. Li & Fung performs lower-value-added middle stages (raw material and component sourcing and managing production) through its network of 7,500 suppliers. Mass customization and virtual production can be easily realized. The chairman of Li & Fung, Victor Fung, argues that borderless manufacturing ensures quick delivery and customizes the value chain to best meet the customer's needs. The primary objectives of borderless manufacturing are flexibility, speed, quality, and differentiation.

Flexible-Integrated Production Systems

Toyota, Honda, Ford, and other global corporations utilize a flexible-integrated system to creatively maintain customer focus. Toyota, for example, localizes its far-flung activities further by integrating operations by region. Toyota implements a system that enables it to integrate across projects as well as within them. The customer focus is sustained through integrative social process (integrative leadership, mutual adjustment, and direct supervision) and forms of standardization (standard skills, standardized work processes, and design standards) (Sobek, Liker, and Ward, 1998). Ford, on the other hand, is using three-dimensional (3D) visualization that enables it to create car components and prototypes on a screen before a car is actually produced. Ford's major suppliers are expected to use 3D technology to design components requested by Ford.

Global Outsourcing

The popularity of outsourcing has increased dramatically in recent years. Globalization increases a firm's sensitivity to flexibility and agility. Traditional benefits of outsourcing that were specified in the previous section are still important, but firms, large and small, are looking for additional benefits that revolve around flexibility, creativity, and meeting customer needs in a timely fashion. These benefits and the necessity of networking in a global context stimulate firms to question the wisdom of engaging in production at all. Some firms recognize that sustaining their competitive advantage requires that they focus on only those activities that are critical to their success (e.g., design, marketing, etc.). Contracting suppliers to perform production, accounting, legal services, and other functions, including research and development, has become the norm. Drug companies, for example, traditionally conducted all their own research activities (e.g., discovery, drug testing, etc.). In recent years, specialized small companies have emerged to design research, contract doctors and patients, analyze data, and process papers and necessary documents for obtaining drug approval. Covance is one of many contract research organizations that performs drug testing for major drug corporations. Furthermore, new companies have sprung up to provide outsourcing services (e.g., Butler International, Comforce, Control Data Systems, Oasis, Thermo Terra Tech Inc.).

* * *

The intensity of competition and the rapid globalization of the world economy accentuate the centrality of strategy in business thinking and action. Traditionally, strategy aimed at focusing organizational efforts and resources on devising goals and giving a sense of direction to those engaged in implementations. These aims are still important in today's business. In fact, they have taken on additional value and urgency. In the past, however, strategy was devised with two assumptions in mind: customers were passive actors relative to what markets offered, and competition was forgiving. Neither assumption is valid in today's global environment. Customers are sovereign and competition is cutthroat. The global strategy, therefore, conveys special meaning both to the company and to its competitors. Put another way, a global strategy represents a firm's commitment to globalization and its active involvement in the global economy. For this reason, strategy becomes a matter of well-thought-out directives and planned actions. If it is utilized creatively, strategy is the sharp edge of the sword that fends off competitors. The absence of adequate strategies leads to catastrophic consequences that ultimately threaten the very survival of the organization.

Chapter 9

Globalization and Competitiveness

Globalization is a long-lasting competitive advantage.

Percy Barnevik
Chairman, ABB, 1991

Those of us in business compete against other companies and firms worldwide. We compete to maintain and build on relationships with existing customers . . . to gain access to new customers, as well as to new and emerging markets.

Albert Bersticker
Chairman and CEO, Ferro Corp., 1997

In the next decade, global competitiveness will separate the leading companies from all the rest.

Caterpillar, 1997

There is an increasing desire in every country for a higher standard of living, and pressure on political leaders to see that that happens. This creates an enormous opportunity and a challenge.

Jack Welch
CEO, GE, 1993

In Chapter 1, globalization is viewed as a process that enhances and strengthens the quality and effectiveness of business, professional, and personal interactions through unrestricted access to world commodities, technologies, and information. Globalization creates a rapid evolution in the economic and financial sectors and subsequently generates unlimited challenges and opportunities. That is, globalization accelerates rapid changes in the priorities and strategic positions of nations and firms alike. The landscape of the relationships among and between nations, regions, and firms has undergone profound alternation. Indeed, jockeying for power and influence has become a tough game. Emerging competitive forces (e.g., regional and international institutions, virtual organizations, NGOs, etc.) display agility and alertness, and inspire global firms to shape the economic and political scene via a complex network of relationships. This chapter addresses issues related to competitiveness at the national and firm levels in the context of globalization. The focus is on how nations and firms seek to improve or sustain their competitive positions in an era when geography and borders appear to be losing their utility. The existing discourse on both globalization and international competitiveness, however, often ignores the vital link between these two factors. Those who are concerned with globalization generally focus on political or trade considerations. Those focusing on the political are generally interested in global hegemony and are probably driven by a view of globalization that appeals to specific interest groups. Those focusing on world trade concern themselves with either the trade balance or the individual firm's efficiency in marketing and distributing particular goods and services on a global basis, regardless of the peculiarity of demand in various markets. Discourses on global politics and commerce, however, often fail to provide any practical link to the issue of competitiveness.

Restoring or maintaining competitiveness will be of primary concern to firms and nations in the twenty-first century. Ultimately, the objective is to survive in a dynamic world. Nations, like firms, that are not relatively competitive are more likely to lose their ability to contribute to improving the welfare of their citizens, therefore endangering their future vitality. Globalization underscores the importance of participating in global action to ensure survival and growth. That is, globalization is a mechanism that highlights the significance of being competitive and creates an environment to reinforce the quest for competitiveness.

CHANGING THE COMPETITIVE LANDSCAPE

Globalization has changed forever the arena of competition and market structures. Competitive players seek to capitalize on emerging events to get a competitive edge. Furthermore, these players appear to converge in a relatively short time around the most competitive practices. The never-ending search for new resources and markets and global networking has expanded the arena and intensified the dynamic of world competition. Competing globally, therefore, is no longer a luxury but a normal practice. The alternative is decline and eventual demise. Recently, the competitive scene has been characterized by notable developments:

- Networking at and across local, regional, national, international, and global levels among organizations is becoming a business norm rather than an exception.
- Investing in particular sites, at home and abroad, is being driven not only by a favorable environment but also by digital infrastructure. Companies that once focused on a stable political environment, tax incentives, low wages, and other economic and regulatory factors in making decisions when selecting sites or relocating are now driven mostly by the availability of high-speed Internet access. That is, the Internet is playing a vital role in decisions about where to locate or relocate. Competitive organizations, more than ever, are relying on digital information to optimally rationalize their operations. Those sites that offer the needed online capacity are given priority. Traditionally, the term "digital divide" was used to describe the gap in technology application between knowledge-based societies and the rest of the world. The digital divide, however, is also likely to be a common phenomenon within nations. That is, the gap between online haves and have-nots among localities in nations such as the United States, Japan, and France will widen, therefore hindering the ability of some communities to attract jobs and companies.
- National competitiveness is not the same as firm competitiveness. Reich (1991) argues that U.S.-based firms maintained their share of world markets even as the United States lost its lead. Similarly, in recent years, Japan-based corporations (e.g., Sony, Sumitomo,

Toyota, etc.) did well despite Japan's overall economic trouble. In other words, competitiveness manifests the importance of skill and knowledge of the workforce, not the ownership of firms.

- A competitive edge is realized by utilizing instant information. This is because globalization creates interdependence among diverse actors and thus intensifies connectivity. Effective competitors are those who obtain, process, and integrate more information than others. John Chamber, president of Cisco Systems, argues that "companies and countries who will thrive in this Internet economy are those who change before the rest of the world realizes that they have to change" (quoted in Friedman, 1998b, p. A27).
- Competitiveness is not confined only to large countries or firms. Small countries and firms may achieve a competitive advantage and can even have an easier time than larger entities in coping with economic shocks and in taking advantage of opportunities. Zachary (1999) asserts that in the information age, innovation gives small corporations and countries an edge over big ones. Small countries (e.g., Iceland, Singapore, Bahrain, and the Netherlands) have, in recent years, outperformed larger national economies. Similarly, small corporations such as Worldonline, Sepracor Inc., and Vantive have made considerable advances in their respective industries, relative to larger firms.
- Companies that are not active participants in the global marketplace have done poorly relative to their globally engaged counterparts. A case in point is Japan-based companies. *Business Week* (Bremner, 1997) reports that Japan has created a two-tier economy: dynamic Japan (highly competitive core industries that are active internationally) and slow-grow Japan (uncompetitive domestic-focus industries). While the first enjoy a competitive business, the second experience productivity and unemployment problems. Similarly, at the country level, nations that lack advanced economic and civil institutions (e.g., Sudan, Congo, and North Korea) are experiencing stagnant economies and low standards of living. The 1999 Index of Economic Freedom indicates that countries with freer economic institutions and public policies (e.g., Hong Kong, Sin-

gapore, Bahrain, New Zealand, and Switzerland) are weathering the current financial and economic turmoil better than countries with less economic freedom (e.g., Angola, Laos, Vietnam, etc.).

- Governments compete globally to attract firms and FDI. Interdependence is a way of life, and growth cannot be achieved, as previously thought, through self-reliance. This is a reflection of two profound changes in public policies worldwide. First, global and international firms are no longer viewed by policymakers, in many countries, as exploitive; rather, they are regarded as indispensable engines for growth. Second, wealth and job creation, rather than ideological conflict, rank high in the priorities of almost all governments. Globalization, therefore, is the key to promoting the welfare of the world community (Wolf, 1994). Likewise, global competitiveness is essential for achieving global citizenship in the twenty-first century (Zahra, 1998).
- Consumers worldwide seek access to the best available commodities and services. Despite differences in economic and social status, consumers prefer commodities that better serve their needs. The Internet and other sources allow consumers to be aware not only of available market options but also of the living standards and marketing habits of people in other parts of the world. That is, consumers, more than ever, are sovereign. To survive, corporations have to recognize consumer needs and adequately meet them.

NATIONAL COMPETITIVENESS

Most of the literature on competitiveness focuses on firms. Porter (1990) advances the proposition that competitive advantage is created and sustained through a highly localized process. He argues that a nation's home environment plays a critical role in sustaining competitiveness. That is, the role of the nation has grown rather than declined in facilitating competitive advantage. Similarly, Reich (1990) stresses the role of the nation in creating an environment conducive to growth and technological breakthrough. Therefore, he asserts that the overriding goals of any government are to induce global corporations to build human capital in the home market and to upgrade the skills and learning of its workforce. Krugman (1994), however, argues that there is no national competitiveness. He asserts that competitiveness at the national level is "elusive" and "meaningless" and that an obsession with it "is both wrong and dangerous." Nevertheless, there is general agreement among trade and international business experts that national competitiveness is not only a useful term but a reality that shapes and influences a nation's position and its relations to others.

As indicated in the preceding chapters, globalization has a far-reaching impact on growth and development. The free movement of capital, commodities, and knowledge, and the ease in the movement of labor enhance opportunities for countries to deepen their global involvement and upgrade their national institutions. In turn, this process helps to accelerate the denationalization of geographic space and reinforce globalization trends. Indeed, increasing worldwide connectivity and the emergence of electronic global networks render territoriality and exclusive geographic organization irrelevant (Kobrin, 1997).

Porter (1990, p. 9) defines competitiveness at the national level as "the ability to export many goods produced with high productivity, which allows the nation to import many goods involving lower productivity." He argues that the only useful concept of competitiveness at the national level is national productivity. The World Economic Forum (1998, p. 2) in its *1998 Global Competitiveness Report* defines competitiveness as "the ability of a country to achieve sustained high rates of growth in GDP per capita." In both cases, competitiveness is defined in terms of productivity or in terms of the ability to achieve high growth in per capita income. Either approach, despite general application, is inadequate. First, the definition of competitiveness is not explicitly linked to globalization. Pursuing and realizing a goal of superior productivity can only be achieved in an open global market. Only in a global competition can the twin forces of competitors and customers exercise their collective influence to ensure continual improvement in the manufacturing and operation processes. Second, the ability of a nation to achieve a high rate of growth in GDP per capita can be sustained only in the dynamic process of global competition. Third, both definitions appear to overlook the paramount importance of the collective welfare of customers/citizens. Customers and citizens are one and the same. Issues of global growth and of customer welfare are vital elements of competitiveness. Furthermore, there are countries (e.g., Bahrain and Saudi Arabia) that have displayed, over the past twenty years, a high per capita income, but have failed to build a civil society that would foster improvement in intellectual capital. National competitiveness, therefore, should be viewed as a nation's ability to improve the economic and social welfare of its people through active participation in the global marketplace. Such a definition of competition is based on the assumption that eroding a nation's position in world affairs has serious political, social, and economic consequences. In addition, the definition focuses on both input and output aspects of competitiveness. Competitiveness encompasses all those factors that are essential for coping with global competition (e.g., vital economic and civil institutions, adequate infrastructure including educational systems, and a skilled and knowledgeable workforce). Improving the welfare of people (e.g., standard of living, safe environment, etc.) constitutes the primary outcome of competitiveness.

Porter (1990) focuses on attributes that enhance national advantages, which are: factor conditions; demand conditions; related and supporting industries; and firm strategy, structure, and rivalry. The *1998 Global Competitiveness Report* (World Economic Forum, 1998) enumerates eight factors to construct national competitiveness: openness, government, finance, infrastructure, technology, management, labor, and institutions. The report ranked fifty-three countries using a combination of qualitative data from a worldwide survey of corporate executives and hard data from authoritative sources. The chosen countries are responsible for 90 percent of the world's industrial output. Countries such as Singapore, Hong Kong, the United States, the United Kingdom, Canada, Taiwan, the Netherlands, Switzerland, Norway, and Luxembourg were judged to be the world's ten most competitive economies.

Cho and Moon (1998) argue that the prevailing models for measuring competitiveness are more useful for countries that share a similar stage of economic development. They suggest a model that links the stage of economic development (less developed, developing, semideveloped, and developed stages) to sources of international competitiveness (physical factors, human factors, and government). The authors, unlike Porter (1990), assert the direct role that government plays in sustaining competitiveness. Cho and Moon focus attention on the government's interventional role in the economy (e.g., protectionism, promotion of exports, stimulation of FDI, and maintenance of world-class business locations where resources are most efficiently allocated). These authors and the *Global Competitiveness Report* overlook the fact that a government's role is not limited to economic affairs. Facilitating the emergence and evolution of civil institutions and building sound political institutions are important. Absence of these institutions hinders the realization of competitive advantage. The *1998 Global Competitiveness Report*, for example, ranked Taiwan, Korea, and Thailand at the top of a list of the world's competitive countries. These countries, however, have weak political institutions. Their economic progress could collapse if these countries face political turmoil. This is because weak political and civil institutions lead to decay, corruption, and instability. The events in Indonesia and Thailand (1997-1999) are cases in point.

A more practical approach to competitiveness is to take into consideration the influence of globalization on national competitiveness. In the preceding chapters, emphasis was placed on information technology and liberalization of economies. Both shape the evolution of competitiveness and provide a strong integrative global force. A nation's position in the world economy and world affairs is determined by its commitment to globalization and knowledge creation. Chambers (1999) and Friedman (1998b) believe that the "new economy is the Internet economy." Countries that are at ease in joining this economy will "beat the slow" to participate. These countries are able to gather, tap, and deploy knowledge to continuously improve their competitive positions. Normally, these countries have the following:

- The capacity of cable, telephone lines, and fiber optics to carry digital communications (bandwidth)
- A degree of connectivity that maximizes PC links to networks within companies, schools, and entertainment sources and ties

them into the Internet and the World Wide Web. For example, Singapore plans to wire "every school, home and business because [it] understand[s] the importance of [the] Internet in this new economy" (Chambers, 1999)

- People who are comfortable in exploiting networks and sharing their knowledge—"business culture"
- A competitive culture that stimulates big corporations to constantly reinvent themselves
- Home-based corporations that are involved globally and have complex partnerships with diverse corporations

FIRM COMPETITIVENESS

Firm competitiveness has been extensively debated in the trade and academic literature. Nevertheless, the debate provides no adequate link to the era of globalization and to the rapid evolution of the global economy.

In addition to rapid change and intense competition that may increase the firm's vulnerability in the market, globalization at the firm level creates specific demands and difficulties, including the following:

- Foreign-based firms directly compete with companies that operate only in domestic markets. Market structure undergoes a profound change. The scope and depth of competition have become global in nature.
- Outsourcing and cooperation among firms has become a worldwide phenomenon, extending the range and intensifying the dynamic of international competitiveness.
- Defining industry boundaries becomes a difficult task because the lines that differentiate among them are blurred. Consequently, competitors can emerge from unexpected economic sectors. Incumbents in a particular industry are often caught off guard.
- Intense cross-border mergers and acquisitions not only change competition landscapes and accelerate cooperation among firms globally, but also increase market volatility.

- Market opportunities, rather than company ownership, largely dictate a firm's investment and operation strategies.
- Alliances become, more than ever, forms of competition and a means to overcome a firm's former limitations.
- Consumers become sovereign, have more options, and are better informed. In addition, their lifestyles and expectations are complex. Firms, like governments, have a tough time satisfying a sovereign consumer.

The literature pertaining to firm competitiveness focuses primarily on improving performance in the market. Factors that are thought to enhance the strategic positioning of firms (e.g., innovation, quality, productivity, work ethics, etc.) have been widely noted. Jack Welch, chairman and CEO of GE, views productivity as the belief that there is "an infinite capacity to improve anything" and that productivity is the foundation of competitiveness. He believes that "[a] company's and country's success is tied to productivity" (Day and LaBarre, 1994). Infinite capacity to improve, however, is broader than the traditional or narrow definition of productivity—"get more output for less input." This "infinite capacity to improve" should, of course, constitute the guiding principle for companies that aspire to realize a competitive position in the world economy. Welch's view of competitiveness, for the most part, is not widely held in academic research, which typically underscores the role of productivity in its narrow sense (e.g., Porter, 1990; Stopford, 1997). For example, Porter defines competitiveness at the firm level in terms of productivity growth.

Academic Perspective

In academia, there are various approaches to achieving competitiveness. Two of the major approaches are discussed in this chapter. The first is advocated by Porter (1985), who focuses on two factors related to the firm (how work actually takes place within a firm and value chain analysis) and the forces within an industry that shape the competitive position of the firm.

The value chain approach attempts to disaggregate a firm into strategically relevant activities. These activities are divided into two broad categories: primary (inbound logistics, operations, outbound logistics, marketing and sales, and service) and support activities (infrastructure, human resource management, technology development, and procurement). Porter indicates that competitive firms are those which perform their strategic activities more cheaply or better than their competitors. The way a firm performs its activities determines not only whether it is high or low cost relative to its competitors but also its contribution to meeting customers' needs.

In addition to identifying its strategic activities, a firm must analyze the forces that shape its industries. These forces determine industry profitability and attractiveness. These forces include potential entrants, suppliers, buyers, and substitute products and services. Understanding these forces and their underlying causes allows a firm to shape its environment and cope with competition.

The second popular approach, advanced by Hamel and Prahalad (1994), focuses on core competence—a bundle of skills and technologies that a company has. The authors argue that competition among firms is a race for "competence mastery" and market position. It is not sufficient for a company to be better and faster; rather, it must be capable of fundamentally reconceiving itself, regenerating core strategies, and reinventing its industry. The starting point for competitive revitalization should focus primarily on the way managers perceive their industry, firm, roles, and the ways in which these perceptions induce them to behave in given circumstances. The authors, therefore, suggest that a firm has to have a point of view about the future (industry foresight) and construct a strategy for getting there (strategic architecture). Both ensure the vitality and survival of the firm in the market. Hamel and Prahalad assert that strategic architecture points the way to the future. Strategic architecture, however, must be supplemented with the emotional and intellectual energy expressed in strategic intent. This is because strategic intent implies a significant stretch for the organization. Strategic intent has three attributes: a sense of direction (the competitive position a firm seeks to build in the years to come), a sense of discovery (exploring new competitive strategies), and a sense of destiny (a worthwhile goal). Unlike Porter, Hamel and Prahalad, in their analysis of and prescription for competitiveness, focus on a firm's position in the global market. The unit of competitiveness analysis is the firm that operates in a dynamic global market. Hamel and Prahalad, as well as Porter, however, fail to highlight the relationship between globalization and competitiveness. Their emphasis is strictly upon market structure and competition. Globalization, the advance of digital technology, and the Internet economy render most of their prescriptions static. Therefore, in the age of globalization, competitiveness at the firm level should be defined as the ability of the firm to be imaginative and agile, either in defining competition or in shaping the existing competitive game to the firm's advantage.

Practitioner's Perspective

Unlike scholars, practitioners and organizations, in their search for a competitive advantage, focus on opportunities globally. For many practitioners, competitiveness is not mere business expansion. Rather, it is a quest to recognize and seize opportunities in a global market. Recognizing and seizing opportunities is not limited only to business involvement in its restricted meaning. It also conveys alertness to ever-changing customer needs and sensitivity to their cultural peculiarities and identities.

Back in 1956, long before Levitt's conceptualization of the globalization of business, Honda developed a global vision that placed considerable emphasis on meeting customer needs on a global scale. Its guiding philosophy reads (quoted in Lida, 1995, p. 114):

> Maintaining an international viewpoint, we are dedicated to producing products of the highest efficiency, yet at a reasonable price for worldwide customer satisfaction.

Companies have adopted various approaches to sustaining their competitiveness, and, naturally, satisfying customers' demands. Usually, firms have a set of priorities. Nevertheless, firms place certain emphasis on one or more priorities to capitalize on global opportunities. Below is a survey of specific priorities advanced by some firms:

- *Recognizing regional difference.* Firms in this category highlight differences and similarities in conducting their global affairs (e.g., Ford, GM, Honda, P&G, PepsiCo, and Unilever).

- *Operating globally by relying heavily on building subsidiaries and acquisitions.* Danfoss, Johnson & Johnson, Motorola, Nestlé, and Roche are leading pioneers.
- *Building alliances and global networking.* AT&T, Caterpillar, Emerson, HSBC, and Merck pursue this approach energetically.
- *Capitalizing on global talent.* Microsoft, Gillette, and Avon are pioneers in attracting and promoting talented individuals wherever they are found.
- *Community partnership.* Nestlé, BT, and Siemens have traditionally established partnerships with local communities on a global scale to strengthen their competitive position and differentiate themselves.

Global firms aim to provide the greatest possible value to customers, which stimulates them to search for worldwide opportunities. Due to their unique operations, histories, and industries, however, firms exhibit different experiences in maintaining their competitive position. The following sections summarize actions and activities taken by four major firms to sustain their competitive positions.

Mitsubishi Electric

Mitsubishi has undertaken specific steps to respond to global change and rejuvenate itself, which were articulated by Takashi Kitaoka (1997), president and CEO:

- Transformation into a global company by maximizing its ability to adjust to the rapidly changing markets. That is, Mitsubishi operates without mental or geographical boundaries.
- Leveraged talent and resources where they work most efficiently and productively. By locating around the world, the company gains the advantage of diversity, local expertise, and local creativity.
- Increased speed and flexibility in operating. This is done by shrinking staff at the headquarters, eliminating bureaucracy, and transferring authority closer to the front lines.
- Became more creative. Mitsubishi has a research facility in Cambridge, Massachusetts, staffed by scientists from China, India, Germany, Poland, Hungary, Brazil, and the United

States. Each scientist brings a unique background and perspective to the work they share. In addition, the company established a reward system in Japan and other parts of the world that recognizes individuals rather than teams.
- Maintained job security. The company espouses a philosophy that "secure employment is the most important social contribution companies . . . can make" (Kitaoka, 1997).

Ferro Corporation

Ferro, a producer of specialty materials used in industry, has been doing business globally for several decades. Its products are sold in over 100 countries. Albert Bersticker (1997), its chairman and CEO, indicates that Ferro follows seven guidelines to compete effectively:

- Rely on experienced international executives.
- Think local, but remember the company's big picture.
- Learn to deal with extreme conditions. Ferro develops contingency plans to deal immediately with crisis situations.
- Measure results in U.S. currency. Results of foreign operations should be translated into dollars.
- Offer the same high level of quality in all markets.
- Focus on customers. Despite the many differences one encounters in other countries, customers all over the world share the same goals.
- Look to the future. All goals must be subordinated to the long-term future prospects of the parent company.

Ryder System, Inc.

Ryder, one of the world's largest providers of integrated logistics and transportation, is innovative in coping with global competition. Anthony Burns (1997), its chairman and CEO, asserts that sustaining a competitive advantage requires moving away from the traditions of the past and embarking on new courses of action (p. 534):

- Away from incremental change
- Away from a "Lone Ranger" approach toward more competitive partnering, alliances, joint ventures, and outsourcing

- Away from functional excellence toward the pursuit of total business excellence
- Away from broad funding of business toward select capital investment
- Away from competition based on price and quality to competition based on time
- Away from top-down management decrees to frequent two-way communication with employees
- Away from a product-driven approach to a market-driven approach
- Away from technological evolution to technological revolution
- Away from U.S.-based competition to global competition
- Away from diversification to a focus on core competencies
- Away from inventory at rest to inventory in motion

Nestlé

Nestlé, long before many other companies, recognized that globalization accelerates the pace of change and competition. Therefore, Nestlé reorganized its production facilities, capitalized on specialized factories and economies of scale, relied on global acquisition, reinforced its regional presence and processing technology for local conditions, and focused on appropriate brand names.

STAYING COMPETITIVE

In the Internet economy, digital connectivity and capacity have altered the rules of competition. To be ahead of competitors, to leap forward, to be imaginative and agile, and most important to shape the competition game, a company must embark creatively on two activities: it must utilize digital tools and refocus its priorities.

Utilizing Digital Tools

Bill Gates (1999), Microsoft's chairman and CEO, argues that in the globalization era firms must have the ability to run smoothly and efficiently, respond quickly to emergencies and opportunities, get valuable information on a timely basis to the people in the company who need it, and to make prompt decisions and interact with customers. Gates provides twelve imperatives for achieving these capabilities:

1. *Insist that communication flow through e-mail.* Personal initiative and responsibility are enhanced in an environment that encourages discussion. E-mail, a key component of any digital nervous system, stimulates initiative. Middle managers who utilize e-mail are more likely to be transformed from information "filleters" to "doers."
2. *Study sales data online to share insights easily.* Gathering business data, in electronic form, at every step of the way and in every interaction with customers and partners, and understanding what the data means can trigger a whole range of positive and new opportunities.
3. *Shift knowledge workers into high-level thinking.* The digital system allows a new level of information analysis that in turn enables knowledge workers to turn passive data into active information.
4. *Use digital tools to create virtual teams.* Digital tools offer the best means for enhancing open communications and adding flexibility. Jacques Nasser, president and CEO of Ford, sends e-mails to Ford employees worldwide, sharing good and bad news with them. In addition, he reads responses and assigns a member of his team to reply.
5. *Convert every paper process to a digital process.* Replacing paper with electronic forms minimizes problems in the administrative process and gives employees the impression that the company values their time and wants them to use it profitably.
6. *Use digital tools to eliminate single-task jobs.* A one-dimensional job can be eliminated, automated, or rolled into a bigger process. Firms should make knowledge workers out of every employee possible and motivate each worker to tackle more challenging tasks.

7. *Create a digital feedback loop.* Companies should have a crisp decision-making process to evaluate change, including a provision for reexamining original project goals.
8. *Use digital systems to route customer complaints immediately.* Companies must focus on their most unhappy customers, use technology to gather information on their complaints related to specific products and what specifications they recommend to be incorporated into product design, and use technology to drive the news to the right people on time.
9. *Use digital communication to redefine boundaries.* Revisiting core competencies and determining which areas are not directly related to the core should be built-in operations.
10. *Transfer every business process into just-in-time delivery.* In the digital age, rapid movement becomes routine for everyone. This makes it possible to meet customer demand quickly enough to avoid sacrificing quality.
11. *Use digital delivery to eliminate the middle man.* The more consumers adopt the Web lifestyle, the easier it will be to "disintermediate" the middleman. Therefore, consumers will be the greatest beneficiaries. Dell, for example, began selling its products online in mid-1996. Initially, the company's online business rose from $1 million a week to $1 million a day. Now it is about $14 million a day.
12. *Use digital tools to help customers solve problems for themselves.* Effective companies combine Internet services and personal contact in programs that give their customers the benefits of both kinds of interaction.

Refocus Priorities

Bill Gates and other major CEOs cited in the previous sections vividly emphasize that the business of their organizations is to provide exceptional service to customers, meeting their needs better than competitors. That is, companies appear to realize that the race for competitiveness in the era of globalization situates the customer as the focal point. It is the customer who drives and determines their business. That is, companies compete to obtain access to customers on a global scale. Therefore, the global company has to build a competitive advantage founded upon discovering and fulfilling, on a timely basis, customers' needs and ever-changing demands. Companies must meet certain structural conditions to sustain their advantage:

- *General conditions.* These are the preconditions that companies have to meet to position themselves on a solid foundation. High-quality products and services, work environment, empowerment of employees, adequate performance, adequate structure, and efficient operations are the areas that firms must attend to in order to compete in the global marketplace.
- *Necessary conditions.* The necessary conditions are those that allow firms to compete adequately in the market. Continuous improvement in productivity, production processes, and innovation strengthen a company's position in the market. The challenge, however, is that companies discover that taking the lead and being ahead of competitors should not be taken for granted. Nobuyiki Idei (1999, p. 31), president of Sony, articulates this point: "We have to be faster than the trends." Innovation and productivity, therefore, become dominant concerns for these firms. Dominant concerns, in turn, sharpen competition and accelerate the search for new strategies for staying in the market race.
- *Sufficient conditions.* Both general and necessary conditions enable firms to compete. However, they are not sufficient to sustain a competitive advantage. Firms must also create conditions sufficient to sustain their competitiveness. Focusing on customers and steering priorities to facilitate this aim are the only conditions that ensure sustainable competitiveness. This point was well expressed by Jurgen Schrempp (1997), chairman of Daimler-Benz. He states, "The primary purpose for this globalizing thrust is to serve our customer . . . by being closer to their needs" (p. 308). In a dynamic and sophisticated global market, a firm must define its market, strengthen and differentiate market segments and regions, and enlarge its base of operation. Certainly, a firm must have an alert customer surveillance system and always look for new opportunities to seize a similar or even different business. Olivetti, for example, managed to reinvent itself as a telecom giant. It has gone,

in two decades, from a typewriter maker, to a computer company, to a provider of telecommunications. Similarly, thirty years ago, the core of Sony's business focused on transistor radios and small televisions. Today, its core business is primarily personal computers and communications. The company is taking advantage of the converging business of consumer electronics, computing, and the Internet to be a leading company for the new millennium. Speed, agility, and flexibility in recognizing customer demands, meeting emerging needs, and anticipating needs place a firm ahead of its competitors and position it to be a major global competitor. Strategic alliances and global connections coupled with maintenance of a talented workforce not only reduce operation costs and enhance speed and flexibility in reacting to changing market conditions but also allow a firm to reach customers in different forms. Microsoft, Dell, McDonald's, Coca-Cola, Nestlé, ABB, Toyota, and DaimlerChrysler are examples of companies that treat the customer as the reason for their business and their drive for excellence: the source of renewal, flexibility, and innovation.

In conclusion, the linkage between competitiveness and globalization is essential. It is true that globalization may not lead, in the short term, to a competitive position for a firm or nation and may even displace labor and capital. In the long term, however, globalization enhances competitiveness and inevitably leads to a more prosperous world. This conclusion is based on the following considerations:

- Knowledge, rather than natural resources, is the source of competitiveness. Consequently, competition in a dynamic global market centers on knowledge creation as intellectual capital.
- A competitive edge results from obtaining instant information; digital connectivity is the basis for positioning the company in the global marketplace.
- Companies are places where thinking and intellectual capital are nurtured and sustained. Intellectual capital is the most important asset.

- Growth and development in any part of the world eventually will contribute to the growth of the rest of the world.
- An open and free marketplace, rather than managed trade, provides the best mechanism to speed and facilitate business growth.
- The global marketplace is the arena where talent and discovery are nurtured.
- Global managers, rather than politicians, are the ones who can strengthen the quest for an inclusive global community and a competitive, yet cooperative, world environment.

Chapter 10

Global Managers

Imagination . . . boldness . . . and enterprise are the qualities that drive the world.

Peter Hellman
President and CEO, TRW, Inc., 1997

Where people previously called on Government to tackle political or environmental problems, they are now directly challenging business to take on these roles.

Cor Herkstroter
Chairman, Royal Dutch/Shell
Group of Companies, 1996

Global interdependence, understanding, and openness have rendered the distinction between "local" and "global," in many cases, obsolete. This is quite accurate in the management world. Globalization has produced two significant developments: changes in management qualities required for effective conduct and widening managerial roles and functions. These developments, if recognized at all, have not been given adequate attention in the management literature. Today's firm is viewed as an ideal chamber, an experimental space within which knowledge workers engage in creative tasks (Webber, 1994). The focus on creative energy combined with the process of globalization is generating new and urgent challenges for managers. These challenges demand agility, foresight, and attention; they are both sophisticated and urgent. Their scope may be domestic and/or international, but, almost always, they have far-reaching cross-function/cross-border implications. Coping with them sets today's managers apart from yesterday's managers. In PricewaterhouseCoopers' 1999 global survey report, it was found that, in the context of management challenge, most CEOs agree on the following:

- Communications technology first drew the world together; now e-business is altering the value propositions upon which a business has been based
- The importance of information technology is transforming the global economy; it is acute and growing
- The management of knowledge has become an important corporate priority

In this chapter, managerial roles and qualities necessary for effective competition in a global dynamic environment are discussed. The emphasis is on the emerging roles and qualities applicable to globalization theory and practice.

MANAGEMENT QUALITIES

Until recently, U.S. scholars produced most of the writing on international management and business. In fact, it is not an exaggeration to suggest that during the 1950s through the 1970s the field of international business and management was the virtual monopoly of scholars residing in the United States (e.g., J. Boddewyn; J. Daniels; R. Farmer; J. Fayerweather; W. Keegan; E. Kolde; L. Nehrt R. Robinson; S. Robock; A. Stonehill; R. Vernon; L. Wells, etc.). In addition, general management theory was developed and advanced mainly by various U.S. scholars (e.g., F. Taylor; C. Chandler; W. Burke; M. McGregor; D. McClelland; R. Likert; L. Porter; W. Bennis; A. Maslow; I. Mitroff; H. Simon, etc.). These researchers and theorists have contributed to the advancement of knowledge that has shaped organizational processes and practices all over the world. In addition, these researchers have created particular ways of thinking and conduct that have tremendously influenced students of management and leaders of business organizations. Their influence is present in contemporary schools of management thought and in the existing body of knowledge. In spite of their stature and influence, however, some have failed to recognize the importance of cross-cultural qualities and adaptations, cultural imperatives, and cultural diversity in their writing. For example, Warren Bennis (1988) cited five leadership qualities (technical competence, people skills, conceptual skills, judgment, and character), but failed to include any specific cross-cultural attributes.

The American contribution to management theory and to the practical orientations of U.S. managers is extraordinary, but it also has severe drawbacks. Simply put, American management theory is a product of the U.S. business environment, an environment that mirrors the reality of the U.S. market during the 1950s, 1960s, and 1970s. The chief characteristics of this market were its large size, relative abundance of resources, strong domestic competitors, and a focus on performance and results. In such an environment, control was essential to ensure conformity among employees and the enterprise's subunits. So the "resulting organizational culture grew passive; with amused resignation, employees implemented corporate-led initiatives that they knew would fail" (Bartlett and Ghoshal, 1995b, p. 134). The basic assumption has been that capital "was the company's most critical and scarcest resource and that labor's role was simply to leverage the company's investment in equipment and machinery" (Bartlett and Ghoshal, 1995b, p. 141). As a result, customers were treated as a passive actor in the marketplace. That is, customers were expected to buy what was offered in the market at a reasonable price. Thus, companies were preoccupied with meeting existing needs. Satisfying current customers needs, however, focuses on short-term results and precludes capitalization on future market opportunities (or creating tomorrow's markets) and the need for genuine interaction with customers. Consequently, firms have viewed their customers in the context of control. They neglected to consider that their employees and customers are their most important strategic resources. Such orientations have stifled the creativity of new employees, hindered progress and growth, and prevented firms from treating their customers as a vital source of creativity and invention. Global competition, however, has rendered this traditional view of employees and customers obsolete.

International competition and the quest for globalization, however, have created two phenomena in the context of international business conceptualization and research: a tremendous growth in international business literature and an increase in the number of European and non-Western scholars resident in the U.S. and abroad who have contributed significantly to theory building (e.g., J. Denning; P. Buckley; G. Hofstede; D. Hickson; A. Nagandi; C. Handy; S. Ghoshal; K. Ohmae, etc.).

Both phenomena have accelerated the process of building sound management and globalization theories while sensitizing scholars and practitioners to the inadequacy of specific terms and concepts that are often used in business and globalization discourse. Concepts represented by terms such as domestic manager, successful manager, sustained competitiveness, and the universality of management theory miss the mark in any serious discourse on management theory applicable to the global environment. In addition, culturally specific words such as "nice," "successful," and "achievers" have been used extensively in the literature without proper attention to their organizational and cultural contexts.

Likewise, in the real business world, U.S. managers have developed neither an appreciation for international competition nor a global mindset (Adler and Bartholomew, 1992; Whitman, 1994; Moran, Harris, and Stripp, 1993). Recently, Doug Ready, CEO of the International Consortium for Executive Development Research, indicated that most U.S.-based companies are still poor at actually cultivating internationally minded managers. In Ready's opinion, U.S. managers appear to have difficulty in adapting to new global cultural realities: "Two generations of economic dominance, combined with a strong domestic market, have contributed to creating a colonial mentality in the U.S. companies" (quoted in Ready, 1995, p. 225). The absence of globally oriented managers, however, is not confined to the United States. For example, in an interview with *Harvard Business Review,* Percy Barnevik (1991), president and CEO of Asea Brown Boveri, one of the most globally driven corporations, has said that his company does not have enough global managers. Propelled by the dramatic growth in international trade and competition, selected U.S.-based business leaders are becoming aware of the necessity of cultivating global managerial qualities. David Whitman (1994), Whirlpool CEO, states:

> An initiative like globalization doesn't acquire momentum just because it is enormous. You have to push hard to overcome the initial inertia. . . .

Whitman, however, acknowledges that most international manufacturers are not truly global. He believes that building a shared base of understanding requires time and endless effort. Similarly, managers from other nations acknowledge that competition today centers on attracting qualified, knowledgeable employees. Emphasis on cultural socialization and adaptation is taking priority. The following quotation from *The 1999 Global Survey* (PricewaterhouseCoopers, 1999) underscores the importance of global thinking and behavior:

> It's going to get less and less important where people come from or where they are located. The great skill will be managing across borders, getting effective, and flexible, virtual teams.
>
> CEO from the United Kingdom

> In the past, the biggest goal of manufacturers was to cut costs and increase profitability by mass production. However, in the future, CEOs will have to understand and adapt to behavioral, cultural and social changes brought on by the development of digital technology.
>
> CEO from Korea

Scholars and practitioners have envisioned general and specific qualities for effective overseas conduct. Researchers, compared to practitioners, describe a wide range of qualities and provide various frameworks for identifying and analyzing management effectiveness. The following sections contain a brief discussion of the perspective of each group.

SCHOLARS' PERSPECTIVE

Because the globalization process has intensified, the quest to understand managers and organizations across nations has become increasingly urgent. Over the last three decades a rich literature dealing with global competition and international human resource management has accumulated. Within the context of managerial qualities and skills applicable to the marketplace, two major classifications of studies have evolved: the international assignment and global competencies.

International Assignment

The major concern of this area of study is foreign assignment in general. This includes expatriates, third-country nationals, and local nationals. Most of the studies in this category focus on ways to enhance the performance of these personnel, thereby improving the competitive position of the parent organization in the global marketplace. In addition, most research in this category is well established, especially in the area of expatriates. Expatriates' selection, training, adaptation rewarding, and repatriation have been investigated extensively. The basic assumption often made by scholars is that corporations have strategic objectives that span the globe, and global assignment plays a significant role in implementing these objectives. Thus, firms must develop people who can successfully design and implement strategies, utilize resources, ideas, and technologies, and effectively process and integrate information in a global context (Black, Gregersen, and Mendenhall, 1992).

Several researchers have examined a wide range of the characteristics needed in international operations. Managerial competence and experience, cultural empathy, ability to face ambiguous situations, communication skills, and the ability to see the world from different points of view are considered the most likely factors to determine success or failure in a foreign environment (Ali and Masters, 1988; Marquardt and Engel, 1993; Doz and Prahalad, 1986; Phatak, 1995).

With regard to the factors critical to expatriate success, Zeira and Banai (1985) find that the most desired criteria in selecting expatriate executives are proficiency in the host country's language, expertise, seniority, and previous success in overseas assignments. The authors indicate that there was substantial consensus on the desired criteria among headquarters officials of MNCs, their subsidiaries' top executives, and host country officials. Ali and Masters (1988) find that the most often mentioned qualities for international assignments are managerial competence and past experience, technical competence, ability to make decisions in an atmosphere of risk and uncertainty, understanding the long-term strategy of the firms, ability to view the world in different ways, and cross-cultural awareness. In the United States, however, most decision makers use domestic performance to predict success in an overseas assignment.

Black and Porter (1991) indicate that U.S.-based firms select typical American managers for overseas assignments and tend to believe that expatriate managers should manage in overseas assignments just as they did back in the United States. Worse, Marquardt and Engel (1993) argue that until recently, U.S.-based corporations have often treated expatriate assignments as a sort of necessary nuisance and have sometimes selected personnel for them without regard to their performance. Indeed, most U.S.-based corporations send American managers for overseas assignment without any preparation or training (Black, 1988; Tang, 1981). Current thinking and reality, however, indicate that such indifferent attitudes toward global assignment on the part of top executives are costly in time and money, and are detrimental to company survival and future growth.

Global Competencies for Success

Studies in this category are concerned with attributes and skills necessary for effective performance at home and abroad. The major assumptions underlying these studies are that: (1) managers should not only manage but also lead, and (2) success comes to the alert and agile, and those who never resign after graduation (Ali, 1993; Kotter, 1995).

Adler and Bartholomew (1992) compare the qualities of transnationally competent managers with those of traditional international managers. They specify the qualities of globally competent managers as follows: (1) understanding the worldwide business environment from a global perspective; (2) learning about many cultures; (3) working with and learning from people from various cultures simultaneously; (4) creating a culturally synergistic organizational environment; (5) adapting to living in many foreign cultures; (6) using cross-cultural international skills on a daily basis; (7) treating foreign colleagues as equals; and (8) willingness to transpatriate for career and organization development. The authors trace the progression of organizations: domestic, international, multinational. They believe that the new global competencies are needed for working in or managing transnational corporations. By limiting these qualities to TNCs, Adler and Bartholomew ignore the fact that even managers in purely domestic organizations need these skills. Today's competition is far-reaching in its scope and effects. Firms operating in a domestic market cannot escape it and are unable to get around it. To survive, these firms must nurture global competencies.

Bartlett and Ghoshal (1992) view global managers as a network of specialists, not single individuals found in TNCs. They believe that in TNCs there are three groups of managers who are highly specialized yet closely linked. The qualities for success in each group are different, but complement the qualities of those in other groups. The three groups are: the business managers, the country managers, and the functional managers, along with the main group, the corporate managers. The identified attributes of the business manager are strategist, architect, and coordinator. Attributes of the country manager are sensor, builder, and contributor. The functional manager displays the qualities of scanner, cross-pollinator, and champion. The corporate manager assumes the qualities of leader, talent scout, and developer. The specification of qualities for each category is useful in the sense that it highlights the most needed skills and focuses the top executive's attention on addressing issues related to motivation, promotion, and global career design and development. In addition, it centers attention on what needs to be done in each category and clarifies roles and expectations. Unfortunately, Bartlett and Ghoshal concentrate only on managing TNCs with their global operations and the complexity of their products and services. Organizations that are not global in their operations still need managers with a global perspective and orientation. These organizations no longer operate in an isolated environment. In a globally integrated economy, these organizations play a significant role in the chain of activities.

Wills and Barham (1994) provide a set of desired behavior competencies for the international manager. They group competencies into three categories: cognitive complexity (cultural empathy, active listening, sense of humility); emotional energy (emotional self-awareness, emotional resilience, risk acceptance); and psychological maturity (curiosity to learn, orientation to time, personal morality). The authors accentuate two important aspects that are often neglected in a discourse on competencies: respecting the equality of human rights and the dignity of individuals, and making sense of life as a complete whole (balancing the demands of work, home, and social life). The authors, however, consider these qualities relevant only to international managers (individuals who are managing across a number of countries and cultures simultaneously).

It is clear from the foregoing that current research and thinking focuses attention on qualities needed for international managers and/or compartmentalizes these qualities among managerial positions in a global organization. There is a need, however, to concentrate on necessary qualities (basic requirements) that each manager should acquire and nurture. Furthermore, it seems that the problems with the preceding studies stem from the fact that most researchers still subscribe to the notion "think globally and act locally," instead of "think and act globally." Different forces are in the process of rendering such a perspective obsolete, including global electronic information and the speed of receiving, processing, and storing information. Global relationships have become essential elements for growth among firms. In fact, local firms have been linked to global webs (Kanter, 1994). Currently there is free movement of skilled people to CDSs and the industrial world and vice versa (skilled human resources used to migrate from emerging and developing nations to the industrial world). Interaction among people of different nationalities has become common. Competition among firms and nations centers on ideas. Human resources, therefore, assume significant roles in enhancing competitiveness, greater than availability of raw materials and capital. Developing and emerging economies are beginning to assume leadership roles as drivers of global growth (Gibbs, 1995). Economic competition is no longer merely among sovereign nations but more and more is occurring among regions within nations or among regional blocs. The traditional role of the nation-state is in decline, but states are assuming new roles (see Chapter 2). The role of corporations, however, is gaining more influence in world affairs; and the world is becoming a knowledge-based society where individual knowledge takes primacy. In this new society, the march of the future is collective and all work emerges through relationships (Webber, 1994). In addition, in the new world economy integration becomes the norm rather than the exception. Therefore, certain universal qualities and attributes (e.g., integrity, sensitivity, cultural empathy, flexibility) are becoming prerequisites for competent managers at home and abroad. Today's manager must be global in his or her orientation and spirit. This does not mean that global managers must have in-depth knowledge of the historical and cultural aspects of other nations. Rather, it means that global managers must have a basic understanding of global events and/or be attentive to the concerns and beliefs of people from other cultures. Ethnocentrism, arrogance, cultural prejudice, and prejudgment hinder managers' progress on local, national, regional, or global levels.

In advocating that today's manager must be global in orientation, there is a need to highlight qualities that managers must display for effective business dealings. Previous research, however, lacks comprehensiveness and often concentrates on either international assignment or competencies for success in the global marketplace. The fact that competition today centers on attracting knowledgeable employees requires that qualities needed for global managers be addressed in the global context. The following are general qualities and skills that are often mentioned:

- Possession of a global perspective
- Effectiveness in dealing with human resource problems
- Maintenance of a flexible attitude
- Achievement of an adequate level of technical literacy
- Comfort with people from different cultures
- Maintenance of a sense of humility in dealing with people from different cultures
- Knowledge of the social, economic, and political environments of other nations
- Creative and imaginative problem solving
- Maintenance of a high level of integrity and ethical conduct
- Willingness to work and live in a foreign environment
- Long-term perspective on business performance
- Ability to think and act in relevant cultural terms
- Ability to voice concerns for any possible human rights violations either at home and/or abroad

- Adaptability and commitment to change
- Conversational proficiency in two or more languages
- Ability to establish and maintain personal relations with influential individuals in foreign countries (e.g., politicians, top businesspeople, social actors)
- Commitment to principles of a civil society
- Ability to deal with delicate and complex issues
- Exercise the same concern for subordinates and their communities worldwide
- Ability to recognize and size up opportunities on a global scale
- Foresight to map business changes and opportunities
- Desire to act fairly and promptly to optimize benefits, business and otherwise, for both their organizations and communities across the globe
- Recognition of the importance of global trade and opportunities
- Effective use of e-business and information technology and familiarity with their implications
- Effective use of networking at home and abroad
- Sense of history of vital world issues
- Balanced view of conflicting concerns and demands

These qualities underscore the notion that in a borderless world global managers should think and act globally. That is, a manager is a world citizen engaging in complex activities and relationships. He or she has allegiance to a constituency that is spread across the globe. Certainly, compartmentalization of these activities into domestic, international, and global is a mere academic exercise. Viewing activities in such a framework abstracts rather than facilitates managerial progress. Therefore, the main concern should be whether a manager is effective in performing these activities. Sensitivity to work and cultural aspects in organizations, therefore, requires courage, confidence, and humility.

PRACTITIONERS' PERSPECTIVE

Unlike scholars, who are more concerned with frameworks and guidelines for capturing qualities necessary for effective conduct, practitioners highlight specific qualities that are relevant to their organizations and industries. Their practical insights have made a significant contribution to theory building in management. Consultants and corporate managers, though they may share a similar perspective, display dissimilarities in their views of effective qualities. For example, Coyne and Dye (1998) of McKinsey & Company underscore the importance of job specific qualities. They state, "managers assigned to a particular type of business unit need to have skills that fit their specific network strategy" (p. 108). S. H. Rhinesmith (1996), president of Rhinesmith and Associates, however, focuses on general qualities. He identifies six attributes of the global mind-set. Competent global managers are said to be knowledgeable, analytical, strategic, flexible, sensitive, and open. D. Ready (1995), of the International Consortium for Executive Development Research, is very specific in terms of needed qualities. Global managers are the ones who celebrate their progress, but never allow themselves to become fully satisfied that they have made it.

CEOs of major corporations have been general in their specification of qualities necessary for global managers. This may reflect an understanding that these qualities are nurtured and developed and that managers exhibit them differently. Cor Herkstroter (1996), chairman of Royal Dutch/Shell Group, for example, accentuates openness and an ability to deal with a multiplicity of changes. Peter Hellman (1997), CEO of TRW, emphasizes imagination, boldness, and enterprise. On the other hand, Percy Barnevik (1994), chairman of ABB, stresses global vision, understanding, leadership, and integrity.

CONFRONTING MYTHS

Several myths exist in both practice and theory regarding global managers. These myths must be confronted in order to refine organization practices and to advance conceptualization. While myths are powerful and take on significant value in the absence of clear understanding, confronting them is the only reasonable way to enhance competencies and minimize cultural blunders. Because the global business literature is in its earliest stage of development and since the globalization process is evolving rapidly, myths often find fertile soil and grow. They appeal to practitioners and researchers who are looking for ready explanations or easy answers for existing global business difficulties. Adler and Bartholomew (1992) and Ali and Camp (1996) observe that many managers and organizations lack global thinking and business strategies. Adler and Bartholomew argue that this is due to prevailing myths—myths that seem to be self-sustaining, thus preventing "firms from acting in a global manner." A review of the literature suggests that various myths are found in business research and practice (for details see Adler and Bartholomew, 1992; Ali and Camp, 1996; Bartlett and Ghoshal, 1995b; Hofstede, 1994; Lobel, 1990; Moran, Harris, and Stripp, 1993). In the following sections some of these myths are identified and discussed.

Myth One: Managers who are working with a company operating in a national market do not need global orientations.

No. To be a global manager one does not have to work overseas or be associated with corporations operating internationally. Today's managers interact with diverse people. Effective relations are not limited to overseas assignments or to international dealings. Similarly, global competition is no longer confined to cross-border activities. Global competition is a reality in virtually all markets whether one works in a small private business or a large publicly owned organization, or whether one works in a small town or a metropolis.

Myth Two: Technical performance in a home market is an indication that managers have global qualities.

No. Success in the home market can be the result of technological literacy or other forces. In addition, success in a results-oriented society (i.e., individualistic culture) has a different meaning from success in a group-oriented culture (i.e., collectivistic). In such a culture, success may indicate that a person is taking care of his or her family and extends a helping hand to those in need. Global qualities are more than numerical achievements and involve interaction and networking with people from various cultural and social backgrounds.

Myth Three: Experience in or visiting a foreign country is adequate for enhancing global orientations.

No. Experience in a foreign country and exposure are necessary but not sufficient qualities. Many who have worked in other countries did not understand the local culture or language. A consultant, for example, who lived in Kuwait for several years did not speak Arabic and displayed a minimal understanding of Arab culture.

Myth Four: Past experience of a firm in foreign countries is evidence that it is managed by globally oriented managers.

No. Conditions in the past may not resemble today's or tomorrow's business environment. Successful overseas operations in an era of growth and opportunity may not be easily realized in an era of global recession or economic fluctuations. Likewise, U.S.-based firms, for example, were successful when products and services were marketed on a global basis (mass manufactured and mass marketed) regardless of the particular needs of customers in other countries. *Fortune* magazine (Ready, 1995) asserts that this practice was driven by a colonial mentality. Global competition, however, has forced companies to pay greater attention to a culture's specific tastes and needs. In this regard, U.S.-based companies have experienced difficulty. Hampden-Turner and Trompenaars (1993, p. 21) argue that "as markets become more customized, more fragmented, more oriented to unique requests, America's difficulties have mounted."

Myth Five: Recruiting international personnel (foreign) to work in the home market indicates that top managers display global qualities.

No. Recruiting international personnel is fine, but not enough to ensure that top managers develop global orientations. International personnel may be hired because there are no others available to perform particular tasks that demand people with special qualities. In any case, developing global thinking is more than recruiting; it is an orientation that managers should exhibit in their strategies, structures, and processes.

Myth Six: Managers working with large organizations are naturally more global than those working in smaller organizations.

No. The size of the company is not a measure of its global intent. Size can be a problem rather than a facilitator. Smaller organizations, because of their missions and cultures, and because of the orientations of their founders and top managers, may nurture global thinking. Such global firms may develop global strategies and have intimate relations with customers and stakeholders from various cultures. Certainly, cultural sensitivity is not confined to large organizations.

Myth Seven: Managers who treat people from other cultures with respect are global.

No. Treating people with respect regardless of their cultural and national backgrounds is essential, but not enough. Respect does not preclude prejudice. Global qualities are broader than mere respect. Competent global managers, however, display a wide range of qualities that are nurtured and developed over the years.

Myth Eight: Familiarity with foreign languages is evidence that managers display global thinking.

No. Knowing one or more foreign languages is important in a global business environment and for furthering one's career. This, however, does not mean that a person espouses global thinking. Someone may learn a foreign language merely to satisfy a school's curriculum requirements. Similarly, a person may learn a foreign language because it is a job requirement (e.g., professional foreign individuals). Furthermore, one may know a foreign language but not nurture qualities of receptivity, empathy, and attentiveness. Thus, a person may acquire some proficiency in a foreign language without knowing the subtleties of the language and the cultural sensitivity that comes with it.

Myth Nine: Today's formal education prepares people to espouse global thinking.

No. This is not necessarily true. Aside from all existing deficiencies in the contents and methods of contemporary educational systems, being an educated person is no longer adequate (Drucker, 1993). Furthermore, it is a mistake to confuse education with knowledge, as many individuals stop learning after graduation.

Education can facilitate global thinking if the desire to change and adapt is combined with high levels of cultural sensitivity, empathy, and curiosity.

Myth Ten: Providing managers with cross-cultural training enhances their global orientation.

No. Training may have a short, but not a long term, impact. Building on newly acquired knowledge, a desire to learn more, and practicing new knowledge and skills are essential for ensuring the benefits of cross-cultural thinking because "increased cognitive understanding does not guarantee increased behavioral effectiveness" (Adler and Bartholomew, 1992, p. 62).

THE MANAGER'S ROLE

International competition, global economic integration, political stability or instability around the globe, and changing social and economic priorities are of immediate concern to managers. Global managers believe that growth will be sustained in the global arena and that a vibrant business environment is essential for a prosperous, peaceful world. Global managers such as Akio Morita, former chairman of Sony, who calls on the leaders of the business community to "think globally and act globally," instead of "thinking globally and acting locally," are possibly the true global leaders. Global managers play significant roles not only in restoring national competitiveness but also in shaping the future of their firms, communities, and the world in general. Improving a specific firm's position in a highly competitive market betters the national standard of living and sets the foundation for a stable world where people of various civilizations live together in dignity and mutual respect. In addition, global managers' actions are not bounded by national borders. A case in point is Percy Barnevik of ABB, who believes that ABB is not Japanese, nor Swiss or Swedish; it is a transnational without a national identity. He holds frequent meetings with ABB's top managers in different countries to foster cultural understanding and global commitment.

In today's global economy managers have come to assume additional responsibility for narrowing the misunderstandings between and among nations and cultures. Some might suggest that managers' roles be confined to their firms and that managers should not engage in culturally partisan politics or global missions. Critics of the new manager's role, however, overlook the fact that in recent years managers have displayed two qualitative aspects related to their roles: distancing themselves from nationalistic attachment and refraining from imposing their views on others. The first represents significant progress in management thinking that is in line with the globalization imperative. The second constitutes a realistic understanding of what the world should be—a place where the use of force and torture, at the national and international levels, is not welcome. Unfortunately, many cannot understand the nature of new management thinking and that globalization, first and foremost, implies a profound transformation in management thinking that focuses on a prosperous and peaceful world community. Friedman (1999) interviewed managers in Silicon Valley and was dismayed at their lack of nationalistic attitudes. He was disconcerted by hearing an executive declare that "We don't even care about Washington. Money is extracted from Silicon Valley and then wasted by Washington. I want to talk about people who create wealth and jobs. I don't want to talk about unhealthy and unproductive people. If I don't care enough about the wealth-destroyers in my own country, why would I care about the wealth-destroyers in another country?" (p. 373). Friedman believes that this is a "disturbing complacency" toward "Washington and even the nation." Friedman appears to be offended by managers who disregard extreme nationalism and who espouse global orientations. He indicates that executives in Silicon Valley say things such as "We are not an American company. We are IBM United States, IBM Canada, IBM Australia . . ." (p. 374). Friedman (1999) and Greider (1993) claim that this thinking reflects a lack of patriotism and a commitment to manage business effectively at the expense of patriotism. These authors, however, miss the point that in the era of globalization, executives view the whole globe as their market and that chauvinistic sentiments are detrimental to the spirit of globalization. Managers of corporations appear to have a realistic understanding of how society and their companies operate free of forces, biases, and resentments toward others. Executives consider world stability a genuine concern and a genuine issue that requires divergent and thoughtful inputs. More important, it requires a down-to-earth, nonethnocentric perspective.

The new development in managers' orientations reaffirms that today's managers often have the skills and ability to deal with complex business and international problems. The essence of their jobs, the type of work they do, their mobility, and their unbiased judgment (e.g., unrestrained by local policies) prepare them to play active but neutral roles in both world business and world politics. Unlike politicians, who are driven by political interests and who think in terms of local constituencies, global managers are imaginative, not conflict driven, and their constituencies are the people of the globe. Likewise, politicians are influenced by lobbyists and interest groups, while global managers are influenced largely by their global customers. In fact, politicians understand neither globalization nor the triumph of the individual (Naisbitt, 1994; Ohmae, 1995). Global managers, on the other hand, treat the globe as the arena of their action and view globalization as a normal progression. Furthermore, global managers exhibit attributes that are not necessarily common among politicians. Global managers display a high level of integrity and humility and are cosmopolitan in their vision, thinking, and behavior. In addition, they are comfortable in dealing with people from different cultures; maintain a flexible attitude, are adaptable and committed to change; and have work experience in more than one culture and have conversational proficiency in two or more languages (Ali and Camp, 1996).

INTERNATIONAL RELATIONS AND COOPERATION

In order to play their vital roles in enhancing global integration and building the global economy where major powers act with justice and integrity and show sensitivity to the aspirations of economically less advantaged nations, managers must assume a new function: international relations and cooperation (Ali, 1992). In this context, various activities rank higher on the agenda of global executives (e.g., negotiation of relationships between communities within and across nations; engagement in activities that minimize the need to resort to war and conflicts, etc.). Indeed, global executives should court multiple goals and courses of action that facilitate global integration and a collective global leadership, as detailed in the following sections.

Fostering a Healthy Economic Environment

Global executives passionately seek and advocate genuinely free-market conditions for international trade. The globalization of business has resulted in a highly competitive but interdependent world where the economies of countries complement one another. Economic competitors (e.g., Japan and Germany) are becoming more like teammates, or, at worst, opponents, rather than enemies (Petre, 1990). Global managers foster the free flow of capital and trade across the globe. Genuine economic competition is a challenge, nevertheless, that eventually enriches and strengthens competitors across the globe. Helmut Maucher (1994), CEO of Nestlé, declares that the freedom to act and operate is essential for the social and economic welfare of any society. He states, "A part of that freedom—and not the least important part—springs from a self-determined exchange of goods and services. When this element of economic self-determination is missing from a society, there is neither freedom nor wealth" (p. 125). Fostering a healthy economic environment demands that senior managers be involved in activities that have external focus and interact with various social and economic agents. Put simply, global managers exercise leadership responsibility in fostering and maintaining a healthy economy at home and abroad.

Increasing R&D Spending in Other Regions of the World

The objectives are to enhance knowledge transfer, capitalize on new discoveries that improve human welfare, facilitate understanding and interaction among world-class scientists from various cultures, and access worldwide talent. For example, SmithKline organized its R&D to become more science-based. In addition, the company negotiated important drug-discovery collaborations with Merck, KGaA in Germany, Synthelabo in France, Schering-Plough in the United States, Takeda Chemical in Japan, and Glaxo Wellcome in the United Kingdom. Executives who are unbridled by a narrow nationalistic view treat innovative development and research involvement in other regions as a normal process.

Forging Strategic Alliances and Cooperation with Others Across the Globe

Strategic alliances have become fundamental for business growth. Strategic collaboration is seen as another form of competition; therefore, joint ventures, along with other types of alliances, should play an increasingly crucial role in international business. IBM, for example, is guided by a strategy that leads to greater global reach. It has created, therefore, an alliance council of senior executives that supervise the activities of more than forty partnerships around the world. Japanese firms, in particular, utilize JVs to serve various strategic goals: entering the foreign market in easier and cheaper ways (e.g., Toyota and GM in the United States, JVC and Thompson in France), dominating particular markets (e.g., Southeast Asia), learning and acquiring new technologies (e.g., Matsushita and Siemens of Germany), and understanding foreign markets and environments. The globalization process has increased reliance on strategic alliances and on networking activities. Mitsubishi Corporation has 73,000 relationships spanning the globe, giving it formidable resources and broad experience. It is likely in the twenty-first century that many industries will be characterized by alliances and networking relations. It was in the 1980s, due to global competitive pressures, that firms resorted to establishing alliances with corporations which would otherwise have been considered traditional competitors. In the twenty-first century, however, alliances will probably be used for achieving economic integration, building a global economy, and enhancing the process of global change and understanding. In this context, alliances are not restricted to business organizations. Rather, managers may find themselves active in promoting alliances among cities, communities, and NGOs across nations. Such alliances strengthen business relations and ensure continuity of a fruitful business environment. In their role as networking champions, CEOs assume a responsibility well beyond their traditional economic roles. This responsibility encompasses activities within and across nations. As Cor Herkstroter, chairman of Royal Dutch/Shell, eloquently puts it, "We have discovered that we have to place a new emphasis on listening and exchanging views. To gain a greater understanding of the changes, we have found that we have to communicate more, both internally and externally" (1996, p. 101). This demand for continuous communication is not the end of the story. Rather, it is the beginning of a profound process that sets in motion a new role for the CEO.

Learning More About Global Stakeholders and Their Cultures

In addition to strategic and analytical skills, global executives must also master the art of politics and social relations. Today's executives are faced with complex situations and have to make sophisticated assessments. Successful or fruitful assessment demands, among other things, political sensitivity. Such sensitivity is a new element that should be included as part of the new international relations function. Egon Zehnder (1993), CEO of Zehnder, argues that political sensitivity allows managers to thrive in extremely complex situations. Executives need to bargain, negotiate, and sell ideas. Effective managers familiarize themselves not only with their counterparts' strategies and orientations, but also with the outlooks, backgrounds, and hopefully the names of influential politicians and social actors. The objective is not to manipulate, but to cultivate long-term relations and identify the best potential partners, employees, and advisors. Personal relationships with social, business, and political actors across boundaries along with some knowledge about the peculiarity of their cultures are essential assets for positioning firms in world markets and for enhancing global understanding.

Renewing Commitment to Cultural Diversity of the Workforce

Recruiting, staffing, and promotion policies should be designed to optimize performance and understanding. Qualified personnel from all over the globe are to be sought. Global managers know that employees' cross-cultural experience is essential not only for business growth but also for improving international understanding and cooperation. It is also important for the international teamwork building process and for cross-cultural conflict negotiation and resolution. Commitment to cultural diversity is a good business practice. In terms of global thinking, however, it takes on additional value. This is because it is closely related to the international relations function and the political sensitivity of managers. Furthermore, commitment to recruiting talent from all parts of the world enhances the firm's competitive advantage. Nestlé conducts seminars aimed at improving its managers' and employees' comprehension of, and tolerance for, different cultures. Similarly, SmithKline has embarked, in recent years, upon a personnel policy that capitalizes on global talent. Their 1996 annual report states: "We will continue to develop as a company of diverse employment, gaining strength from a culture that is open to talented people, without regard to ethnic background, religion, age, disability or gender" (SmithKline, 1996, p. 31). Likewise, Siemens follows a human resource strategy that key positions will be staffed only by managers with international experience. Their 1996 annual report states: "To ensure that we can draw on a strong global pool of talent, we opened a management training center in the United States in addition to our facility in Germany. A third center will follow in Southeast Asia" (Siemens, 1996, p. 9).

Renewing Commitment to Ethical and Moral Objectives

Although commitment to social justice is important, in the coming decades the commitment to wider distribution of opportunities and economic development among regions and localities across the globe will take priority. As people get control over their destinies, politics will be less important. Furthermore, the economic and social welfare of individuals should be a guiding principle for global managers. Caterpillar, P&G, and Nestlé are leading global corporations that are serious about advocating social and economic justice. In fact, Nestlé "is racing across the developing world building brands, roads, farms, factories, and whatever else it needs to capture new markets" (Rapoport, 1994, p. 147). Social and economic injustices are not only a source of instability, but also a manifestation of bad business practices. Alleviating them is a sign of a healthy economy. Balanced economic and social programs are top priorities for global managers. In this context, global managers strive to check the widening gap between the haves and have-nots (Hoadley, 1998).

Renewing Commitment to a Peaceful World

Global managers treat this commitment as an integral part of fostering world economic prosperity. Politicians have dominated the global scene for a long time. Traditionally, their actions have had devastating consequences (e.g., the First and Second World Wars, the Holocaust, the Cold War and nuclear race, economic sanctions, regional wars, etc.). The cost has been high in terms of human suffering and economic tragedy because politicians often thrive on conflict and are handicapped by their chauvinistic views. In contrast, business managers function best in a peaceful and cooperative environment. The globalization era signals the rise of the manager's role and the decline of the politician's role in world affairs. In fact, managers are more in tune with the goals and spirit of globalization (e.g., prosperity, cooperative conduct, and peace) than politicians. Managers, unlike politicians, are neither imperialists nor relativists. Therefore, they are at ease with global conduct and globalization goals. Indeed, global managers, free from extreme nationalism and the urge for domination, are capable of strengthening collective actions and advancing common goals.

WHO IS THE GLOBAL MANAGER?

Global managers are defined in terms of their qualities and roles. In their orientations and conduct, they add tangible value to their firms, communities, and the world. Certainly, global managers stand in contrast to ethnocentric, parochial managers. To have a better grasp of what it means to be a global manager, it is essential to refer to current thought in the literature. Alkhafaji (1995, p. 237) states that global managers take "ideas and concepts from the environment and use them in the more complex world of global management." Similarly, Lane and DiStefano (1992, p. 49) hold that the term global manager means "reorganizing the way one thinks as managers and as students of management." Both definitions lack accuracy as they emphasize the mechanical aspects of perceiving and transmitting events. Global managers do not act on a particular stimulus with the assumption that it is globally neutral. Rather, global managers receive proposals and determine whether they are culturally relevant. Global managers do not simply try to figure out where they came from in order to understand their underlying assumptions, but process them by critically evaluating their appropriateness in terms of culture and new organizational realities. Global managers seek to process, integrate, and coordinate thought to generate synergy and a responsive system that enhances global understanding and interaction. Global managers have a mind-set, outlook, and orientation that treat the world as the arena where the action is and believe that people, regardless of their origin, are capable of growth and can contribute in a meaningful way. The global manager is not a passive actor who receives ideas; rather, he or she is able to refine and act on them in a way that optimizes the welfare of the organization and the society where it operates.

Certainly, "true" global managers display qualities that are needed for effective performance. It is worth noting that the true global manager is not what Reich (1991, p. 78) defined as one who is "driven by the irrefutable logic of global capitalism to seek higher profits, enhance market leadership, and improve stock prices." This definition focuses the role of global manager on financial performance, thereby reducing the desired attributes to those which are measurable and quantifiable. Global managers seek to increase corporate value but not at the expense of any stakeholder. In addition, this definition attempts to project U.S. values on the rest of the world. In many countries, global managers are neither preoccupied with short-term profits nor with the immediate reaction of Wall Street. Similarly, capitalism has various faces (e.g., collective, humanistic, etc.), and the free market system is the main concern of global managers.

The essence of the global manager is his or her orientation and conduct, the inner qualities that set him or her apart from those who are parochialistic and unconcerned about the consequences of their activities on the lives of other people either abroad or at home. In this book, therefore, global managers are viewed in terms of their orientations and actions. Both outlook and action focus on the world in its entirety. That is, managers, in performing their tasks, are attentive to world reality and to the conditions and consequences of their acts. Unlike other global players, global managers match words with action. More important, they treat globalization not merely as an intellectual exercise, but also as a practical outreach that opens new avenues for growth and prosperity worldwide. In other words, global managers understand globalization's imperative and reality. In their spirit and conduct, they aim at generating and expanding benefits to stockholders, employees, and communities across the globe. Figure 10.1 depicts managers in terms of global thinking and action. Managers at the bottom left depict those who maintain indifferent attitudes toward globalization. Those at the top right represent managers who are at ease with globalization and corporate integration in the world economy. The matrix underscores the fact that in a global environment, managers espouse various orientations based on their understanding of and inclination to participate in global affairs. These orientations are manifested in different patterns of behavior. Though the range of possible behavior is wide, the focus here is on the most common patterns that encompass the complexity of thinking and acting on a global scale.

The Global Manager Matrix demonstrates the variation in types of managers that is common in the globalization era. Though the global manager is still in an early developmental stage, some com-

FIGURE 10.1. Global Manager Matrix

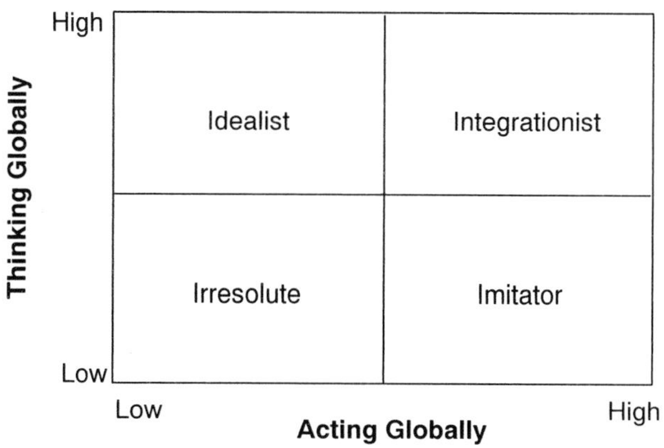

panies may have more of these managers than other companies. Resources, capabilities, and culture give specific organizations the opportunity to upgrade their human resources at the right time, thereby realizing a competitive edge in the global marketplace. The following sections are descriptions of each type of manager in the matrix.

Idealist

Theoretically, the idealist manager gives the appearance of understanding the demands of the global environment. Thus, this manager gives the impression that he or she has what it takes to be a global manager. Nevertheless, infatuation with the globalization trend does not ensure that such a manager is capable of acting in a reasonably global manner. Youthful prejudice and lack of cultural empathy, for example, are real roadblocks to translating aspirations into actions that resemble true global behavior. The liberalization of trade and investment and the openness of the U.S. market, along with aggressive promotion by academic and professional institutions of the economic necessity of globalization, stimulate many U.S. managers to publicly advocate the advantages of globalization. Internalization of globalization principles, however, is still a distant goal.

Irresolute

The irresolute manager still thinks and acts as if the world has not changed that much since the 1950s-1970s era (the era of rising nationalism, decolonialization, and predeterminism). He or she is contained by the situation and is not inspired to move ahead. He or she is indecisive and unable to change his or her outlook and behavior. This type of manager constitutes a serious stumbling block to the organization's ability to integrate into the global economy because these managers think that globalization is neither good nor inevitable. They are primarily found in countries that are not yet opened to the world economy and in many quarters of the globe that are not actively involved in world trade and investment.

Imitator

The imitator is a manager who is not consciously able to comprehend the complexity and speed of global change. The imitator manager believes that globalization is inevitable, but has not yet internalized its benefits. Nevertheless, he or she is following the trend. Other managers advocate and act globally and he or she does not want to be left out. That is, global involvement is done out of necessity rather than conviction. This type of manager could create some obstacles for his or her company's entry into the global economy. Nevertheless, it is easier to educate imitators and induce them to understand the principles and the spirit of globalization than irresolute managers. Imitators are likely to be found in any organization. Their presence is a manifestation of prevailing conformity in organizational life, rapid organizational transformation, and pressures to join a global action.

Integrationist

Managers at the integrationist stage believe that globalization is inevitable and good. They are sensitive and aware of their global situations and the impact of technology and world economic integration on the global positions of their firms. Integrationist managers internalize the challenge of globalization and have a balanced view of both the constructive and destructive aspects of globalization. Possible minefields and setbacks in business conduct are treated as normal, and the road to integration into the global economy is not seen as always even. These managers actively promote free trade systems, open access to opportunities everywhere in the world, and sustaining world development and the welfare of the global community. Undivided allegiance to consumers is the hallmark of their managerial careers.

All four types of managers are found in organizations. Globalization is contested daily by those who are not yet convinced that it is both inevitable and beneficial. Building a global organization and developing global managers require fundamental changes in orientations, priorities, and resource allocation. Corporations, however, should map the consequences of information technology, economic globalization, and democratization around the world for their employees. Internalization of these consequences and changes is the foundation for global transformation.

Chapter 11

Global Leadership

I believe there is a need for France to assert itself more on the international scene, not because of its power or wanting to teach anybody lessons, but because it has a different way of seeing a certain number of international realities.

Lionel Jospin
Prime Minister of France
(in Whitney, 1999a)

Ultimately, however, the peace we seek . . . is one that reflects the lessons of our terrible history: that peace is not true or lasting if bought at any cost; that only peace with justice can honor the victims of war and violence; that without democracy, tolerance and human rights for all, no peace is truly safe.

Kofi Annan
UN Secretary General, 1999a

In this time of accelerated change, American leadership must remain constant. We must be clear-eyed and vigilant in pursuit of our interests.

Warren Christopher
U.S. Secretary of State, 1996

The journey of humankind, over the last few decades, has been full of contradictions: aspirations for peace and tragic wars; astonishing prosperity and widespread misery and poverty. Taken collectively, these contradictions, along with many others, reflect, to a large degree, an absence of visionary global leadership. In modern history, global leadership has been a complex necessity for securing world stability and development. Columbus's voyage of 1492 marked the beginning of the ascendancy of European power and the subsequent colonization of most parts of the world by European countries. Portugal, the Netherlands, and Spain were the dominant powers on the world stage in the sixteenth century. Their rise and decline were an epoch in world history that could shed light on the use and abuse of power in pursuing national goals to the detriment of other nations' interests. The industrial revolution, which began in the last quarter of the eighteenth century, was the hallmark of Western civilization. Since that time, modern technology has emerged as the vital factor for enhancing one's position of power in world affairs. England, with its new economic clout and naval power in the nineteenth century, came to play a decisive role in world events for many years. The birth of the Soviet Union in 1917 and the rise of the United States as a world economic and military power after World War II marked the emergence of a global tension between these world superpowers. Their ideological conflicts and their domination in various parts of the world polarized countries into capitalist and socialist camps. The collapse of the Soviet Union and the "self-resignation" of Russia as a superpower have left the United States the sole global power for the immediate future. The end of the Cold War is considered by many international relations experts as a blessed turning point in the history of humanity that coincides with the globalization era. In fact, for a few years, there was an optimism that the world was on the verge of peaceful transformation and prosperity. This optimism appeared, however, to be premature. Small-scale conflicts, regional instability, and economic and financial crises are a reminder that the world's problems are serious and require thoughtful leadership. In a startling acknowledgment of the deep problems the world faces, Klaus Schwab and Claude Smadja (1999), the president and managing director of the World Economic Forum, respectively, state:

> We must demonstrate that globalization is not just a code word for an exclusive focus on shareholder value at the expense of any other consideration; that the free flow of goods and capital does not develop to the detriment of the most vulnerable seg-

> ments of the population and of some accepted social and human standards. We need to devise a way to address the social impact of globalization, which is neither the mechanical expansion of welfare programs nor the fatalistic acceptance that the divide will grow wider between the beneficiaries of globalization and those unable to muster the skills and meet the requirements of integration in the global system.

Furthermore, critics argue that the abatement of the Cold War initiated the beginning of a new world system, a system characterized by at least three aspects. First, the plights and tragedies of many people in the CDSs are either ignored or not publicized. The seriousness of starvation, civil strife, foreign interventions, and wars, for example, in Rwanda, Colombia, Angola, the Sudan, and the Congo have been given little attention by the leading powers. Second, the unipolar world has become mostly hierarchical. The United States is the supreme power, and other economically powerful countries are reduced to client-state status (e.g., Canada, Russia, Germany, and England). The client states, however, have some degree of freedom in pursuing their national interests internationally. Third, nationalism and strong nationalist sentiments have become the driving force beyond the supreme power's foreign policy. Yet, the supreme power denounces the same tendencies in other nations as manifestations of extremism and dangerous behavior.

This chapter is designed to address the issue of world leadership in the globalization era. The major theme is that global change demands that the world's leaders have a coherent vision based on peace, justice, and prosperity, and that they must display an unwavering commitment to principles of democracy and self-determination for people across the globe and a commitment to equity and the quality of human life. This proposition is based on four premises. First, business leaders and corporations are actively engaged in defending human rights. In addition, they play leading roles in building global consensus. These new actors find that it is not only a matter of principle, but good business practice to denounce violations of human rights and abuses of power. Second, because of the information technology revolution, powerful nations can no longer dictate events in most parts of the world. Events can be influenced by powerful actors, but it would be difficult to control them. Third, people in the age of globalization have less tolerance for abuse than previously. Many people across the globe have experienced a taste of freedom. Indeed, freedom empowers them to denounce brutality and abuse. Last, NGOs have broadened their worldwide activities and are inspired to assume the role of guardians of principled conduct. Their active campaigns and well-organized information networks may deter some powerful nations from continuing their abuse and misuse of resources.

NECESSITY OF GLOBAL LEADERSHIP

Modelski (1987) argues that the global system needs leadership for three reasons: because all political systems have it, because it performs a set of basic functions at the global level, and because the role has been successfully practiced in the modern world for several centuries. These reasons are not quite accurate; leadership is needed, not because all political systems have it, and certainly not because it has been successfully practiced, but simply because political systems differ in their forms and natures. There are democratic and autocratic systems in transition. The existence of each system does not ensure the existence of leadership. Leadership requires specific qualities and is a multidimensional process. Responsible leadership fosters diversity and stimulates creativity in political, business, and social conduct. Dictatorship suppresses both. In addition, the experience of past centuries evinces, at best, an imposition of hegemony rather than leadership. The memory of colonization and exploitation of the African, Asian, and Latin American peoples by Western nations evokes bitter feelings and outcries among these people. The arbitrary rules and decisions that were made by the colonial powers tragically paralyzed many of the colonized nations politically, socially, and economically. This practice can be termed anything but leadership.

The necessity for global leadership should stem from the essence and essential functions of leadership. The essence of leadership is the ability to steer events in such a way as to minimize damage especially to the less fortunate members of the global community. Responsible global leadership must articulate vision, strengthen the collective behavior, and shoulder responsibility morally and financially. The functions of global leadership, using Benne and Sheats' (1948) terminology, encompass task and maintenance functions. In the global context, maintenance functions (e.g., standard setting and following, consensus taking, harmonizing, and tension reducing) take priority. Performing them ensures the continuity of the global community, its progress and prosperity. The essence and functions of responsible leadership accentuate that the threat or use of force is counterproductive to world peace and wealth creation.

JOCKEYING FOR WORLD LEADERSHIP

For the near future, there does not appear to be a viable challenge to the United States as a supreme world power. Yet the United States has to direct substantial resources toward domestic growth and in the meantime sustain its position as an international leader. In addition, several countries are competing and aspire to assume leading positions in world affairs.

Thurow (1992) and Ohmae (1991), among others, project that the world will be most influenced by three regions: the United States and its domain, North America; Germany and its sphere of influence, the European Union; and Japan and the East Asia region. These areas are presumed to represent the world's most powerful economic and political units. Certon and Davies (1991) argue that each region will be heavily influenced by its largest member, but will act primarily by consensus in all matters of common interest. The rest of the world (e.g., the Middle East, South Asia, Africa, and Latin America) will be left out of this interlocking arrangement and be reduced to serving, on occasion, the interests of the major powers. Toffler and Toffler (1993) assert that the media-drenched nations that rely on a complex electronic infrastructure (e.g., the United States and Japan) are the dominant world powers. The authors, however, predict that the great powers may decline; tiny states may become shooting stars, and nonstates (e.g., transnational corporations in alliances with city-regional governments) may dominate the real decision-making powers of the future.

Three major assumptions are advanced in support of the above schemes. First, the next few decades will be marked by fierce economic competition among the three regions. Second, other regions or nations are not expected to make major economic leaps. Third, the world appears to be nearing a point where military power is not needed to resolve conflicts. In addition, the above classifications of world leadership, while asserting a global division of labor according to specific economic and technological stages, ignore or minimize the likelihood of a clash of civilizations and the possible conflict within existing economic superpowers (e.g., China, India). Furthermore, the conflict in Kosovo and the use of force by NATO is a reminder that military power is still a potent factor. In the context of a clash of civilizations, it is important to note that the twenty-first century will be the time when the world moves from economic and possibly technological competition with other countries toward a competition between ideas and values. Recently, Huntington (1993), among others, fears that the clash of civilizations is a possibility in today's world. This fear will be amplified in the digital age if the gap between digital haves and have-nots is not reduced.

Furthermore, conflicts among existing economic superpowers (the United States, Japan, and the European Union) are not unimaginable possibilities. As Wright and McManus (1991) indicate, an economic cold war between the United States and its allies is quite possible. A *Wall Street Journal* (1993a, p. A20) editorial observes that trade conflicts almost resemble cold war disputes. It states "like the old superpower rivalry, the trade order seems to offer much insecurity and requires a costly preoccupation with denying the other side any advantage." The United States-European banana fight in February-March 1999 is an example of how a trade war, even between close allies, can get out of hand. The U.S. government announced that it would impose 100 percent tariffs on $520 million worth of European goods. This action was taken because the EU preferred to buy bananas from former European colonies in the Caribbean rather than from Latin America, where U.S.-based fruit companies operate.

POSSIBLE WORLD POWER RIVALS

Several countries are jockeying for power in the globalization era. Some of these countries assert their right to influence because of their economic, military, and/or technological advantages. Other countries still yearn for world influence because of their imperial traditions and histories. Mitchell (1992) argues that there is a leading power index—GNP, military expenditure, and manufacturing production. He believes that a leading power, at any given time, is capable of forging global hegemony if it dominates in all three dimensions of the power index. He suggests that the United States has a considerable advantage in all three dimensions.

Modelski (1987) argues that a nation must meet four conditions to successfully perform as a global leader (pp. 219-225):

- *Insularity.* Geographic isolation is the clearest and most easily observable qualification for world power. Being surrounded by an ocean provides higher security than being land-locked.
- *Stability and openness.* Stability and freedom from strife and revolution marked all the world powers during their periods of dominance.
- *Economic leadership.* GNP, along with its composition and the proportion given to innovative projects, distinguishes the world powers.
- *Politico-strategic organization for global reach.* The ability to fight and to win global wars decides the issue of world leadership.

Modelski's conditions are general. Furthermore, they are not sufficient for global leadership. Militaristic hegemony and economic clout, along with geographic location, may sustain a powerful position, but they are never enough for commanding leadership. The following is a brief discussion of several countries that are competing to position themselves on the global stage.

Japan

Japan's economic miracle, its success in applying technology to the high-value-added industries, and its leadership in the world financial market represent significant achievements that prepare Japan to be a power with which to reckon. Despite its 1990s economic problems, Japan still has the largest Asian economy and has a savings pool of $9 trillion.

Lincoln (1992) argues that in contrast to the United States, Japan is unlikely to push large ideological or moral issues as part of its national interest. In fact, Japan has always negotiated "its way out of most international problems and learned to live with (or financially insure against) international loss rather than use military force" (p. 14). Japan may be willing, nevertheless, to exercise influence in the international arena proportional to its economic power (Ali, 1992). For example, Tsutomu Hata, a former Japanese foreign minister, calls for equal partnership between the United States and Japan. He states, "I don't think we can call our relations 'big brother/little brother' any longer" (quoted in Schlesinger and Forman, 1993). Likewise, The Japan Federation of Economic Organization issued a report that put forth Japan's position relative to that of the United States. The report states, "It is important that the United States should learn from other countries and harmonize its system with international norms . . ." (quoted in *Tokyo Business Today,* 1992). Similarly, Ishihara (1991, p. 55) asserts that Japan has the power and knows how to be independent in its actions, and it "no longer needs America's military protection." Japan, however, does not have the potential to compete militarily with the dominant military powers in the Pacific region: China and the United States. Furthermore, Japan's role may be to "ameliorate the hegemonic tendencies of the two" (Funabashi, 1998, p. 34).

Germany

Germany appears to favor a collective approach to solving international problems. In February 1999, German Chancellor Gerhard Schroeder argued: "that there is a danger of unilateralism, not by just anybody but by the United States, is undeniable" (Whitney, 1999b). Unlike Japan, Germany has sought, whenever possible, to assert its leadership on the global stage. In recent years, Germany has made its concerns vividly known regarding Chechnya, Bosnia, and Iraq and has called for observing international norms and laws evenhandedly. Furthermore, Germany does not hesitate to project itself as a global power that should be taken seriously by the United States. Likewise, Germany represents a real challenge to U.S. leadership in world economic affairs. Germany played a significant role in establishing the EU and the Euro. A unified EU gives Germany the necessary backbone to make its voice heard globally. Its economic and intellectual powers should enable it to operate on the international stage with confidence and maturity. Recently, Kissinger (1994, p. 821) asserted that Germany "will insist on the political influence to which its military and economic power entitles it." German President Roman Herzog (1999) outlined eight maxims that would promote world peace and understanding:

- Promotion of democracy
- Protection of fundamental human rights
- Renunciation of nationalism
- Avoidance of cultural and religious conflicts
- Better use of international and regional institutions to enhance economic and social stability
- An end to selfish "beggar thy neighbor" commercial policies and "social dumping"
- More effective communications
- Global intercultural learning and research communities

France

The most vocal of international critics of the United States and its foreign policy, France has long resisted U.S. domination in Europe and NATO. France sees that the United States is dominating economic, military, technological, and cultural areas on a global scale, prompting French Foreign Minister Hubert Vedrine to state that this phenomenon "is not comparable, in terms of power and influence, to anything in modern history" (Whitney, 1999b). Since France is incapable of being a major superpower, it has resorted to strengthening EU institutions and multilateral arrangements.

England

Naval power and a strong aristocratic and imperial view have helped England for many decades to be a powerful world nation. These historical attitudes and behaviors have made it difficult, in recent years, for England to play a major or even independent role in world affairs. For this very reason, England has closely allied itself with the United States to protect its interests abroad and to maintain what is left of its international prestige.

England, under both labor and conservative governments, is still a force that protects reactionary and autocratic governments in the Middle East and other parts of the world. It is these governments, with U.S. support, that perpetuate England's influence on the global stage.

Russia

Russia has serious potential as a world leader. It has a strong military establishment and a rich arsenal of nuclear weapons. It aggressively makes its voice heard. Despite its economic problems, Russia, time and again, has asserted its role as a global power. In the postcommunist era, Russia is gripped by fear and uncertainty. Therefore, it has engaged world events with less confidence and maturity than that exhibited by the Soviet Union. Nevertheless, Russia still clings to its past glory.

Andrei Kozyrev (1994), Russia's foreign minister, declares that the notion of U.S. hegemony is a dangerous dream. He states that "Russia is destined to be a great power, not a junior one. Under a communist or nationalist regime, it would be an aggressive and threatening power, while under democratic rule it would be peaceful and prosperous. In either case, it would be a great power." Recently, Prime Minister Yevgeny Primakov, remarked that Russia is willing to play by international rules: "I believe it's possible to combine a number of things. One, protect the national interests of Russia. Two, do it without slipping toward confrontation. Three, to develop relations with every country" (quoted in Perlez, 1999). The future of Russia as a superpower, however, is uncertain. It has more than fifty ethnic groups, all yearning for some type of freedom from Moscow; therefore, its unity is questionable. In addition, its handling of the recent Chechen uprising hurts its image abroad and casts doubt on its commitment to human rights principles. This, coupled with its severe economic problems (e.g., capital outflow, low productivity, and high unemployment) and the ascendancy of oligarchs in its political and business affairs, may reinforce turmoil rather than foster progress in the future. In short, Russia currently lacks discipline and coherence.

Emerging powers (e.g., China, India, Indonesia, Korea, etc.) are expected to yearn for international leadership and influence. Some of them may assume global power far more aggressively than anticipated. The dynamics and complexity of global politics, while enhancing the demise of a traditional superpower, may accelerate the rise of a new star.

China

One of the competitive global players with the most potential is China. China's huge GNP, its annual growth rate (dropped from 13 percent in 1993 to 7 percent in 1999), and its market make it a potential power. In 2015, China's GDP will be between $11 and $12 trillion, almost equal to that of the United States. Nevertheless, its military capital ($410 billion) will be less than half that of the United States (Wolf, 1997). In addition, overseas, the Chinese have done well economically. Their presence in East Asian countries and their entrepreneurial spirit enhance the future role of China in world affairs. The overseas Chinese own many large corporations. Drucker (1994) calls this group of Chinese entrepreneurs "the new superpower." China is a potentially important giant, though attempts to revitalize it have not been successful. In addition, China has carefully shied away from publicly asserting its ideas and values. The major principles guiding China's international relations are:

1. *Operational flexibility*—retaining the option of accommodation and using force only as a last resort, to protect its territory and immediate Pacific interests (Cohen, 1997).
2. *Global status*—measured by economic strength, not military strength (Tyler, 1999).

In addition, China, unlike Russia, has not projected itself as an intellectual international actor. China still faces formidable challenges in alleviating poverty, utilizing its scarce resources, and modernizing its backward industries. In fact, China is torn between the desire to move ahead and a strong tradition of fearing the unknown consequences of free markets, decentralization, and democracy. Hopefully, economic forces and the experience with individual freedom will eventually propel China into a new era of prosperity. Until then, China is expected to maintain a low profile in the international arena.

Indonesia

Indonesia is destined to be a major economic power in East Asia and perhaps the world. Nevertheless, Indonesia is not, at this time, aspiring to be a global power. It might realize significant importance in foreign trade, but not in foreign policy. The possibility, however, of an Asian free trade pact could give it more weight in world affairs. The Asian economic crisis of 1997 and political turmoil in Indonesia have had a tremendous impact on its clout in the region and in the world. Potential exists, however, once Indonesia manages to straighten out its political and economic problems. The transformation to democracy is a powerful stimulus for the realization of Indonesia's aspiration to be a powerful regional actor.

India

India is one of the most promising countries to play a leading role in shaping global events in the twenty-first century. It is the second most populous country after China and has the fastest growing middle class (over 220 million people). In addition, India has a large stock of highly skilled people, especially engineers. India has played an influential role in the formation and development of the nonaligned nations and has been active in mediating conflicts in Asia, the Arab world, and Africa. India has the experience and the propensity to assume a world leadership role. Unfortunately, in recent years India has suffered from religious and ethnic conflicts and many analysts have suggested that its democratic system may be in jeopardy. Before it can move forward, India has to dismantle its central planning and its reliance on its huge, bureaucratic public sector. Recently, India has started to liberalize its economic and investment policies; nevertheless, analysts suggest that speed in transformation is essential to ensure faster growth in the economy.

Despite the fact that India is a nuclear power and has sophisticated military weapons, its political leaders have refrained from any reference to using force to pursue India's national interests. Indian politicians, on the global stage, have tended to use persuasion and dialogue for solving international disputes. This quality and the inclination to emphasize soft, personal approaches give India the potential to be one of the major international players in the twenty-first century.

Other nations or actors may rise to power on the global scene. It is a tragic mistake to dismiss the possibility of rising stars among the former European colonies in Africa and Asia. In addition, the traditional superpowers may experience erosion of their positions in world affairs. This is largely due to the dynamic of global change and the formation of new alliances and partnerships. But most important, in the era of globalization, two factors contribute to a faster decline of the traditional powers. First, knowledge, rather than endowment of natural resources, has become the most important factor in sustaining competitive advantage. Knowledge and skills travel easily across borders and become the most significant base of power. Upgrading and advancing knowledge, especially in areas of Internet networking and digital communications, therefore, prepare nations and actors to exercise significant power in shaping world events. Second, in a knowledge-based world, the use of force and brutality is less tolerated by large segments of the world's populations. Traditional mechanisms of power not only lose their appeal, but eventually their utility.

This brief discussion of the nations that have the potential to shape global events reveals that for the near future, the United States is the supreme global power. To gain a better understanding of the world's reality, and the status of the United States in it, two issues need to be addressed: the nature of global conflicts and the challenge for the United States in the years ahead.

THE NATURE OF GLOBAL CONFLICT

Traditionally, most of the conflicts in the world have been driven by the urge to expand and to control new sources of wealth and raw materials. By the end of the nineteenth century, the conflict was centered on economic and political hegemony. Yergin (1991) provides an interesting story of behind-the-scenes manipulation and struggle among economic and political elites in and across nations for access to and control of a vital natural resource (oil). Yergin indicates that oil was seen (and still is) as a commodity intimately intertwined with national strategies and global politics and power.

Yergin produces evidence of how oil provides the point at which the interests of the superpowers converged in this century. The following four examples are indicative.

San Remo Agreement

When the French and British governments signed the San Remo Agreement in 1920 to divide Mesopotamian (Iraqi) oil, the accord was denounced in Washington as "old-fashioned imperialism." The United States, however, changed its position when the British government signaled a new "openness to American participation in Mesopotamia" (Yergin, 1991, p. 196).

Japan's Expansion in Southeast Asia

In 1923, Japan decided to align its interests with Anglo-American postwar military orders due to its need for oil. The Great Depression, however, brought hardship to Japan and disclosed its vulnerability to Western oil firms. Sixty percent of Japan's oil market was held by two Western corporations—Rising Sun and Standard-Vacuum. To reduce its vulnerability and its reliance on U.S. oil, Japan decided to solidify its geographic control through expansion in Southeast Asia and in the East Indies. This attempt initiated the first U.S.-Japan struggle for economic and military domination on a worldwide scale. Specifically, this was reflected in the U.S. government's stand against Japan's interest in China. Japan's elite believed that controlling oil resources in the Far East would make it impregnable. Years later, Japan's attack on Pearl Harbor was motivated mainly by its need to secure its oil supply.

Hitler's Invasion of the Soviet Union

The rise of Hitler in Germany sparked new thinking: oil as a strategic weapon. Hitler made it clear that "an economy without oil is inconceivable in a Germany which wishes to remain politically independent" (Yergin, 1991). In his quest for German economic independence, Hitler initiated programs for "recovering" the German domestic market from Standard Oil, Shell, and other foreign oil companies. Hitler saw oil as the vital commodity of the industrial age and for economic power. Therefore, he was determined to have access to the oil of the Caucasus. The invasion of the Soviet Union was seen by German elites as a strategic move for economic and military domination.

The Gulf War

During the Cold War era, a common understanding between America and Western Europe and the Soviet Union regarding the magnitude of the world's resources was maintained. Oil, again, provided the point at which the interests of the superpowers converged. At the end of the Cold War, the Gulf crisis (August 1990-March 1991) demonstrated again that any potential threat to oil supplies would not be tolerated and force would be used, as before, to ensure American hegemony. In fact, analysts suggest that the American militaristic response to the Gulf crisis was an attempt to gain a stranglehold on all oil supplies to Japan, Germany, and the rest of Europe (Ridgeway, 1991). If true, this aim is not different from the old goal (control of oil resources).

Current Trends

Today's tactics and strategies, however, are different from the old ones. Traditionally, the colonial powers boldly stated their goals: political and economic domination. In contemporary conflicts these goals are only on occasion made public, and new dimensions are added to them: cultural and domestic political manipulation. The cultural dimension involves spreading a superpower's plan to other areas in the world. Cultures that display pride and strong identity are treated unfavorably and probably punished. George Shultz (1997) former U.S. Secretary of State, expresses that when other nations do not "play by the rules . . . then they will hear from us." Domestic political manipulation is often addressed by experts, but like the cultural dimension, it has never received adequate coverage. In 1956, for example, "Britain's international finances were precarious; its balance of payments, fragile. Its gold and dollar resources were sufficient to cover only three months of import"

(Yergin, 1991, p. 485). It was time to divert domestic attention to problems abroad. Therefore, Britain, along with France and Israel, organized an invasion of Egypt. Likewise, Yergin indicates, President Nixon was always "searching for some political spectacular [sic] involving oil and the Middle East to try to divert the country from its obsession with Watergate and each new revelation in the scandal" (p. 619). Therefore, the "October War," "oil embargo," and "energy crisis" had to be induced or fabricated. All were valuable tools for domestic politics, especially for their destructive utility, that is, their value in diverting attention from important issues. In contemplating a war, the public is often bombarded with nationalistic or emotionally charged terms such as "national interests," "human rights," "naked aggression," "implementation of the UN Security Council Resolutions," etc. In such an environment, intervention has been justified and the issue of political, cultural, or economic domination is rarely debated.

The preceding discussion raises two questions: Do post-Cold War conflicts differ from previous conflicts? Can globalization and world interdependence proceed smoothly? The answer to the first question is certainly no. Today's conflicts, in their nature and motivation, are very similar to those of the past two centuries. The methods might be different, but the goals are the same. For example, in the Caspian Sea region, the United States has invested money and time to exert influence and control in Central Asia. The motive for this is eloquently stated by Stanley Escudero, U.S. Ambassador to Azerbaijan: "We are at the beginning of what will be a massive oil boom" (quoted in Kinzer, 1999a). Another U.S. official indicates that the United States "wants every country except Iran to prosper," and the United States is "involved in a modern version of the nineteenth-century Great Game, in which Britain and Russia competed for dominance there" (quoted in Kinzer, 1999a). For this very reason, the United States opposes the oil companies' attempts to have a cheaper and shorter Caspian oil pipeline through Iran. Instead, the U.S. government lobbied for a pipeline route from Azerbaijan across Georgia and Turkey to the Mediterranean. Bill Richardson, U.S. Energy Secretary, defends this action as an effective means for strengthening U.S. national interests. Richardson argues that this is not only a matter of energy but "also about preventing strategic inroads by those who don't share our values." He stated (quoted in Kinzer, 1998):

> We're trying to move these newly independent countries toward the West. . . . We would like to see them reliant on western commercial and political interests rather than going another way. We've made a substantial political investment in the Caspian, and it's very important to us that both the pipeline map and the politics come out right.

Clearly, then, today's conflict is not completely different from previous conflicts. The issues of controlling natural resources and maintaining trade and political influence are still powerful motives that dictate certain actions and strategies. In addition, the new conflict focuses on projecting particular values and preventing those who do not espouse them from benefiting from the fruits of globalization. This point touches on the second question about whether or not globalization and interdependence can proceed smoothly. The conflict between the United States and China about the latter's participation in the WTO, protecting its national interests in Taiwan, and conflicts in the Middle East, Africa, Latin America, and the Balkans suggests that the immediate future is not as rosy as one would expect. That is, in the absence of agreed-upon global leadership, competing powers manifest their interests and disagreements in various innovative forms. Nevertheless, some evidence exists that peace may be more than a distant possibility and that conflicts can be solved through dialogue and multilateral institutions.

THE U.S. ROLE

The United States has enjoyed a unique position in world affairs. Its economic, technological, and military powers have been vital in shaping and designing world realities. In fact, the United States in the last few decades has been the undisputed power that manages to steer events to serve its world interests. Over the years, political leaders and foreign policymakers in the United States have developed various visions of what the world should be. President Woodrow Wilson, for example, was largely interested in pursuing moralistic foreign policy. In Mobile, Alabama, in October 1913, he declared that it is unacceptable to design a foreign policy in terms of material interests: "It is not only unfair to those with whom you are dealing, but it is degrading as regards your own actions. . . . We dare not turn from the principle that morality and not expediency is the thing that must guide us" (quoted in White, 1996, p. 7). President Jimmy Carter was an ardent supporter of a foreign policy founded on protecting and promoting human rights all over the world. This was not followed, however, by his successors (Reagan, Bush, and Clinton).

In terms of international involvement and vision for the U.S. global role, three schools of thought are common among policymakers:

1. *The Moralist School.* This school asserts that humanitarian principles, rather than material goals, should guide the pursuit of world leadership. Defenders of this thought (e.g., Cyrus Vance, George Ball, and Edmund Muskie) believe that national interests are best served through respect and commitment to human rights, freedom, and democracy. Dialogue and accommodation are viewed as essential means for advancing global understanding and national interests.
2. *The Nationalistic School.* Advocates of this school (e.g., James Baker, John F. Dulles, and George Schultz) treat the globe as a new frontier that the United States must exploit to secure its national interests. Accordingly, the United States should use any means at its disposal to maximize its wealth and enhance its prestige. For example, James Baker (1999), in commenting on the agreement on March 16, 1999, between the United States and North Korea that allows the former to inspect an underground site suspected of housing nuclear weapons, shows strong resentment, as he thought the agreement failed to strengthen the U.S. role in the Pacific region. In a militaristic-nationalistic tone, he said: "Most important, we should have reminded the North Koreans that we kept the peace in Europe for more than forty years against an overwhelming Soviet conventional force and did so by virtue of our strategic nuclear deterrent. And we should have told them

that we fully intended to honor our security agreements with South Korea and Japan, and that, if necessary, we would not rule out the use, again, of nuclear deterrence."

3. *The Opportunistic School.* Promoters of this school advocate using any available means to realize their goals. History is viewed as a series of events that were precipitated by a few unique individuals. Therefore, opportunists are interested in making their marks on history. Members of this school are masters of public relations and have developed friendly relations with major media outlets (e.g., Madeleine Albright, Lawrence Eagleburger, Alexander Haig, Richard Holbrooke, and Henry Kissinger). International crises and public promotion of American leadership abroad, along with tough talk, are utilized to secure their places in history. Cohen (1995) describes Richard Holbrooke, for example, as having always sought to lead a major international negotiation and as thirsting to make a historical mark; the rest for him is marginal and infinitely malleable. United States economic and military power has been used as an instrument for translating their projections of the world into reality. Like the nationalist school, this school views small-scale conflicts and managed wars as practical ways of advancing their international goals.

There is agreement that the United States will probably retain its status, for the time being, as the sole superpower. Two questions, therefore, need to be addressed. First, given the dramatic social and economic changes in the world, how long can the United States reasonably expect to maintain its superpower status? Second, is the United States willing to be a leader among peers? Possibly the answer to both questions is "it depends." Indeed, there are internal forces and considerations that may restrain the United States from shouldering the burden and reaping the consequences of a highly interdependent world. The quest to defeat communism and the preoccupation with preventing its spread throughout the world have made it possible to overlook the contradictory aspects of U.S. global politics and the magnitude of internal problems. Likewise, at the international level, the Cold War era and the efforts of most nations to pull themselves from the miseries of poverty and/or colonialism have contributed to their tolerance for a global power's mistakes. In the information age and in the age of prosperity, however, a Cold War style of leadership is no longer valid.

Critics of U.S. involvement abroad point out that U.S. foreign policy needs a major overhaul. Robert Reich (1998), Secretary of Labor in the first Clinton Administration, argues that the United States has no coherent foreign policy:

> America used to have a real foreign policy . . . and an apparatus for setting it: a State Department run by people knowledgeable about the politics and societies of places around the globe, as well as a national security adviser and congressional foreign affairs committee. But now our foreign policy depends largely on global flows of money, and our apparatus for influencing them is almost totally removed from democratic oversight.

Likewise, Sanger (1999a) indicates that the U.S. government has failed in its duty to set foreign policy priorities and articulate them to the American people and to the international community. Foreign policy observers indicate that for years U.S. foreign policy was dominated by Eastern internationalists (Clough, 1994; Thompson, 1981). Today's foreign policy establishment, however, is dominated by new elites, or what Brzezinski (1995) called "Mediterraneans"—the Slavs, the Jews, and the Italians. Most of these foreign policymakers have been drawn exclusively from think-tank institutes (e.g., Council on Foreign Relations, Center for Strategic and International Studies, and the Washington Institute for Near East Policy). This tendency not only prevents qualified Americans from assuming responsibility in conducting a balanced foreign policy, but also puts an end to the cherished traditional American practices of participation, inclusion, and equal access. The most important concerns raised by experts regarding U.S. foreign policy are:

1. *Resorting to intimidation and force in dictating its wishes.* Rohter (1994) argues that the United States has a tendency to intervene in other countries' affairs, even though those interventions "have almost uniformly failed to produce the results that policy makers in Washington had hoped for." Richard Haass (1994), a senior director on the National Security Coun-

cil (1989-1993), points to the centrality of using force against other nations to achieve goals deemed important to U.S. national interests.

2. *Reliance, more than any other nation, on a defense industry and weapon sales to stimulate its economy.* The United States has become the dominant arms merchant to the world. In 1986, the United States accounted for only 13 percent of the world's weapons exports. In 1993, the United States' share of the weapons market was an overwhelming 70 percent (Thompson, 1994).
3. *A tendency to use military force to deter a potential rival.* The Defense Department in 1992 issued a report on preventing the emergence of a new rival. The report states, ". . . the U.S. must show the leadership necessary to establish and protect a new order that holds the promise of convincing potential competitors that they need not aspire to a greater role or pursue a more aggressive posture to protect their legitimate interests" (quoted in Ali and Camp, 1992, p. 16). Ehrenreich (1991, p. 125) argues that because of the inclination to use force, "We are in danger of becoming a warrior nation in a world that pines for peace, a high-tech state with the values of a warrior band."
4. *A nonparticipatory foreign policy.* U.S. foreign policy is characterized as undemocratic (Clough, 1994); and it has lagged behind the other advanced democracies in recognizing the moral and political imperative of promoting a more equitable world order (Brzezinski, 1993).
5. *A tendency to be preoccupied with personality and lack of interest in history* (Brzezinski, 1993).
6. *Selective in promoting democracy and freedom.* In principle, the United States always stands for liberty and democracy at home and in the world. Critics, however, suggest that the foreign policy elite ignore this principle more often than not. For example, the Historical Clarification Commission, an independent commission established as part of the United Nations, which supervised the peace accord in Guatemala, released a report that concluded that the United States "gave money and training to a Guatemalan military that committed 'acts of genocide' against the Mayan people" (Navarro, 1999). It is important to note that President Clinton, on March 10,

1999, apologized for this involvement: "For the United States, it is important that I state clearly that support for military forces and intelligence units which engaged in violence and widespread repression was wrong, and the United States must not repeat that mistake" (Clinton, 1999a). Similarly, in Central and West Africa, the foreign policy elite supports dictators and "play[s] down concerns over issues such as democracy, human rights and good governance in the name of energy security and corporate profits" (French, 1998). Robinson (1996) argues that the foreign policy elite actively promotes "low-intensity democracies" in CDSs so as not to disturb the social and political tensions produced by undemocratic status quos, and to suppress "popular and mass aspirations for more thoroughgoing democratization of social life in the twenty-first century international order" (p. 6).

7. *Relying on economic sanctions to achieve political goals.* Business leaders have always voiced concern that trade should not be used as an instrument for advancing political goals. For example, the National Foreign Trade Council was formed by a coalition of more than 650 business organizations to promote alternatives to economic and trade sanctions. According to James Perrella (1998, p. 682) chairman and CEO of Ingersoll-Rand Company, "unilateral sanctions have become our country's foreign policy 'fix-it' tool of choice."
8. *A tendency by foreign policymakers to stand against multilateral agreements when other nations do not follow their dictates.* Critics point out that the United States objected to establishing the international criminal court and international agreements to ban land mines (DePalma, 1999), and rejected a global treaty to regulate trade in genetically modified products (Pollack, 1999). Even in cases where the United States is the major founder (e.g., the WTO), it invokes a new tactic in the international system: "multilateral unilateralism." That is, U.S. policymakers pursue their interests "with vigor inside the framework of the trade system, but not in conformity with the intentions of the system" (Moller, 1997, p. 67).

Most aspects of U.S. foreign policy stated previously are products of the Cold War era. As Gelb (1991, p. 50) states, "Indeed, few people today, in or out of government, have the background or skills to grasp, let alone direct, the new agenda." Most of the existing policymakers are captives of an era of conflict, suspicion, and espionage. In today's world, however, there is a need to attract people to foreign policy work who are experts rather than ideologues, who are motivated by the desire to build a global economy rather than reinforce antagonism and trade wars.

Most of the critics cited here are more likely motivated by the hope that the United States will utilize its potential and capability to be a world example, to be a catalyst for change and an instrument for world stability. Perhaps the widespread criticism also reflects a belief that there is a gap between the ideals articulated by the American founding fathers and the reality of today's politicians. Criticism may also stem from the fact that many people in the world have high expectations of the United States and hold the U.S. foreign policy elite to a high standard.

Over the years, the United States has shown a remarkable ability to revitalize itself and leap ahead. This is especially true in the economic arena. In international relations and in global affairs, the difficulties are not overwhelming. The youthful and entrepreneurial spirit prevailing among U.S. business leaders can be emulated by foreign policymakers. In fact, there are many lessons to be learned from business executives. New perspectives and a clear vision that emphasizes free trade principles and the interdependence of the world economy will ensure that the United States enters the new era as a vital force for world peace and prosperity. Traditional American values that were advocated by George Washington, Benjamin Franklin, and John Adams, among others, stress civilized political values, rather than hegemony. Once these values are internalized and once policymakers face the realities of the new nonhegemonic world, they can overcome weaknesses and ethnocentric policies. The following steps are often recommended by foreign affairs experts to facilitate this goal:

- Defending justice and asserting morality abroad irrespective of special interest groups and their agendas (Brzezinski,

1993). That is, the United States should be an integral part of historic global justice.
- Attract people to foreign policy work who are experts rather than ideologues (Ali and Camp, 1992; Gelb, 1991).
- Enlarge the ethnic, religious, and geographic diversity of people appointed to foreign policymaking circles. African Americans, Hispanics, Asians, and people from the Midwest have been, at best, nominally represented. Recruiting people from these backgrounds is not only a legal requirement, but a condition for having a participative foreign policy that is in tune with the composition of the U.S. population and the need to build a global civil society.
- Take seriously inputs received from global managers regarding foreign policy, especially those inputs that stress nondiscriminatory policy.
- Promote free trade and democratic values as underlying principles for strengthening relations with other nations. That is, stress civilized political values, not mere order (Ali and Camp, 1993).

HEGEMONY AND LEADERSHIP

A futile mistake in the literature on leadership is the tendency to treat global leadership in terms of power and being "number one." As a consequence, experts often equate hegemony with leadership (e.g., Gray, 1997; Kagan, 1998; McGrew, 1992; Mengisteab, 1996; Mitchell, 1992; Talbott, 1998). In fact, Gray views global leadership as a burden that requires security, financial, and economic hegemonies. He argues that the United States made a conscious choice to seek the role of a hegemony. Strobe Talbott (1998), the U.S. Deputy Secretary of State, declares that while taking into account the "foreign sensitivities to American assertiveness," we must be proud of being a hegemony. Talbott, like Kindleberger (1981), believes that hegemonic leadership is essential to stabilize world order.

Viewing leadership as a hegemonic function, however, overlooks the essence and meaning of leadership. In spirit and in practice, hegemonic power forces its will on others. The latter are considered insignificant and their wishes and interests are marginalized, if not discredited. Hegemony conveys domination and a deterioration of moral standards. This is because the hegemonic power demands and rewards submission and reduces interaction with other parties to mere mechanical relations. These parties are obliged to comply with the hegemonic power's orders; noncompliance is punished and submission encouraged. This point was articulated by Mengisteab (1996). In the context of African experience, he states (p. 152):

> The U.S.-led camp of the capitalist countries essentially applied the carrot and the stick to attract and keep African countries in its sphere of influence. It provided some incentives in the form of economic and military aid to the countries under its influence. The price for siding with the U.S. camp was maintaining the socioeconomic structures left behind by the colonial system. The interests and ideological orientation of this camp, by and large, did not allow fundamental changes in the existing social order.

Therefore, hegemony is a process in which the powerful actor dictates its wishes to the less powerful parties through coercion, seduction, manipulation, and inducement. The hegemonic power seeks to create the world according to its image. Madeleine Albright (1997), U.S. Secretary of State, quite eloquently expresses the essence of hegemony when she says, "Our vision must encompass not one, but every continent."

In the business world such a proclamation is unwelcome and is viewed as an obstacle to globalization. For example, Caterpillar (1992, p. 13) asserts:

> It isn't our aim to remake the world in the image of any one country or philosophy. Rather, we hope to help improve the quality of life, wherever we do business, by serving as a means of transmission and application of knowledge that has been found useful elsewhere. We intend to learn and benefit from human diversity.

Similarly, Cor Herkstroter (1996), chairman of the Royal Dutch/ Shell Group, argues that "[t]hose who would impose one standard on the whole globe, the moral imperialists are clearly wrong" (p. 105). Global managers, unlike politicians, are not comfortable with hegemony. William Holland (1996), chairman and CEO of United Dominion Industries, asserts that business people should "question the so-called 'facts' that politicians and media send out" (p. 504). He called for nurturing understanding among citizens of the world rather than dominating others. This signifies a fundamental difference between hegemonic and global managers' orientations toward global affairs. Global managers perceive globalization as an inclusive process that maximizes participation and induces access to global economic and technological benefits. They believe that the future is shaped by those who think and act with speed and agility to adjust and learn, and have the means to generate wealth and jobs on a global scale. In a hegemonic environment, the political elite and think-tank intellectuals seek to maintain a monopoly on the direction and the shape of world affairs.

Table 11.1 highlights major differences between global leadership and hegemony. Global leadership is distinct in spirit and approach from hegemony. Leadership is the capacity to influence and inspire others through an effective, two-way, interactive process to reach a common understanding of principles and norms relative to world affairs. The objective is to sustain global growth and cooperation. Global leadership focuses on devoting time and resources to address global challenges and offers direction at the multilateral level to "advance the cause of social progress, democratization and human rights" (D'Aquino, 1996, p. 109). That is, power reinforces and strengthens the tendency among global leaders to work through multilateral institutions. In contrast, power emboldens the hegemony and induces it to marginalize multilateral institutions. Practically, hegemony offers plentiful opportunities for dominant nations to pursue their interests internationally at considerable costs to others, thereby creating winners and losers. Global leadership minimizes this situation and allows the maximum participation possible in world affairs.

The primary differences between hegemony and leadership center on at least three aspects. First, in a hegemonic environment, power takes the form of coercion while in leadership it is derived from consent. Indeed, hegemony undermines faith in global institu-

TABLE 11.1. Contrasting Global Leadership and Hegemony

Dimension	World hegemony	Global leadership
• Base of power	• Military, financial, and economic resources	• Knowledge and reference
• Goal	• Military, economic, and cultural domination	• Devising collective principles to focus on world affairs, peace, and economic prosperity; offers directions for change
• Means for achieving goals	Mostly coercion, force, and manipulation	• Dialogue and negotiation via well-structured multilateral institutions
• Vision	• Creating a world according to its own image	• Appreciates diversity within the framework of the world community
• Underlying motives	• Nationalistic superiority	• Collective understanding and the welfare of the world community
• Actors	• A few dominant nations	• Leading nations, NGOs, global corporations, and influential individuals
• Frame of reference	• National experience	• A sense of history and the collective experience of the world community
• Decision style	• Erratic and authoritarian	• Systematic and participative
• Orientations	• Generally conflict oriented and secretive in nature; less inclined to play by the global rules	• Consensus building, transparency, and commitment to play by the agreed-upon rules
• Faith in capabilities and future	• Pessimistic and no confidence in followers' ability to contribute meaningfully to world affairs	• Optimistic and strong faith in collective judgements
• Tolerance for uncertainty	• Low tolerance and high fear of uncertainty	• High tolerance
• Procedures for solving conflicts	• Arbitrary, secretive, and exclusive	• Rule of law, openness, and inclusion
• Treatment of followers	• Discriminatory in nature, preferences are determined by economic and cultural interests and domestic political priorities	• Relatively nondiscriminatory and influenced by the need to maintain consensus and coherence of the world community
• Attitude toward change	• Maintains status quo and views change as a last resort. Change, however, is highly guarded; it is a destabilizing factor	• Encourages change; a necessary means for understanding global trends and improving quality of life

tions and obstructs the development of global peace. Second, hegemonic power does not tolerate deviation and seeks to maintain the status quo; change is viewed as a threat to national interests. Therefore, change is only reluctantly pursued. Leadership, on the other hand, creates an environment conducive to genuine change. Third, the dominant actor in a hegemonic environment is a powerful nation or a selection of nations; centralized power. Under leadership, the actors are nations, global corporations, NGOs, and so on. These actors are not obsessed with the urge to dominate. That is, power is diffused globally.

GLOBAL LEADERSHIP IN THE TWENTY-FIRST CENTURY

Lester C. Thurow (1996b) predicted that at century's end, there would be no clear dominant economic power in view. The dominant power manages the world economic system and takes responsibility for dealing with crises. He stresses that leadership involves more than being "number one." His argument, of course, focuses on global leadership and describes neither the United States nor Japan as a dominant economic power. Thurow views global leadership in terms that encompass not only economic and military power, but also the psychological willingness to play the role.

The psychological aspect of global leadership is often neglected in globalization research, but consulting personal psychology may provide the insight essential for understanding world realities. A 1996 *Time* magazine article points out an important distinction between power and influence (*Time,* 1996). This distinction is relevant to the globalization debate and to the quest for a practical and theoretically sound conceptualization of global leadership. As *Time* points out, "influence is not the same as power." The report in *Time* demonstrates that power "gets its way," while influence "makes its way." Although the distinction was made in the context of United States social, political, and economic structure and concerned micro implications at individual and organizational levels, it has a profound message for the globalization discourse. First, influence is viewed as "a vision" that inspires people or nations to discard their doubts and "an ability to connect with people" across the globe and comprehend the way they look at and react to events. Second, yesterday's dominant powers such as Rome, Spain, Great Britain, and the contemporary dominant power, the United States, have relied on a single view of their own leaders and elite. This view is shaped by domestic political considerations, and is often ethnocentric in its orientations and approaches. A political elite seldom pursues a vision that takes into account the aspirations and goals of other nations. These two distinctions have several implications for global leadership. First, powerful nations, who lack vision and resort to coercion in their relations, are not influential as they cannot attract a following and build the confidence and trust necessary for stability and global growth. Second, power, if used unilaterally, creates friction, conflict, and resentment. In the information age, in an integrated world economy, relying merely on power will impair the quest for a civilized global society. Third, in a highly interdependent world, global decisions must reflect, in general terms, the collective aspirations of world citizens, not just those of the G7 elite. Global actions have far-reaching impacts, and the need to avoid global backlash demands that inclusion, rather than exclusion, be the mode for international relations. Certainly, this will enhance global understanding and progress toward a civilized global society. Fourth, militaristic power may bring international visibility and exposure; it may not, however, ensure influence because influence requires compassion and a special touch that arouses, inspires, and energizes people to do their best. In fact, actors who are influential have a sense of history and insight with which to probe the future and act accordingly. It is essential that the twenty-first century is guided by global leadership—a coalition of leading powers rather than a single power. The coalition should encompass "leader nations" and "surrogate leaders." Currently, the latter are attacking global problems, but the approach has been largely ad hoc and random (Tarantino, 1998). Nevertheless, surrogate leaders can set priorities and develop plans pertaining to global challenges.

To take charge of the twenty-first century, the leader nations must have a relatively collective vision—free of any hegemonic tendencies—and must be a catalyst for integration and collaboration and must not rely on coercive seduction. In addition, these leader nations should advocate avoiding the use of force and economic sanctions to achieve foreign policy objectives. Furthermore, leader nations should have a deep understanding of human conditions in all countries and communities where people yearn for peaceful coexistence, the alleviation of poverty, and social and economic justice. Twenty-first century global leadership must focus on integrating all social and economic forces at the city, state, and regional levels and on a global basis. The leader nations must work closely with and stimulate surrogate global leaders such as global development and social agencies, regional and multicultural organizations, and global corporations. These surrogate leaders are destined to assume greater roles in facilitating relationships among global forces and in setting moral and ethical standards to minimize social suffering while strengthening the foundation for cooperative utilization of existing resources. Thus, the global leadership of the twenty-first century leads by example. It should be viewed in terms of its economic, cultural, intellectual, and moral contributions aimed at liberating the mind and soul from distrust and greed.

Chapter 12

Global Backlash

Ensuring that low-income countries do not miss out on the benefits of globalization is a crucial moral challenge, but it is also in the self-interest of developed countries to confront global poverty aggressively.

Peter Sutherland
Chairman, Goldman Sachs International, 1998a

We must address the issues of long-term equitable growth, on which prosperity and human progress depend. . . . We must focus on social issues. . . . Because if we do not have the capacity to deal with social emergencies, . . . there will be no political stability. And without political stability, no amount of money put together in financial packages will give us financial stability.

James Wolfensohn
President, The World Bank, 1998b

Ignoring serious conflicts in Africa and other underdeveloped regions deprives these people of justice and equal rights.

Jimmy Carter
Former President of the United States, 1999

I am not sure at all that we have learned from experience, and I worry that we will end up making the same mistakes again and again.

Robert McNamara
Former U.S. Secretary of Defense, 1999

In an astonishing acknowledgment, Klaus Schwab and Claude Smadja, the World Economic Forum president and managing director, respectively, wrote in 1996 that a mounting backlash against globalization's effects, especially in the industrial democracies, is threatening to have a very disruptive impact on economic activity and social stability in many countries. Later, in 1999, the authors sounded the alarm again and cautioned that globalization needs a human face (Schwab and Smadja, 1999):

> We are confronted with what is becoming an explosive contradiction. At a time when the emphasis is on empowering people, on democracy moving ahead all over the world, on people asserting control over their own lives, globalization has established the supremacy of the market in an unprecedented way. . . . The forces of financial markets seem to be running amok, humbling governments, reducing the power of unions and other groups of civil society, creating a sense of extreme vulnerability for the individual confronted with forces and decision-making processes way beyond his reach.

These concerns are also shared by leading investors and executives. Peter Sutherland, George Soros, and James Wolfensohn, the world's most eminent investors, have repeatedly raised the prospect of globalization's destructive aspects. Their arguments assert that there are serious threats to the very stability of the world. Sutherland (1998a) argues that ensuring that low-income nations do not miss out on the benefits of globalization is a crucial moral challenge. He asserts that there is a disturbing tendency to look at the world's poverty with indifference. Addressing human suffering, he adds, is essential to fulfilling the world's growth potential, and it is in the self-interest of developed nations to address global poverty aggressively. Similarly, Wolfensohn (1998a) declares that development should be viewed as a totality of effort—a balanced economic and social program. "We must go beyond financial stabilization. We must address the issues of long-term equitable growth, on which prosperity and human progress depend." Soros (1998), furthermore, finds that the global capitalist system is coming apart at the seams and that there is an urgent need to rethink and reform it. He suggests that market discipline "needs to be supplemented by another discipline: maintaining stability in financial markets."

The above concerns have been debated by civil, business, religious, and political groups for about two decades. Many of these groups acknowledge that the future has unlimited opportunities. Nevertheless, they argue that the unchecked consequences of globalization can lead to global disasters. Burbach, Nunez, and Kagarlitsky (1997), for example, assert that the globe is mired in an unprecedented era of misery, alienation, and turbulence, and that only a few beneficiaries enjoy a "grand banquet." A wide range of issues and problems has been identified ranging from poverty, pollution, and child labor to politics and technology. It is important, however, to point out that most of the problems that critics have attributed to globalization have been in existence for a long time. That is, some of these problems are not the direct result of globalization. Rather, globalization has brought these issues to the public's attention with intensity and energy due to the availability of instant information, world connectivity, and worldwide sensitivity to the necessity of civilized behavior and action.

SOURCES AND NATURE OF GLOBAL BACKLASH

Sanger (1997) asserts that a backlash against "market worship" is inevitable. What is surprising these days, he argues, comes from some of the world's confirmed capitalists and from the oligarchs who see that globalization is causing instability that could unmake the market revolution. That is, the criticisms of globalization are not coming entirely from radical groups or civic, consumer, or human rights activists. In fact, objections to globalization originate from diverse sources. Just after the abatement of the Cold War, many international relations experts voiced their concerns about a world dominated by a single superpower. In many quarters of the world, globalization is viewed as the projection of American culture abroad (see Chapter 3). In addition, labor unions and civil and religious groups, along with environmental activists, have identified and highlighted a wide range of issues they claim are associated with regionalism and globalization. Most of these issues (pollution, wage disparity, labor displacement, political domination, etc.) have a long-term impact and urgently need solutions. In fact, these are problems that the majority of the world's population is facing, and they incite fear, apprehension, and anger. These issues alarm globalization advocates because they contradict the essence of globalization and its cherished objectives (e.g., worldwide prosperity, stability, and harmony). Well-informed advocates of globalization, however, believe that globalization offers opportunities for firms and countries to better their positions and the welfare of their members. Therefore, they view criticisms of globalization and its possible negative consequences as an opportunity for constructive engagement that will eventually lead to minimizing obstacles, to identifying blind spots, and to fostering coherent directions.

The primary objections to globalization can be grouped into five categories: economic, cultural, political, technological, and ecological. These general categories encompass a wide range of concerns and claimants. Each category represents claimants that have various interests and expectations. These concerns are valid from each claimant's perspective and should be taken into consideration when engaging in globalization processes and anticipating their constructive and destructive consequences. In the economic context, unions and social activists, for example, fear labor displacement, unemployment, and drops in the real wage. Culturally, citizens and policymakers in many parts of the world are frightened by the prospect that their way of life is about to be disrupted. Some politicians expect that their nations will eventually lose their independence and that globalization is a new code word for "recolonization" or submission to Western powers. Likewise, some politicians and conservative businesspeople in Western nations believe that globalization represents an end to national sovereignty and the rise of world governance (e.g., Patrick Buchanan and Ross Perot in the United States). In the context of technology, there is a fear that technological innovation and the priority of profit will take precedence over human considerations and compromise national interests. Environmentalists fear that globalization will have a drastic impact on the environment and the ozone layer, thereby endangering the welfare of future generations.

Individuals from different social and political spectrums voice common fears. For example, Peter Sutherland (1998b), of Goldman Sachs International, identifies the following challenges to globalization:

1. Throughout emerging market economies unemployment is soaring, businesses are collapsing, wages are dropping, and prices for basic commodities are rising.
2. Low-income countries will be further marginalized as these countries lack the human capital, the institutions, the physical infrastructure, and the policies necessary to seize the trade and investment opportunities of globalization.
3. Workers in advanced countries are forced to bear a higher share of the costs of improved benefits, and globalization's processes reduce their bargaining power relative to employers. The result is greater job insecurity and downward pressure on wages and benefits.
4. The policy capacity of governments at all levels of development is being challenged by the growing disjunction between national, political, and economic space.
   a. Globalization of production makes it difficult for governments to pursue national trade, industrial, and competition policies.
   b. The growth of intrafirm transactions is complicating the work of national authorities responsible for taxation and economic policy.
   c. Governments have difficulty in managing electronic transactions facilitated by new digital technologies.
   d. Governments find it harder to achieve social welfare goals.
   e. Liberalization and changes in the structure for production generate new trade disputes over policies and practices that have traditionally been regarded as domestic.
5. Globalization is imposing new pressures on key international institutions. Furthermore, it exposes weaknesses in the current system of global leadership.

George Lodge (1995), of Harvard Business School, identifies four conflicts that globalization has exacerbated: the destruction of old and cherished ways, tensions between environmentalists and trade specialists and economists, gaps between rich and poor, and clashes resulting from the impact of migration and culture. Lodge believes that globalization has its winners and losers, creating a world full of surprises. Like Sutherland, he stresses the urgent need to advance new thinking and paradigms to address the reality of globalization.

Pope John Paul (1999) underscores the moral obligation to seriously address the negative consequences while acknowledging the fruits of globalization. In his message to the Roman Catholic Church in the Americas, he states:

> There is an economic globalization which brings some positive consequences, such as efficiency and increased production, and which, with the development of economic links between the different countries, can help to bring greater unity among peoples and make possible a better service to the human family. However, if globalization is ruled merely by the laws of the market applied to suit the powerful, the consequences cannot but be negative. These are, for example, the absolutizing of the economy, unemployment, the reduction and deterioration of public services, the destruction of the environment and natural resources, the growing distance between rich and poor, unfair competition which puts the poor nations in a situation of ever-increasing inferiority. . . .
>
> And what should we say about the cultural globalization produced by the power of the media? Everywhere the media impose new scales of values which are often arbitrary and basically materialistic, in the face of which it is difficult to maintain a lively commitment to the values of the Gospel. . . .
>
> More and more, in many countries of America, a system known as neo-liberalism prevails; based on a purely economic conception of man, this system considers profit and the law of the market as its only parameters, to the detriment of the dignity of and the respect due to individuals and peoples. At times this system has become the ideological justification for certain attitudes and behavior in the social and political spheres leading to the neglect of the weaker members of society. Indeed, the poor

are becoming ever more numerous, victims of specific policies and structures which are often unjust. . . .

UNIT OF ANALYSIS

Concerns about and fear of the globalization process are likely to be in a state of flux for a long time. In fact, hoping for the disappearance or demise of the globalization backlash is unrealistic. Given the complexity of the world community, diversity in thinking and backgrounds, and differences in countries' states of historical and technological evolution across the globe, backlash and resentment are part of the world reality. Globalization does not mean or imply an absence of conflict. In addition, globalization does not imply or convey conformity to a particular approach or view.

The list of concerns and complaints about globalization is extensive, making it almost impossible to reach a practical and comprehensive view of globalization backlash. However, by organizing criticisms according to the unit of analysis—a firm, a nation, and the globe (see Figure 12.1)—we are better able to discuss the destructive aspects of globalization.

Firm Level

Most of the criticisms and outrage against globalization are leveled at business organizations. This is because global firms are seen as the instruments for creating, promoting, and advancing globalization. While there is general agreement that global firms are the engine for generating wealth and jobs, there are some who advocate that firms are primarily motivated by profit and therefore tend to overlook environmental and human issues. Critics of firms' involvement in the globalization process claim that firms:

- Get all the benefits generated by liberalization and globalization (Burbach, Nunez, and Kagarlitsky, 1997; Korten, 1997).
- Spread their power globally, thereby marginalizing governments and other organizations (Mander, 1993).
- Spread Western values and cultures to other countries (Khor, 1993; Nader, 1993).

- Impose unfavorable conditions on CDSs and contribute to the erosion of their natural resources and environments (Khor, 1996; Morris, 1993; Nader and Wallach, 1996).
- Produce economic and income inequality in their global conduct (Korten, 1996; Morris, 1993).
- Recolonize CDSs through their economic and business conduct (Goldsmith, 1996; Mander, 1996).
- Contribute to diminishing the viability of traditional cultures (Barnet and Cavanagh, 1996).
- Create obstacles to democracy and democratic transformation in CDSs (Nader and Wallach, 1996).
- Increasingly function as agents of a global financial system that has become the world's most powerful governance institution (Korten, 1996).
- Contribute to the rapid elimination of work opportunities worldwide and destroy family-oriented business (Lehman and Krebs, 1996).
- Create "technological unemployment" as they build state-of-the-art, high-tech production facilities, and shed millions of unskilled workers who can no longer compete with cost efficiency, quality control, and the speed of delivery achieved by automated manufacturing (Rifkin, 1996).
- Become more interested in maximizing their profits at the expense of human and environmental considerations (Lehman and Krebs, 1996; Greider, 1993).
- Are effectively governing the lives of the vast majority of people on Earth (Clarke, 1996).
- Use information technology to invade customers' privacy and to monitor and record employees' correspondence and conversations (*The Economist,* 1999d).
- Are able to hijack information democracy and establish information tyranny to the detriment of citizens' welfare and rights (Frankel, 1999).

These claims and arguments, in general, tend to ignore the fact that in the last two decades firms have engaged in actions to reduce many of the adverse consequences resulting from those firms' global operations. Serious, but gradual, progress is in the making and

FIGURE 12.1. Major Globalization Challenges

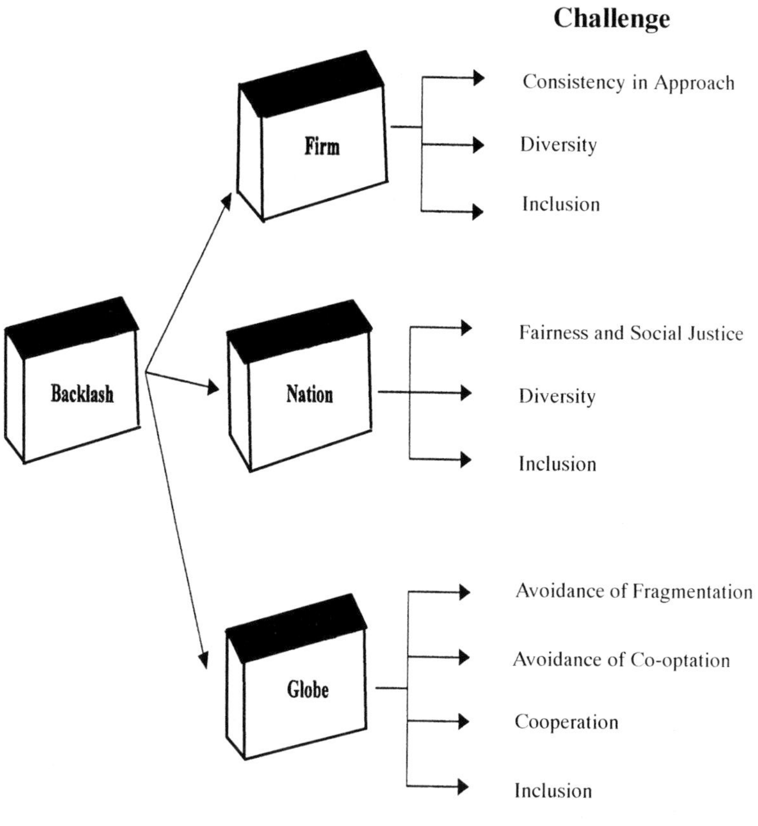

should be transformed into normal conduct. Corporations such as Nike and Phillips-Van Heusen, for example, have taken steps to end child labor abuses and establish a work environment that is consistent with generally accepted moral standards. Likewise, corporations such as the Body Shop have been pioneers in advancing human rights globally and in minimizing damage to the environment. In addition, more and more corporations are joining the Caux Round Table and World Business Council for Sustainable Development to increase their sensitivity to problems associated with globalization conduct and contribute to world development. Companies, nevertheless, face several challenges: consistency in approach, diversity, and inclusion.

Consistency in Approach

The most important challenge facing corporations is to be consistent in their approach to opportunities worldwide. A nondiscriminatory approach in site selection is a high priority. That is, corporations allocate FDI based on economic opportunities available and business environment. It must not be based on political ideology or cultural preference; no community should be excluded based on these considerations.

Diversity

Globalization reinforces, rather than represses, diversity in orientation, religion, ethnicity, and so on. Global corporations and global executives have been up front in claiming and advocating the pluralistic aspects of life and work. Other firms should do the same to ensure full participation and transformation in global affairs.

Inclusion

Globalization in spirit and outlook means inclusion. A major aspect of any global corporation is its ability not to discriminate against any economic actor (e.g., supplier, employee, customer, or community). Inclusion is a safety valve that ensures vitality and continuity in the globalized world. Firms that discriminate against these actors may reduce their long-term viability.

National Level

Concerns at the national level focus on the opportunities that globalization will make available to governments and influential groups to marginalize some segments of the society, overlook their welfare, and limit their freedom of choice to get access to the benefits of globalization. Specifically, critics raise the following issues:

- Government programs designed to accelerate integration in the global economy destroy many civil institutions in the MDSs, and the family itself has increasingly become an extension of the market (Burbach, Nunez, and Kagarlitsky, 1997). In the CDSs, the urge to participate in the global economy increases alienation, resentment, and anger (Norberg-Hodge, 1996).
- Economic restructuring to sharpen national competitiveness produces a regressive redistribution of income and concentration of productive resources in the hands of smaller groups (Robinson, 1996; Teeple, 1995).
- Rapid privatization and liberalization programs accelerate social tension and intensify grievances among millions of people. In Argentina, for example, about 42 percent of the population became unemployed in 1998, and angry people blocked twenty-one provincial highways for several days. In Latin America, in general, the rush for liberalization has induced widespread corruption and mismanagement (Cohen, 1998a, b).
- Globalization destabilizes communities in CDSs and endangers their traditional economic bases and ways of living. Worse, it increases food insecurity in many countries (UNCTAD, 1997c).
- Political and other influential elites in emerging markets find it easier to steer most of the benefits of liberalization to themselves. In Russia, for example, oligarchs underwrote Boris Yeltsin's reelection campaign in 1996. Through their influence on Yeltsin, they invented a scheme to auction off choice state-owned enterprises and took control of the most lucrative privatized firms (see Hoffman, 1999).
- Liberalization induces governments in CDSs to relax laws and regulations related to child labor (see Greenhouse, 1997).
- Globalization reinforces rather than minimizes economic nationalism in the powerful nations. These nations now privilege outcome over process, and interfere in the marketplace to ensure desirable outcomes (Gummett, 1996).
- The triumph of globalization is seen as a victory of the Western world; hence, it encourages political and influential elites

within these nations to dominate other nations and cultures (see Rothkopf, 1997).

- Globalization encourages governments to compete to attract FDI by giving incentives to companies. This weakens a government's ability to adequately meet the social needs of their citizens (Burbach, Nunez, and Kagarlitsky, 1997).
- Information technology enables governments to invade personal privacy more than ever. For example, in the United States a law was passed in 1994 to aid law enforcement in gathering information. This law requires telecom firms in the United States to install equipment that permits the government to intercept and monitor all telephone and data communication (*The Economist*, 1999d). *The Economist* reports that Britain, Canada, Australia, New Zealand, and the United States jointly monitor all international satellite-telecommunications traffic.

Nations face three challenges in adapting to a global reality, which are more serious than those at the firm level. This is because states are less amenable to change than firms, and state apparatuses and layers of bureaucracy are likely to resist outside stimuli. In addition, powerful think-tank intellectuals and politicians are probably more inclined than business executives to maintain a monopoly over power, display narrow interests, and exhibit loyalty to a specific constituency. These elites lack the qualities and worldwide experience and outlook exhibited by corporate executives. Three primary challenges stand out, as discussed in the following sections.

Fairness and Social Justice

Building a civil society is a prerequisite for vital participation in global affairs. A civilized society is one in which individual rights are respected and where the concerns and the interests of disadvantaged groups are not ridiculed. Fairness and social justice allow citizens to utilize their full potential, discard their prejudice, and be free of fear. Therefore, citizens are more likely to view globalization and global involvement as a worthwhile endeavor. Unfortunately, many nations have been slow to create the necessary institutions that provide the foundation for a civil society. The absence of equity and justice induce social misery and corruption. In societies where the elite live in prosperity and the majority barely survive, there is fertile ground for corruption.

Diversity

Societies that have built civil institutions have made remarkable progress in advancing and institutionalizing diversity in ethnicity, beliefs, lifestyles, and so on. Acceptance of diversity represents societal maturity and civility. Its absence promotes discrimination and a lack of spiritual strength. In many of today's societies, respect and appreciation for diversity are far from a reality. Certainly, the slow acceptance of diversity, socially and legally, hinders participation in the globalization process and minimizes globalization's benefits.

Inclusion

This challenge is closely linked to those discussed previously. Inclusion has three primary aspects: free flow of information, access to sources of power and decision making, and access to economic and other opportunities. Exclusion of any group automatically prohibits its contribution of significant and creative resources. Likewise, preventing some individuals and groups from participating in the decision process leads to injustice and discrimination. Both are impediments to social progress and economic development. Free access to financial and other kinds of opportunity means that everyone is entitled to prosper in an open, civilized society. It conveys a belief that the society benefits more from enlarging than from limiting the "economic pie." A realization of this aim minimizes prejudices, resentments, and insecurities. In addition, it enables people to treat participation in the global economy and its affairs as a normal activity.

Two examples show the complexity and consequences of globalization in the context of inclusion. The first is the displacement of workers resulting from companies locating some or all of their plants overseas. This is common in the United States, Germany, and other industrial countries. In these countries, both the state and firm have established training programs to upgrade workers' skills. This, along with financial assistance, has made it easier for some workers to overcome their psychological and economic difficulties resulting from losing their jobs. In emerging and other poor countries, the suffering is deeper. The rapid adoption of liberalization and privatization left some segments of the society very poor while enriching a few. The liberalization allows those with some skills and those who work with corporations participating in the global economy to improve their welfare substantially compared to those who do not work with such firms. Likewise, powerful politicians in emerging countries (e.g., Russia, Indonesia, Thailand, etc.) use privatization to get monopolies over the most attractive and vital privatized institutions. They and their associates, therefore, accumulate wealth in a short period while most of the population struggles to survive. The absence of civil, legal, and sound economic institutions in many emerging and other countries has compounded the inclusion problem.

Global Level

At the global level, the backlash has been leveled specifically at the world political and economic institutions and at the prevailing superpower. Most of the ills that have existed for a long time have suddenly been attributed to globalization. Moreover, international observers and critics of globalization mistakenly fail to distinguish between globalization as a process and concept and the dominant superpower's behavior and goals. This makes it impossible, on many occasions, to isolate facts from illusions and to have a rational and productive dialogue. Boutros Boutros-Ghali (1996), former UN Secretary General, characterizes globalization as the world's long-term problem, offering prosperity to some and simultaneously driving many into deeper poverty. Similarly, Wilkin (1996) asserts that global inequality in the last two decades is greater than at any period in history. Robinson (1996) argues that the dramatic growth under globalization of socioeconomic inequalities and of human misery in nearly every part of the world is a consequence of the "unbridled operations of transnational capital." Experts often attribute such consequences to three major factors:

1. The market economy and democracy are more likely to undermine than support one another (Attali, 1997). Attali argues that the ascendancy of market economy over democracy allows powerful

minorities to control resources who view the collective democratic decisions of the majority as intolerable burdens. Concentration of capital in the hands of small groups leads to instability and conflict. Moreover, depriving some people of the ability to meet their basic needs will likely result in disenfranchising and alienating them.

2. Elites in the world's institutions ascribe to most nations a type of capitalist system that is a reflection of U.S. capitalism (Kristof and Sanger, 1999). Realistically, several types of capitalism can and do exist in the world. The type that evolved in the United States is evangelical capitalism. Many observers attribute this type of capitalism to the peculiarities of U.S. political and societal development, and to the individualistic nature of the American society. In such a society, the willingness to further one's interests and to accumulate wealth takes priority. Despite many positive aspects of this system, applying or advocating it abroad may backfire and lead to undesirable consequences. Furthermore, international observers indicate that emerging markets have lost their independence as the IMF increasingly extends its agenda at the command of the United States (Bhagwati, 1998). In addition, elites at the world's institutions appear to be more concerned with fiscal measures and budgeting rules to the detriment of human needs. In an editorial on June 9, 1999, *The New York Times* reported that in 1996 the World Bank and the IMF began a program that aimed to help poor countries escape their debt traps. The program was not adequate, and many of these nations have spent up to "60 percent of their budgets for interest on foreign debt that will never be retired—leaving little for the basic health care and education needed to reduce poverty." Economic hardship and misery lead, moreover, to social and political instability (Schwab and Smadja, 1999; Wolfensohn, 1998a).

3. The dominant superpower (the United States) tends to interfere arbitrarily in world affairs irrespective of the desires of other people and nations (Burbach, Nunez, and Kagarlitsky, 1997; Robinson, 1996). Mengisteab (1996) argues that the primary interest of the United States is to solidify its hegemonic dominance and to maintain the status quo in the international division of power. In the case of Africa, Mengisteab argues, the United States applied the carrot and the stick to attract and keep African countries under its sphere of influence. Likewise, Evans (1997) declares that in the

current global power structure, Anglo-American ideological prescriptions have been transcribed into formal rules of the game to which other nations must submit or risk becoming economic pariahs. In a series of articles written by a team led by Nicholas Kristof that appeared in *The New York Times* (Kristof and Sanger, 1999), the authors concluded that the global financial crisis that began in 1997 resulted largely from Washington's desire to accelerate financial liberalization and freer capital flows in emerging markets, thereby allowing foreign money to stream into these countries and domestic money to move out. Indeed, the authors assert that "Washington helped supply the blueprints" for weak foundations in emerging markets that eventually led to the global crisis. Furthermore, some experts claim that the dominant superpower uses its military and economic power to expand its cultural influence all over the world. Elliot (1999) states:

> The dominant fact of international relations since 1989 has been the extent of American might. Only the United States has possessed a combination of political, military, economic and cultural power—Silicon Valley, stealth bombers, and "Star Wars" all rolled into one force with the ability to set a global agenda. (From *Newsweek,* May 24, 1999. ©1999 Newsweek, Inc. All rights reserved. Reprinted by permission.)

Critics argue that there is a serious attempt by the world's superpower, the United States, to homogenize the global culture (Barlow and Robertson, 1996; Barnet and Cavanagh, 1996; Norberg-Hodge, 1996). Norberg-Hodge asserts that people in traditional societies feel pressured to conform and live up to idealized images—to American symbols. She indicates that in these societies the gulf between reality and the American ideal is very wide, resulting in deep and serious psychological disruptions.

The list of complaints at the global level is very long indeed. The following catalog includes only those voiced most frequently:

- Enlarges the gap between rich and poor nations. In the peripheries, global capitalism creates dramatic conditions at economic (growing poverty), social (massive marginalization), and cultural (frustrations) levels (Amin, 1997). Indeed, it excludes those without the necessary social, economic, and political power from either control over or consumption of the very products that are generated by capitalism (Wilkin, 1996).

- Reinforces dependency as industrial societies maintain technological advantage over other countries (Modelski, 1987). In addition, dependency is compounded as globalization reinforces the debt epidemic among CDSs (Bhagwati, 1998; Johnson, 1991).
- Destabilizes civil institutions and shatters the traditional ways of life in CDSs (Angotti, 1996; Johnson, 1991; Barnet and Cavanagh, 1996). In addition, in MDSs, such as in the United States, globalization accelerates the "feminization of poverty" as many women and children have no adequate or stable income (Burbach, Nunez, and Kagarlitsky, 1997).
- Redefines citizens as customers and disciplines their energies so they can function in the market (Sauer-Thompson and Smith, 1996).
- May lead to a slow decline in quality of life (Thurow, 1997). In addition, it contributes to the decay of inner cities worldwide (*Washington Spectator*, 1997).
- Spreads American cultural values and norms; therefore, others gradually lose their cultural identities and traditions (Norberg-Hodge, 1996; Sauer-Thompson and Smith, 1996).
- May spread corruption and bribery because many countries accelerate liberalization and privatization without having sound economic or legal foundations (Leiken, 1996-1997; Spero, 1996). Leiken indicates that a climate that provides hard times for some amid boom times for others opens not only a wage but also a credibility gap, making intolerable the easy money that is collected by senior officials.
- Helps transform local drug operations into global enterprises. The most unregulated "multi-trillion pool of money in supranational cyberspace, accessible by computer twenty-four hours a day, eases the drug trade's toughest problem: transforming huge sums of hot cash into investments in legitimate business" (Mathews, 1997, p. 58).
- Reduces the power of nation-states (Evans, 1997; Laxer, 1993).

- Fosters digital divide among nations, as poor nations find it almost impossible to have access to advanced technology.
- Increases anxiety and fear among traditional segments of the population, thereby giving rise to extreme groups in various parts of the world. Juergensmeyer (1996) calls this phenomenon "religious nationalism" and indicates that it is found among Christian, Jewish, Muslim, and other religious communities. Tommy Lapid, a member of the Israeli parliament, describes Israeli fundamentalists as "part of the global phenomenon of the poor and the uneducated turning toward fundamentalist religion. . . . They abhor modernism, technology" (quoted in Hockstader, 1999).
- Is an instrument for dominant superpowers to reshape and recolonize other countries (Attiga, 1997; Laxer, 1993).
- Generates pressures for integration into a single political regime or "polygarchy"—"a process of the exercise of hegemony within and between countries in the context of transnationalization" (Robinson, 1996, p. 42).

Four major challenges must be faced at the global level to ease integration and advance worldwide prosperity. Each is briefly discussed in the following sections.

Avoidance of Fragmentation

Globalization is aimed at integrating world communities and simultaneously increasing religious and ethnic identity. On the surface, this seems contradictory. This, however, is not the case. A global outlook and participation in global affairs do not force groups or communities to lose their identity. It is the violent reaction to events and an arrogance in conduct, rather than cultural or ethnic identity, that are against the spirit and aim of globalization. Some observers believe that the real threat to an integrated and stable world comes from the attempts of dominant superpowers to intentionally marginalize other members of the international community, to deny them full participation in global affairs, and to ignore their aspirations for liberty, freedom, and human rights. For example, the economic sanctions against North Korea, Cuba, Iraq, Sudan, etc. have contributed to the economic paralyses of these countries, intensifying their suffering, and limiting the freedoms of existing and future generations. According to a UN report in 1998, 30 percent of North Korean children under age two are acutely malnourished and 67 percent of all children are physically stunted (World Food Programme, 1998). Likewise, China, despite its economic and political clout, is not allowed to be a member of the WTO unless it meets certain conditions set by the United States. In terms of national aspirations for freedom, the United States never "really thought Arabs were entitled to human liberty in their own nations" (Rosenthal, 1999). Similarly, *The New York Times* stated, "Even the United States, which raises the question of democracy with great frequency elsewhere, has shied away from that in the Arab world" (Crossette, 1998). It is these actions and attitudes that lead to world fragmentation, turmoil, and instability.

Avoidance of Co-optation

Political maneuvering to sustain power, maintain and enlarge coalitions, and advance one's national interests is a fact of life and is not expected to vanish in the foreseeable future. Coercive seduction and co-optation have been employed effectively by superpowers to maintain conformity and submission. This, however, stands against the spirit of globalization since it marginalizes the democratic process and overlooks the desires and aspirations of others. Two examples underscore the dysfunctional nature of co-optation. Kofi Annan, the UN Secretary General in a speech delivered to the "Appeal for Peace" Conference at the Hague on May 15, 1999, criticized the decision by NATO to take action in Kosovo without seeking explicit Security Council authorization. "Unless the Security Council is restored to its preeminent position as the sole source of legitimacy on the use of force," warned Annan, "we are on a dangerous path to anarchy." Annan cites the "emergence of the single superpower and new regional powers" and the desire to marginalize the UN as the reasons for overstepping the authority of the Security Council. Despite the severity of starvation and food shortages in North Korea, the Clinton administration is not willing to lift sanctions against the country unless several major concessions, including an agreement to end North Korea's long-range missile program, are met (Sanger, 1999b). Using food as an instrument for co-optation prolongs human suffering. Worse, co-optation and coercive seduction, unlike open war, repress feelings and legitimate concerns. This may lead to deep resentments and international terrorism, thereby fostering a vicious cycle of global violence and instability.

Cooperation

Enhancing cooperation on a global level is a necessary condition for encouraging the flourishing of the world community. Sutherland (1998a) argues that the powerful nations are not willing to adopt a more inclusive decision-making process. Superpowers have consistently resisted solutions that are not determined by them and have shown a tendency to rely on forced submission and domination, instead of constructive engagement, to ensure compliance. Martin Indyk (1999), U.S. Assistant Secretary of State, vividly explains this tendency relative to the Middle East:

> We must maintain our ability to contain those states and those forces who threaten those [our] interests. . . . In May of 1993, almost six years ago, I outlined the Clinton administration's dual containment policy toward Iraq and Iran. This policy reflected the geopolitical reality at the time: the recent conclusion of three wars—the Cold War, the Iran-Iraq war, and the war to liberate Kuwait—had left the United States the dominant power in the region. It also had left both Iran and Iraq, while war-weary and economically weakened, still militarily ambitious and clearly hostile to the United States and our interests in the region.
>
> Dual containment was premised on the notion that the United States needed to shift away from our earlier policy of relying on one of these regional powers to balance the other, a policy we had followed throughout the previous decade with disastrous results.

Inclusion

This is the most serious challenge on the global level. Inclusion implies an absence of discrimination, willingness to listen, and attentiveness to contributions from the less powerful partners. Reconciling national interests among nations is an impossible task that further complicates the inclusion goal. "National interests" is a vague term and political elites have often utilized it to justify aggressive actions that are initially unpopular domestically, are abhorred internationally, and are unconscionable morally. Indeed, so long as there is no agreement on the conceptualization of national interests, the inclusion challenge will persist. This ultimately paralyzes international institutions. For example, in 1990 the UN Security Council initially imposed economic sanctions on the Iraqi regime to induce it to withdraw from Kuwait. Iraq was forced to withdraw from Kuwait in March 1991, but the sanctions are still in force. Several UN agencies reported that the sanctions created a human catastrophe as more than 1.5 million Iraqis died and more than 6,000 children continue to die monthly. Mueller and Mueller (1999, p. 51) report that "economic sanctions may well have been a necessary cause of the deaths of more people in Iraq than have been slain by all so-called weapons of mass destruction throughout history." Despite the urgency of the need to stop human suffering, the five permanent members of the Security Council are divided: France, China, and Russia have many times circulated resolutions to lift the sanctions, but they are always vetoed by the United States and Britain. Each group in the council invokes "national interests" as a guise for its indifference to a serious human problem.

When national interests are pursued aggressively and without regard to the interests of other parties, the world's institutions will lose their viability. A case in point is the U.S. rejection of any role for the World Court in solving a trade dispute with the European Union over the legality of certain American sanctions against Cuba (Greenberger, 1997). The Clinton administration claims that the WTO "has no competence to proceed" in a matter that is important to American "national interests." Clinton's attitude is surprising since many experts in international trade consider denial of a role for the World Court in settling trade disputes to be a major setback for those who believe in the free market economy and in the role of the WTO in solving trade disputes. The United States was the major player in establishing the WTO. In addition, the United States "files far more complaints about foreign trade practices at WTO than are filed against it" (Sanger, 1997).

The United States and British governments also use other international organizations (e.g., World Bank, IMF) to serve their interests. Sutherland (1998b) and other business executives have called for an end to the marginalization of the poorer nations and for strengthening global governance to translate the goal of inclusion into reality. Additionally, the inclusion goal accentuates the need to broaden and strengthen the role of NGOs, place priority on constructive engagement, and treat nationalistic prejudices as obstacles for world peace and stability.

MINIMIZING THE BACKLASH

The preceding discussion of the destructive aspects of globalization highlights the most important concerns voiced in various quarters of the world. In any discourse, especially a productive one, diversity of thinking and argument is a healthy sign. Familiarity with these concerns underscores the vitality of globalization in the human journey toward a better tomorrow. In this challenging journey one should not lose sight of two realities. First, globalization is irreversible, and it is the way to an improved future if its destructive aspects are minimized. Second, the benefits of globalization have multiple and far-reaching impacts at individual, corporate, and societal levels. That is, spreading the benefits of globalization is also a commitment to the vitality of the world economy and promotion of a healthy environment. The question, therefore, is, how can these benefits reach all parts of the world while limiting the disruptive outcomes? Four general approaches are outlined below. These approaches are not mutually exclusive, and taken together, they provide useful insights.

Ruth Dreifuss (1999), Swiss president, reiterates the linkage between democracy and economic health. She states that "we should use democracy for the individual, communities and cultures to see that all players have their say, thus ensuring that our material prosperity reflects the richness of our diversity." Dreifuss believes that respect for human dignity is important for a safe environment, combating child labor abuses, and guaranteeing the quality of life.

Similarly, Schwab (1999) has called for devising new frameworks and procedures for responsible globality. These frameworks should focus on simple but fundamental moral values: a sense of responsibility of caring for our neighbors in the global village and for ecological integrity. He argues that the most crucial value in the era of globalization is tolerance for differences in religion, ethnicity, ideology, and history. The underlying assumption is that any rules and agreements that do not stem from a common and shared understanding are doomed to failure.

Cox (1994) suggests that changes are not likely to come about as a result of moral inducement or idealistic schemes of institutional reform. He provides a general framework for reform in economic practices. Cox recommends that global actors:

- subordinate competitiveness to forms of regulation aimed at managing economic growth in a manner consistent with ecological balance and social equity;
- change consumption patterns to ones that are more respectful of ecological balance; and
- regulate finance to serve the real economy and to curb speculation, destructive asset stripping, and corruption.

Spero (1996) indicates that successfully spreading the benefits of a global economy depends on promoting macroeconomic stability, trade and investment, human capital formation, and good governance. She suggests that advanced countries should continue providing substantial flows of development assistance to alleviate poverty and to encourage economic reform in CDSs.

Realistically, however, the above guidelines are virtually impossible to translate into action at the national and global levels. This is not to suggest that these proposals are inadequate or deficient. Rather, in a world that is shaped by powerful forces and is characteristically complex, a profound change would not come about without shaking the foundations of prevailing outlooks and programs. The forces that currently shape the globalization process have vested interests in maintaining the status quo and maximizing their benefits. Eliminating obstacles to "globalization with a human face" requires restructuring of the power foundations in a way that facilitates economic and social growth in every part of the globe.

Certain conditions must be met in order to spread the advantages of globalization and make them accessible to communities across the globe. These conditions include reducing the influence of political elites and think-tank intellectuals, solidifying business executives' involvement and roles, and reducing central governments' roles.

Limiting the Power of Political Elites and Think-Tank Intellectuals

Chapter 3 examined the role of political elites in globalization. Observers of globalization have long scrutinized the role of political elites and think-tank intellectuals, and most observers focus on the attempts of these groups to design and shape realities. The political elites, in particular, work against tolerance and diversity. Because of their narrow constituencies and their distrust of open societies, they fear globalization with a human face. They are obsessed with power and control, and most of them are preoccupied with leaving their marks in history regardless of the destructive nature of their actions, especially in the world arena. These leading politicians have relied on threat and intervention in world affairs to impose their own agendas. Harris (1996) contends that the appointment, for example, of Madeleine Albright as U.S. Secretary of State epitomizes a belief in the virtue of uninhibited American intervention, as signaled by her predilection for using adjectives such as "combative," "forceful," and "abrasive." Similarly, Tony Blair of Britain rose to prominence by aggressively calling for intervention and the use of force abroad. He emphasizes having "the capability to make a difference" globally (Hoge, 1998).

The drive to win at any expense by leading politicians, be it in Britain, Pakistan, or the United States, is a threat to peaceful world integration and business growth. Not only are economic opportunities sacrificed, but human and economic miseries are also needlessly extended. For example, Madeleine Albright (1996), on the CBS program *60 Minutes*, maintained that the death of 5,000 children in Iraq each month was worth the price. Many civil and business leaders, however, reject Albright's views and consider what is happening in Iraq a human tragedy.

Think-tank intellectuals are powerful players in any modern society. Originally, think tanks were formed to legitimize politicians by providing a theoretical underpinning for dominant groups (Robinson, 1996). In recent years and in most Western countries, especially in the United States, these elites have acquired extraordinary power to shape events. Their search to solidify their power and position themselves as indispensable actors has often led them to exaggerate threats to "national interest" and to incite global instability. In recent years, for example, leading intellectuals at the Brookings Institute, the Heritage Foundation, the Council on Foreign Relations, the American Enterprise Institute, the Center for Strategic and International Studies, etc. have constantly furnished the media with information about threats coming from China, including Chinese-American citizens, as well as citizens having ties to Russia, Libya, North Korea, Iran, and Lebanon. These intellectuals (for example, Richard Haass, Michael O'Hanlon, James Fallows, Michael Ledeen, Steven Emerson, Richard Perle, D. Rothkopf, R. Kagan), continously bombard the public with information that is intended to arouse fear and anxiety. Unfortunately, such activities often drain people emotionally, create intolerant attitudes, and foster prejudice, rendering cooperation and peaceful coexistence among nations impossible tasks.

Both political elites and think-tank intellectuals:

- Seek to limit or slow down world economic integration that benefits all economic actors, and to inhibit the smooth integration of the poorer nations into the global economy. For example, David Mulford, U.S. Undersecretary of the Treasury in the Bush administration, stated that "The countries that do not make themselves more attractive will not get investors' attention. This is like a girl trying to get a boyfriend. She has to go out, have her hair done, wear makeup" (quoted in Robinson, 1996, p. 374). This remark conveys the message that the less powerful nations will not be welcomed as partners in globalization without submitting to the wishes of the most powerful actors.
- Capitalize on their access to power, technology, and knowledge to further their monopoly on information and other sources of domination. They use trade restrictions and sanctions to pro-

hibit the sale of technology to other nations, thus prolonging domination.

- Seek to limit the participation of business leaders and NGOs in world affairs under the pretext that these matters are related to national interests. For example, former U.S. President Jimmy Carter (1999) argues that political elites have a tendency to exclude NGOs from peacemaking, thus missing real opportunities for resolving disputes.

Various steps must be taken to limit the negative impact of leading politicians and think-tank intellectuals. One of the most important activities involves the participation of management and organization scholars, in particular, along with business executives in shaping social theory of life and international events. Management and organization scholars have the capacity and the necessary knowledge to contribute to furthering economic and organizational integration on a global scale. Their skills and resources are vital instruments for profound global changes.

Enhancing the Global Executive's Role and Involvement in Global Affairs

Global executives show remarkable flexibility and attentiveness in dealing with international issues. Their cross-cultural perspectives, global experience, commitment to civil societies, and their capacity to integrate matters qualify them to play a pivotal role in enlarging and sharing globalization's benefits. In fact, global executives, in the current environment, provide the only counterbalance to the power of the political elites and think-tank intellectuals. The following examples underscore the differences in priorities between business leaders and politicians:

- Many business executives support China joining the WTO and having strong trade relations with it. The political elite in the United States, however, seeks the revival of the Cold War environment and the prevention of China from joining the WTO (see Blustein and Mufson, 1999; Sanger, 1999c).
- Many business leaders promote democratic systems all over the world. Politicians in the Western world, however, support

dictatorships in the Arab world, Latin America, and Africa. Recently, in Indonesia, for example, the Clinton administration trained the police force there in riot control (see Shenon, 1999). Likewise, politicians in the United States knew about military abuses in Guatemala and Chile but maintained good relationships with the dictators in power there (see Farah, 1999). Furthermore, global corporations such as Body Shop and Caterpillar, contrary to the designs of politicians and think-tank intellectuals, believe that it is not their purpose "to remake the world in the image of any country or philosophy" (Caterpillar, 1992, p. 13).

- Business leaders are against using economic sanctions as a foreign policy tool (see Armstrong, 1997; Perrella, 1998). Politicians, however, utilize economic sanctions in pursuing their political goals. In the case of Iraq, for example, pencils, notebooks, medicines, chlorine, fertilizers, and insecticides, along with other necessary items, are banned under the sanctions, resulting in a massive death toll among Iraqi civilians (Kinzer, 1999b; Mueller and Mueller, 1999). Politicians in Britain and the United States believe in sanctions though they publicly call for improving the welfare of other people. President Clinton, in a speech to the International Labor Organization Conference in June 1999, stated that "we must . . . give life to our dream of an economy that lifts all our people. . . . Every single day tens of millions of children work in conditions that shock the conscience. . . . We will not tolerate children being used in pornography and prostitution." However, according to UN reports, the U.S.-led sanctions in Iraq contribute to human misery and poverty in Iraq, and deterioration of educational, economic, health, and environmental systems. More important, sanctions force children to leave school and work as prostitutes (see Kinzer, 1999b).
- Oil and gas companies planned to construct a Caspian oil pipeline through Iran. The Clinton administration, however, objected to the plan for political reasons. In fact, U.S. officials applied every form of pressure they could muster to persuade oil companies to construct the pipeline through Turkey instead (Kinzer, 1999a).
- Business executives are more inclined than politicians to reduce the digital divide between and across communities. They

pursue opportunities wherever they are available. In contrast, politicians aim at maintaining social and economic inequality. Export controls and regulations on advanced technology are always pursued by political elites as strategic tools.

Reducing the Role of Central Governments

Central governments are widely recognized as inefficient and conflict oriented in their relations with other governments. They are inclined toward secrecy and regulation. In their hunger for power they mistrust civil institutions, especially NGOs. Many observers assume that globalization diminishes the role of central government. This, however, is not the case at the present, nor will it be in the near future.

Globalization demands openness, flexibility, and rapid response to changing events. This accentuates the need to diffuse power by empowering local governments and communities. In addition, it demands more involvement of NGOs in global and international affairs. Mathews (1997) points out that in the era of accelerated change, NGOs can respond more quickly than governments to new demands and opportunities.

In conclusion, globalization offers unlimited opportunities for worldwide communities to utilize their full potential to fight poverty, disease, and corruption, and to upgrade educational and health systems. In fact, globalization is a challenging stimulus for individuals, firms, and communities to better themselves while participating in world affairs. That is, globalization has a far-reaching practical and intellectual impact that does not discriminate among peoples or regions. Nevertheless, there is always a risk that globalization processes may produce destructive consequences. The challenge is to minimize these consequences and build on human creativity to make jobs and wealth accessible to all people while preserving ecology. Globalization may take several paths. The hope is that the adopted path is the one that strengthens world peace, stability, and prosperity. The unbridled ambition to control globalization's benefits leads to destruction and ruin. A belief in a free trade system, viability of other civilizations' contributions, and a commitment to principles of justice and liberty are the means for enhancing benefits to all parties involved.

Bibliography

Abrams, E. (1995). The national prospect—A symposium. *Commentary,* November 24-25.

Adam, C. (1998). Internationalization and integration of financial and capital markets. In A. Levy-Livermore (Ed.), *Handbook on the globalization of the world economy* (pp. 557-581). Northampton: Edward Elgar.

Adelman, I. (1997). The genesis of the current global economic system. In A. Levy-Livermore (Ed.), *Handbook on the globalization of the world economy* (pp. 3-28). Northampton: Edward Elgar.

Adler, N. and Bartholomew, S. (1992). Managing globally competent people. *Academy of Management Executive,* 6(3), 52-65.

Ahtisaari, M. (1997). Globalization and its implications for Europe: Europe and the United States must work together. *Vital Speeches of the Day,* 64(4), 104-107.

Airbus (no date). *And our search landed us here.* Herndon, Virginia: Airbus.

Albright, M. (1996). Interview. *60 Minutes.* CBS, May 12.

Albright, M. (1997). Calls for activist foreign policy. Speech at Harvard, June 6.

Albrow, M. (1990). Introduction. In M. Albrow and E. King (Eds.), *Globalization, knowledge and society* (pp. 3-13). London: Sage Publications.

Ali, A. (Ed.) (1992). *How to manage for international competitiveness.* New York: Haworth Press.

Ali, A. (1993). The incompetent crowd. *Competitiveness Review,* 3(1), 4-8.

Ali, A. and Camp, R. (1992). Competitiveness: No quick fix solutions. *Competitiveness Review,* 2(1), 14-18.

Ali, A. and Camp, R. (1993). Competitiveness and global leadership. *Competitiveness Review,* 3(1), 21-33.

Ali, A. and Camp, R. (1996). Global managers: Qualities for effective competition. *International Journal of Man Power,* 17(6/7), 5-18.

Ali, A., Chaubey, M., and Camp, R. (1994). The storm over NAFTA. *Competitiveness Review,* 4(2), 3-14.

Ali, A. and Masters, B. (1988). Management perceptions of the qualities needed for international success. *International Journal of Management,* 5(2), 287-295.

Al-Jabiri, M. A. (1998). Globalism and cultural identity: Ten theses. *Arab Thought Forum,* 5(21), 1-5.

Alkhafaji, A. F. (1995). *Competitive global management: Principles and strategies.* Delray Beach: St. Lucie Press.

Allianz (1997). *Horizons.* Munich: Allianz Aktiengesellschaft.

Allianz (1998). *Annual report 1997.* Munich: Allianz Aktiengesellschaft.

Alvesson, M. (1990). A flat pyramid: A symbolic processing of organizational structure. *International Studies of Management and Organization*, 19(4), 5-23.

Amin, A. and Thrift, N. (1992). Neo-Marshallian nodes in global networks. *International Journal of Urban and Regional Research,* 16(4), 571-587.

Amin, A. and Thrift, N. (1995). *Globalization, institutions, and regional development in Europe*. Oxford, UK: Oxford University Press.

Amin, S. (1997). Reflections on the international system. In P. Golding and P. Harris (Eds.), *Beyond cultural imperialism* (pp. 10-24). Newbury Park, CA: Sage Publications.

Angotti, T. (1996). Confronting globalization: The role of progressive planners. <www.pratt.edu>.

Annan, K. (1999a). Walking the international tightrope, January 19. <www.um.org/doc>.

Annan, K. (1999b). Ultimate crime to miss chance for peace and condemn people to misery of war. Speech to "Appeal for Peace" conference, Hague, Netherlands, May 15. <www.un.org/doc>.

Armstrong, C. M. (1997). International trade and the American dream. *Vital Speeches of the Day,* 63(11), 330-333.

Artzt, E. L. (1990). Strategies for global growth. Speech delivered at a meeting for leading financial analysts at Procter & Gamble, Cincinnati, Ohio, May 21.

Attali, J. (1997). The crash of Western civilization: The limits of the market and democracy. *Foreign Policy,* Summer, 54-64.

Attiga, A. A. (1997). Globalism: A new kind of empire. *Arab Thought Forum,* 4(1), 1.

Baker, J. A. 3rd (1999). North Korea wins again. *The New York Times on the Web,* March 19. <www.nytimes.com>.

BankAmerica (1996). *BankAmerica 1996 Annual Report.* San Francisco: BankAmerica.

Barlow, M. and Robertson, H. (1996). Homogenization of education. In J. Mander and E. Goldsmith (Eds.), *The case against the global economy* (pp. 60-70). San Francisco: Sierra Club Books.

Barnet, R. J. (1994). Lords of the global economy. *The Nation,* December 19, 754-765.

Barnet, R. J. and Cavanagh, J. (1995). *Global dreams*. New York: Touchstone Book.

Barnet, R. J. and Cavanagh, J. (1996). Homogenization of global culture. In J. Mander and E. Goldsmith (Eds.), *The case against the global economy* (pp. 71-77). San Francisco: Sierra Club Books.

Barnevik, P. (1991). The logic of global business. Interviewed by W. Taylor. *Harvard Business Review,* March-April, 91-105.

Barnevik, P. (1994). The ABBs of competition. Interviewed by McClenahen. *Industry Week,* June 6, 20-24.

Barth, S. (1997). U.S. stands alone on Burma sanctions. *World Trade,* July, 13.

Bartlett, C. A. and Ghoshal, S. (1992). What is a global manager? *Harvard Business Review,* September-October, 124-132.

Bartlett, C. A. and Ghoshal, S. (1995a). *Transnational management.* Chicago: Irwin.
Bartlett, C.A. and Ghoshal, S. (1995b). Changing the role of top management: Beyond systems to people. *Harvard Business Review,* May/June, 132-142.
Benne, K. and Sheats, P. (1948). Functional roles of group members. *Journal of Social Issues,* 4(2), 41-49.
Bennis, W. (1988). Presidents as CEOs. *Los Angeles Times,* March 6, Part IV, 3.
Berenbeim, R. (1996). Board and directors' assessment. *Vital Speeches of the Day,* 63(9), 280-281.
Bergsten, F. C. (1996). Globalizing free trade. *Foreign Affairs,* 75(3), 105-120.
Bersticker, A. C. (1997). A guide to global competitiveness. *Vital Speeches of the Day,* 63(17), 519-523.
Bhagwati, J. (1998). The capital myth: The difference between trade in widgets and dollars, *Foreign Affairs,* 77(3), 7-12.
Birnbaum, J. H. (1998). Capitol clout: A buyer's guide. *Fortune Magazine,* October 26, 177-186.
BIS (1998). *International banking and financial market development.* Basle, Switzerland: External Services Section, Bank for International Settlement.
BIS (1999). *Consolidated international banking statistics.* Basle, Switzerland: External Services Section, Bank for International Settlement.
Black, J. (1988). Work role transitions: A study of American expatriate managers in Japan. *Journal of International Business Studies,* 19(2), 277-294.
Black, S., Gregersen, H., and Mendenhall, M. (1992). *Global assignments.* San Francisco: Jossey-Bass Publishers.
Black, S. and Porter, L. (1991). Managerial behaviors and job performance: A successful manager in Los Angeles may not succeed in Hong Kong. *Journal of International Business Studies,* 22(1), 99-114.
Blumenthal, W. M. (1986). The World Economy and Technological Change, *Foreign Affairs,* 66(3), 529-550.
Blustein, P. and Mufson, S. (1999). Clinton urges against cold war with China. *Washington Post,* April 8, A2.
Bora, B. (1998). The role of multinational corporations in globalizing the world economy: Evidence from affiliates of US multinational companies. In A. Levy-Livermore (Ed.), *Handbook on the globalization of the world economy* (pp. 147-167). Northampton: Edward Elgar.
Bossidy, L. (1997). The American advantage: Where we are in the world economy. *Vital Speeches of the Day,* 64(2), 37-40.
Boudreau, M. C., Loch, K. D., Robey, D., and Straud, D. (1998). Going global: Using information technology to advance the competitiveness of the virtual transnational organization. *Academy of Management Executive,* 12(4), 120-128.
Boutros-Ghali, B. (1996). Global leadership after the cold war. *Foreign Affairs,* 75(2), 86-98.
Brauchli, M. W. (1996). Echoes of the past. *The Wall Street Journal Classroom,* September 26. Lesson Plan #2. New York: Ed. Dow Jones and Company, Inc.

Brecher, J. (1993). Global village or global pillage? *The Nation,* December 6, 683-688.

Bremner, B. (1997). Two Japans: The gulf between corporate winners and losers is growing. *Business Week,* January 27, 24-29.

British Petroleum (1997). *Annual report and accounts 1996.* London: British Petroleum.

British Telecommunications (1997). *Organization.* London: British Telecommunications.

Broder, J. M. (1998). Clinton, in final China speech, calls for defense of personal freedom. *The New York Times on the Web,* June 29, <www.nytimes.com>.

Brzezinski, Z. (1993). *Power and principle.* New York: Farrar, Straus, and Giroux.

Brzezinski, Z. (1995). The national prospect—A symposium. *Commentary,* November, 38.

Buckley, P. J. (1996). Cooperative forms of transnational corporation activity. In United Nations. *Transnational corporations and world development* (pp. 473-496). Boston: International Thomson Business Press.

Burbach, R., Nunez, O., and Kagarlitsky, B. (1997). *Globalization and its discontents.* London: Pluto Press.

Burgess, P. M. (1995). From partnership to restoration. *Vital Speeches of the Day,* 62(4), 108-109.

Burns, A. (1997). Gaining a competitive edge. *Vital Speeches of the Day,* 63(17), 533-538.

Burt, R. (1993). More power to the powerful. *The New York Times,* May 14, A31.

Business Week (1999). Man on the spot. May 3, 142-151.

CARE (1997). *World Development Statistics 1997. CARE Web page:* <www.care.org>.

Carter, J. (1999). Have we forgotten the path to peace? *The New York Times,* May 27, A21.

Caterpillar (1992). Code of worldwide business conduct and operating principles. Peoria: Caterpillar.

Caterpillar (1997). *1996 annual report.* Peoria, IL: Caterpillar.

Caux Round Table (1998). *The critical role of the corporation in a global society.* Position Paper, <www.cauxroundtable.org>.

Cavanagh, R., Broad, R., and Weiss, P. (1993). The need for a global deal. *The Nation,* December 27, 794-798.

Center for International Business Studies (1998). *Internationalization of business education is a journey, not a destination.* College Station, TX: College of Business, Texas A&M University.

Certon, M. and Davies, O. (1991). 50 trends shaping the world. *The Futurist,* September/October, 22-29.

Chambers, J. (1999). A presentation at the Churchill Club, February 16, Santa Clara, CA.

Chichilnisky, G. (1998). Trade regimes and GATT: Resource-intensive versus knowledge-intensive growth. In A. Levy-Livermore (Ed.), *Handbook on the globalization of the world economy* (pp. 226-249). Northampton: Edward Elgar.

Cho, D.-S. and Moon, H. C. (1998). A nation's international competitiveness in different states. *Advances in Competitiveness Research,* 6(1), 5-19.

Chomsky, N. (1993). The masters of mankind. *The Nation,* March 29, 412-416.

Christopher, W. (1996). Leadership for the next American century. Speech at Harvard University, January 18, <www.state.gov>.

Clarke, T. (1996). Mechanisms of corporate rule. In J. Mander and E. Goldsmith (Eds.), *The case against the global economy* (pp. 297-308). San Francisco: Sierra Club Books.

Clinton, W. (1997). China stands at a crossroads. *Vital Speeches of the Day,* 64(3), 66-69.

Clinton, W. (1998). Remarks to the Arab world. December 19, <www.pub.whitehouse.gov>.

Clinton, W. (1999a). Remarks in roundtable discussion on peace efforts. Guatemala City, March 10, <www.pub.whitehouse.gov>.

Clinton, W. (1999b). Remarks to the International Labor Organization conference. Geneva, Switzerland, June 16, <www.pub.whitehouse.gov>.

Clough, M. (1994). Grass-root policymaking. *Foreign Affairs, The Year Ahead,* 73(1), 2-7.

Cohen, R. (1995). Taming the bullies of Bosnia. *The New York Times Magazine,* December 17, 58-71.

Cohen, R. (1998a). Brazil pays to shield currency, and the poor see the true cost. *The New York Times on the Web,* February 5, <www.nytimes.com>.

Cohen, R. (1998b). Argentina grapples with downside of globalization. *The New York Times on the Web,* February 6, <www.nytimes.com>.

Cohen, W. I. (1997). China's strategic culture. *Atlantic Monthly,* March, 103-105.

Cohen, W. S. (1998a). *Remarks at Fortune 500 Forum dinner keynote.* Pittsburgh, PA, October 16. *Defense Issues on the Web,* <www.defenselink.mil>.

Cohen, W. S. (1998b). U.S. must remain active in post-cold war foreign affairs. *Defense Issues on the Web,* <www.defenselink.mil>.

Collins, G. (1996). Global Pepsico units set for snack foods and drinks. *The New York Times,* March 12, D5.

Collins, P. (1998). Regional trading blocks and foreign direct investment flows and stocks. In J. Dunning (Ed.), *Globalization, trade and foreign direct investment* (pp. 28-48). Oxford: Elsevier.

Cooper, R. N. (1991). Prospects for the future world economy. In R. K. Smith (Ed.), *Facing the future: American strategy in the 1990s.* Lanham, MD: University Press of America.

Cooper, R. N. (1994). Considerations for the future of the world economy. Remarks to annual meeting of the Academy of International Business, Boston, November.

Cowell, A. (1999). Annan fears backlash over global crisis. *The New York Times on the Web,* February 1, <www.nytimes.com>.

Cox, R. (1994). The crisis in world order and the challenge to international organization. *Cooperation and Conflict,* 29(2), 99-113.

Cox, K. R. (1997). *Spaces of globalization: Reasserting the power of the local.* New York: Guilford Press, 1-18.

Coyne, P. C. and Dye, R. (1998). The competitive dynamics of network-based business. *Harvard Business Review,* January-February, 99-109.

Crawford, C. J. (1997). Major trend in global communication. *Vital Speeches of the Day,* 63(17), 538-541.

Crossette, B. (1997). UNICEF chief says 80,000 North Korean children may die of starvation. *The New York Times,* August 7, E1.

Crossette, B. (1998). A rising tide of freedom bypasses the Arab world. *The New York Times on the Web,* April 26, <www.nytimes.com>.

Daimler-Benz (1997). *Annual Report 1997.* Stuttgart, Germany: Daimler-Benz AG.

Danfoss (1998). *1997 Annual Report.* Nordborg, Denmark: Danfoss.

D'Aquino, T. (1996). Globalization, social progress, democratic development and human rights. *Vital Speeches of the Day,* December 1, 107-110.

D'Aquino, T. (1998). The global economic hurricane—The challenge to Canadian and international business. *Vital Speeches of the Day,* 65(6), 164-166.

Dawkins, K. and Muffett, C. (1993). The free trade sellout. *The Progressive,* January, 18-21.

Day, C. and LaBarre, P. (1994). *GE.* Penton Publishing, Inc. Reprint from *Industry Week,* May 2.

Depalma, A. (1994). Trade back spurring Mexican deals in U.S. *The New York Times,* March 17, D1.

Depalma, A. (1999). A Canadian rousts diplomacy (and ruffles the U.S.). *The New York Times on the Web,* January 10, <www.nytimes.com>.

Deutsche Bank (n.d.). *Outline: Activities and structure of the Deutsche Bank Group.* Frankfurt: Deutshe Bank AG.

DeVellis, R. (1991). *Scale development.* Newbury Park, CA: Sage Publications.

Dicken, P. (1994). Global-local tensions: Firms and states in the global space-economy. *Advances in Strategic Management,* 10B, 217-247.

Dolny, M. (1996). The think tank spectrum. *Extra,* 9(3), 24.

Dolny, M. (1997). New survey on think tanks. *Extra,* 10(3), 24.

Dolny, M. (1998). What's in the label. *Extra,* 11(3), 9-10.

Doremus, P. N., Keller, W. W., Pauly, L. W., and Reich, S. (1998). *The myth of the global corporation.* Princeton, NJ: Princeton University Press.

Dreifuss, R. (1999). *Partnership with business for stronger democracy in globalized world.* Live 99, World Economic Forum. Davos, Switzerland, January 28. <www.Live99.weforum.org>.

Drobis, D. R. (1996). Borderless believability. *Vital Speeches of the Day,* 63(9), 281-285.

Drucker, P. (1993). Interviewed by G. Harris. The post-capitalist executive. *Harvard Business Review,* May/June, 114-122.

Drucker, P. (1994). Multinationals and developing countries: Myths and realities. *Foreign Affairs*, Fall, 121-134.

Dunn, H. S. (1995). *Globalization, communications and Caribbean identity.* New York: St. Martin's Press.

Dunning, J. H. (1996). The nature of transnational corporations and their activities. *In United Nations, Transnational corporations and world development* (pp. 27-43). Boston: International Thomson Business Press.

Dunning, J. H. (1997). A business analytic approach to governments and globalization. In J. H. Dunning (Ed.), *Governments, globalization, and international business* (pp. 114-131). New York: Oxford University Press Inc.

Dunning, J. H. and Sauvant, K. P. (1996). Introduction. In United Nations (Ed.), *Transnational corporations and world development* (p. xi). Boston: International Thomson Business Press.

DuPont (1996). *Annual report.* Wilmington, Delaware: DuPont.

DuPont (No date). *The world of DuPont.* Wilmington, Delaware: DuPont.

The Economist (1995). World: The nation-state is dead. Long live the nation State. December 23, 15-18.

The Economist (1996). The miracle of trade. January 27, 61-62.

The Economist (1997). Trade winds. November 8, 85-86.

The Economist (1998a). A new approach to financial risk. *The Economist Web Page,* October 13-23, <www.economist.com>.

The Economist (1998b). The risk business. *The Economist Web page,* October 17-23. <www.economist.com>.

The Economist (1998c). Turmoil in financial markets: The risk business. Editorial, October 17. *The Economist Web page,* <www.economist.com>.

The Economist (1999a). Business last year, 1-8. *The Economist Web Page,* January, <www.economist.com>.

The Economist (1999b). China and the WTO. Editorial, April 1. *The Economist on the Web,* <www.economist.com>.

The Economist (1999c). FDIs. *The Economist on the Web,* <www.economist.com>.

The Economist (1999d). The surveillance society. *The Economist on the Web,* <www.economist.com>.

Egon Zehndar International (1988). *A lack of creativity* (Appeared in *The Wall Street Journal,* January 15, 1995, p. 19).

Ehrenreich, B. (1991). The warrior culture. In J. Ridgeway (Ed.), *The march to war* (pp. 124-127). New York: Four Walls Eight Windows.

Elliot, M. (1999). A world of trouble. *Newsweek on the Web,* May 24, <www.newsweek.com>.

Emmerij, L. (1992). Globalization, regionalization and world trade. *Columbia Journal of World Business,* 27(2), 7-13.

Evans, P. (1997). The eclipse of the state? Reflections on stateness in an era of globalization. *World Politics,* 50, October, 62-87.

Fallows, J. (1993). Japan's moment and ours. *The New York Times,* August 1, E15.

Farah, D. (1999). Papers show U.S. role in Guatemalan abuses. *The Washington Post,* March 11, A26.

Ferdows, K. (1997). Making the most of foreign factories. *Harvard Business Review,* March-April, 73-88.

Fischer, S. (1998). *Reforming world finance.* IMF. <www.imf.org>.

FitzGerald, N. (1999). A giant reawakens. Interviewed by Deborah Orr. *Forbes,* January 25, 52-54.

Flux, A. W. (1899). The flag and trade: A summary review of the trade of the chief colonial empires. In J. Foreman-Peck (Ed.) (1998), *Historical foundations of globalization* (pp. 206-239). Northampton: Edward Elgar.

Fonton, F. M., Fong, K. T., and Mizrahi, A. (1993). Design and development for a global market. *AT&T Technical Journal,* March/April, 2-5.

Food and Agriculture Organization. (1998). *Large gap in food availability between rich and poor countries.* Press Release No. 98/70, <www.fao.org>.

Fortune Magazine (1995). Don't be an ugly-American manager. October 16, 225.

Foust, D., Smith, G., and Rocks, D. (1999). Nowadays, things go tougher at Coke. *Business Week,* May 3, No. 3627, 142-151.

Frank, R. and Friedland, J. (1996). How Pepsi's charge into Brazil fell short of its ambitious goals. *The Wall Street Journal,* August 30, B1.

Frankel, J. (1997). *Regional trading blocks.* Washington, DC: Institute for International Economics.

Frankel, M. (1999). The information tyranny. *The New York Times Magazine on the Web,* June 13, <www.nytimes.com>.

Franklin, B. A. (1997). The bridge to the 21st century leads to gridlock in and around decaying cities, *Washington Spectator,* 23(12), 4.

French, H. W. (1997). France fears Anglo-Saxons are usurping it in Africa. *The New York Times,* April 4, A3.

French, H. W. (1998). Competition heats up for West Africa's oil wealth. *The New York Times on the Web,* March 7, <www.nytimes.com>.

Friedland, J. (1998). U.S. phone giants find Telmex can be a bruising competitor. *The Wall Street Journal,* October 23, A1.

Friedman, T. (1996). Big Mac II. *The New York Times,* December 11, A27.

Friedman, T. (1998a). Techno-nothings. *The New York Times,* April 18, A27.

Friedman, T. (1998b). The Internet wars. *The New York Times,* April 11, A27.

Friedman, T. (1999). *The Lexus and the olive tree.* New York: Farrar, Straus, and Giroux.

Fujita, K. and Hill, R. C. (1995). Global Toyotaism and local development. *International Journal of Urban and Regional Research,* 19(1), 7-22.

Funabashi, T. (1998). Tokyo's depression diplomacy. *Foreign Affairs,* 77(6), 27-37.

Gardner, R. N. (1988). The case for practical internationalism. *Foreign Affairs,* 66(4), 827-845.

Garten, J. E. (1998). Needed: A Fed for the world. *The New York Times on the Web,* September 23, <www.nytimes.com>.

Gates, B. (1999). *The speed of thought.* New York: Warner Books.

Gelb, L. (1991). Fresh face. *The New York Times Magazine,* December 8, 50-54.

Gibbs, M. (1995). Organizational optimistic culture: The prescription and trend for the 21st century. Presented at the American Society for Competitiveness Conference, Dallas, October.

GM (No date). *A look at General Motors today.* Detroit: General Motors.

GM (1996). *Annual report.* Detroit: General Motors.

Goldsmith, E. (1996). Global Trade and the Environment. In J. Mander and E. Goldsmith (Eds.), *The case against the global economy* (pp. 78-91). San Francisco: Sierra Club Books.

Grant-Wisdom, D. (1995). The economics of globalization. In H. S. Dunn (Ed.), *Globalization, communications and Caribbean identity* (pp. 2-17). New York: St. Martin's Press.

Grasso, R. A. (1997). The best is yet to come: Globalization, America and the NYSE. *Vital Speeches of the Day,* January 15, 215-219.

Gray, H. P. (1997). The Burdens of global leadership. In K. Fatemi (Ed.), *International Trade in the 21st Century* (pp. 17-27). New York: Pergamon.

Gray, H. P. (1998). International trade and foreign direct investment: The interface. In J. H. Dunning (Ed.), *Globalization, trade and foreign direct investment* (pp. 19-27). New York: Elsevier Science Ltd.

Greenberger, R. (1990). Calls for democracy in the Middle East are creating a dilemma for White House. *The Wall Street Journal,* October 8, 4.

Greenberger, R. S. (1997). Commerce department plays more cautious role in promoting U.S. business interests overseas. *The Wall Street Journal,* April 8, A24.

Greenhouse, S. (1997). Sporting goods concerns agree to combat sale of soccer balls made by children. *The New York Times,* February 14, A12.

Greider, W. (1993). The global marketplace: A closet dictator. In R. Nader (Ed.), *The case against free trade: GATT, NAFTA, and the globalization of corporate power* (pp. 195-217). New York: Earth Island Press.

Griffin, R. W. and Pustay, M. W. (1996). *International business: A managerial perspective.* New York: Addison-Wesley.

Gummett, P. (1996) (Ed). *Globalization and public policy.* Cheltenham, UK: Edward Elgar.

Haass, R. N. (1994). Military force: A user's guide. *Foreign Policy,* 96, Fall, 21-37.

Haass, R. N. and Litan, R. E. (1998). Globalization and its discontents: Navigating the dangers of a tangled world. *Foreign Affairs,* 77(3), 2-6.

Halliday, D. (1998). Sanctions have an impact on all of us. Speech delivered on Capitol Hill, Washington, DC. *Middle East Report,* Winter (209), 3-7.

Hamel, G. and Prahalad, C. K. (1994). *Competing for the future.* Boston: Harvard Business School Press.

Hampden-Turner, C. and Trompenaars, A. (1993). *The seven cultures of capitalism.* New York: Currency Doubleday.

Harris, O. (1996). Madeline Albright's "Munich Mindset." *The New York Times,* December 19, A29.

Harris, R. G. (1993). Globalization, trade, and income. *Canadian Journal of Economics,* November, 755-775.

Hattmann, U. (1997). Letter to our shareholders. In VEBA, *1996 annual report,* pp. 8-11. Dusseldorf, Germany: VEBA.

Hedlund, G. (1996). Organization and management of transnational corporations in practice and research. In United Nations, *Transnational corporations and world development* (pp. 123-144). Boston: International Thomson Business Press.

Hellman, P. (1997). Erasing boundaries: Globalization. *Vital Speeches of the Day,* 64(2), 57-60.

Herkstroter, C. (1996). Dealing with contradictory expectations: Dilemmas facing multinationals, *Vital Speeches of the Day,* December 1, 100-105.

Herzog, R. (1999). Programme for better global relations, speech at World Economic Forum Annual Meeting, Davos, Switzerland, January 28. *The World Economic Forum on the Web,* <www.live99.weforum.org>.

Hewlett-Packard (1996). *1996 Annual Report.* Palo Alto, CA: Hewlett-Packard.

Higgott, R. (1996). Beyond embedded liberalism: Governing the international trade regime in an era of economic nationalism. In P. Gummett (Ed.), *Globalization and public policy* (pp. 18-45). Cheltenham, UK: Edward Elgar.

Hoadley, W. E. (1998). Needed: Change in business priorities. *Caux Round Table Web Site,* July, <www.cauxroundtable.org>.

Hobson, J. A. (1919). *Richard Cobden.* London: Ernest Benn Limited.

Hockstader, L. (1999). Israel's most unorthodox politician. *Washington Post,* June 4, C1.

Hoffman, D. (1999). The fall of the financiers. *Washington Post*, April 8, A21.

Hofstede, G. (1983). The cultural relativity of organizational practices and theories. *Journal of International Business Studies,* Fall, 75-89.

Hofstede, G. (1994). The business of international business is culture. *International Business Review,* 3(1), 1-14.

Hoge, W. (1998). Blair says use of force is "global reality." *The New York Times on the Web,* December 21, <www.nytimes.com>.

Holland, W. R. (1996). Citizens of the world—Building bridges across boundaries. *Vital Speeches of the Day,* 62, May 12, 562-64.

Honda (1997a). *The environmental challenge.* New York: Honda North America, Inc.

Honda (1997b). *Annual report.* Tokyo: Honda Motor.

Honda (1997c). *Corporate profile.* Tokyo: Honda Motor.

Honda (1997d). *Factbook.* Tokyo: Honda Motor.

Hormats, R. (1994). Making regionalism safe. *Foreign Affairs,* 73(2), 97-108.

Hout, T., Porter, M., and Rudden, E. (1992). How global companies win out. In C. Bartlett and S. Ghoshal (Eds.), *Transnational management* (pp. 334-344). Chicago: Irwin.

Huntington, S. (1993). The clash of civilizations. *Foreign Affairs,* 72(3), 22-49.

Husseini, S. (1998). Brookings: The establishment's think tank. *Extra,* 11(6), 21-23.

Idei, N. (1999). Sony's new game. Interviewed by B. Schlender. *Fortune,* April 12, 30-31.

IMF (1998). *World economic outlook.* Washington, DC: IMF.

IMF (1999a). *World economic outlook.* Washington, DC: IMF.

IMF (1999b). Responding to the challenges of globalization. *IMF—Survey,* January 11, p. 16.

Indyk, M. S. (1999). Remarks at the Council on Foreign Relations. New York, April 22, Web page, <www.state.gov>.

ING (1996). *Annual report 1996.* Amsterdam: ING.

Inzerilli, G. (1990). The Italian alternative: Flexible organization and social management. *International Studies of Management and Organization,* 20(4), 6-21.

Ishihara, S. (1991). *The Japan that can say no.* New York: Simon and Schuster.

Ito-Yokado (1997). *Ito-Yokado Co., Ltd. 1997 annual report.* Tokyo: Ito-Yokado Co.

Johansson, J. K. (1997). *Global marketing: Foreign entry, local marketing, and global management.* Chicago: Irwin.

John Paul II (1999). *Ecclesia in America.* <www.catholic-pages.com>.

Johnson, H. J. (1991). *Dispelling the myth of globalization* (pp. 1-16) New York: Praeger.

Joint Statement by the heads of the International Monetary Fund (IMF), the World Bank and the World Trade Organization (WTO) (1998). Washington, DC, October 3.

Jones, G. (1996). Transnational corporations—A historical perspective. In UNCTAD, *Transnational corporations and world development* (pp. 3-26). Boston: International Thomson Business Press.

Juergensmeyer, M. (1996). Religious nationalism: A global threat. *Current History,* 95(604), 372-376.

Kagan, R. (1998). The benevolent empire. *Foreign Policy,* Summer, 24-35.

Kahn, J. (1998). Global corporations. *Fortune,* October 26, 206-208.

Kanter, R. (1994). Change in the global economy: An interview with Rosabeth Moss Kanter. Conducted by P. Stonham. *European Management Journal,* 12(1), 1-9.

Kanter, R. (1998). Good for them and us. *The New York Times,* May 12, A21.

Kawamoto, N. (1997). Progress in step with the world and its people. In Honda, *Corporate Profile* (p. 3). Tokyo: Honda Motor.

Khor, M. (1993). Free trade and the Third World. In R. Nader (Ed.), *The case against free trade: GATT, NAFTA, and the globalization of corporate power* (pp. 97-107). New York: Earth Island Press.

Khor, M. (1996). Global economy and the third world. In J. Mander and E. Goldsmith (Eds.), *The case against the global economy* (pp. 47-59). San Francisco: Sierra Club Books.

Kilman, S. and Cooper, H. (1999). Monsanto falls flat trying to sell Europe on bioengineered food. *The Wall Street Journal,* May 11, A9.

Kindleberger, C. (1981). Dominance and leadership in the international economy. *International Studies Quarterly,* 25(3), 242-254.

Kinzer, S. (1998). On piping Caspian oil, U.S. insists the cheaper shorter way isn't better. *The New York Times on the Web,* November 18, <www.nytimes.com>.

Kinzer, S. (1999a). Caspian competitors in race for power on sea of oil. *The New York Times on the Web*, January 24, <www.nytimes.com>.

Kinzer, S. (1999b). Smart bombs, dumb sanctions. *The New York Times on the Web,* January 3, <www.nytimes.com>.
Kirdar, U. (1992). *Change: Threat or opportunity for human progress?* New York: United Nations.
Kissinger, H. (1994). *Diplomacy.* New York: Simon and Schuster.
Kitaoka, T. (1997). Rejuvenating Japan. *Vital Speeches of the Day,* 63(17), 516-519.
Knight, C. (1996). Emerson Electric letter to shareholder—annual report (pp. 2-8). St. Louis: Emerson.
Kobrin, S. J. (1997a). The architecture of globalization: State sovereignty in a networked global economy. In J. Dunning (Ed.), *Government, globalization, and international business* (pp. 146-172). Oxford: Oxford University Press.
Kobrin, S. J. (1997b). Electronic Cash and the end of national markets. *Foreign Policy,* Summer, 65-77.
Kobrin, S. J. (1998). The MAI and the clash of globalizations. *Foreign Policy,* Fall, 97-108.
Komansky, D. and Allison, H. (1998). To our shareholders and clients. In Merrill Lynch, *Merrill Lynch 1997 annual review* (pp. 3-17). New York: Merrill Lynch.
Koopman, A. (1994). *Transcultural management.* Oxford: Blackwell.
Korten, D. (1996). The failures of Bretton Woods. In J. Mander and E. Goldsmith (Eds.), *The case against the global economy* (pp. 20-32). San Francisco: Sierra Club Books.
Korten, D. (1997). Economies of meaning. *Tikkun,* 11(2), 17-18.
Kotter, J. (1995). The new rules. New York: The Free Press.
Koudal, P. (1998). International wage inequality and convergence: The impact of transnational corporations. In F. Contractor (Ed.), *Economic transformation in emerging countries* (pp. 233-246). Oxford: Elsevier.
Kozyrev, A. (1994). Don't threaten us. *The New York Times,* March 18, A29.
KPMG (1999). Global M&A exceeds record volume. International Media Release, December, <www.Kpmg.com>.
Krauer, A. (1996). Management letter. In *Novartis Operational review 1996* (pp. 7-9). Basel, Switzerland: Novartis.
Kristof, N. D. (1998a). As free flowing capital sinks nations, experts prepare to "rethink system." *The New York Times on the Web,* September 20, <www.nytimes.com>.
Kristof, N. D. (1998b). Japan sees itself as scapegoat of Washington in Asia crisis. *The New York Times on the Web,* September 21, <www.nytimes.com>.
Kristof, N. D. and Sanger, D. E. (1999). How U.S. wooed Asia to let cash flow in. *The New York Times on the Web,* February 16, <www.nytimes.com>.
Krugman, P. (1994). Competitiveness: A dangerous obsession. *Foreign Affairs,* 73(2, March/April), 44.
Krugman, P. (1997). How fast can the U.S. economy grow? *Harvard Business Review,* July-August, 123-129.

Lake, A. (1994). The reach of democracy. *The New York Times,* September 23, A35.

Lane, H. W and DiStefano, J. J. (1992). *International management behavior.* New York: Blackwell Publishers.

Laxer, J. (1993). *False god: How the globalization myth has impoverished Canada.* Toronto: Lester Publishing Limited.

Lee, S. and Foster, C. (1997). The global hand. *Forbes,* April 21, 85-94.

Lehman, K. and Krebs, A. L. (1996). Control of the world's food supply. In J. Mander and E. Goldsmith (Eds.), *The case against the global economy* (pp. 122-130). San Francisco: Sierra Club Books.

Leiken, R. S. (1996-1997). Controlling the global corruption epidemic. *Foreign Policy,* Winter, 55-73.

Levitt, T. (1983). The globalization of markets. *Harvard Business Review,* May-June, 92-102.

Levy-Livermore, A. (1998). *Handbook on the globalization of the world economy.* Cheltenham, UK: Edward Elgar.

Lewis, B. (1996). The wealth of a nation. *The Wall Street Journal,* June 7, A12.

Lewis, C. and Ebrahim, M. (1993). Can Mexico and big business USA buy NAFTA? *The Nation,* June 14, 826-839.

Lida, O. (1995). Becoming a global company. *Vital Speeches of the Day,* 62(4), 114-117.

Lincoln, E. (1992). Japan in the 1990s. A new world power. *Brooking Review,* Spring, 12-17.

Lobel, S. (1990). Global leadership competencies: Managing to a different drumbeat. *Human Resource Management,* 29(1), 39-47.

Lodge, G. (1995). *Managing globalization in the age of interdependence* (pp. 61-93). San Diego: Pfeiffer and Co.

Lussier, R. N., Baeder, R. W., and Corman, J. (1994). Measuring global practices: Global strategic planning through company situational analysis. *Business Horizons,* September-October, 56-63.

Magretta, J. (1998). Fast, global, and entrepreneurial: Supply chain management, Hong Kong style—An interview with Victor Fung. *Harvard Business Review,* September-October, 103-114.

Mair, A. (1997). Strategic localization: The myth of the postnational enterprise. In K. R. Cox (Ed.), *Spaces of globalization: Reasserting the power of the local* (pp. 64-88). New York: Guilford Press.

Mandela, N. (1999). Farewell. World Economic Forum Annual Meeting, January 28-February 2, 1999. Davos, Switzerland. *The World Economic Forum on the Web,* January 29, <www.live99.weforum.org>.

Mander, J. (1993). Megatechnology, trade, and the new world. In R. Nader (Ed.), *The case against free trade: GATT, NAFTA, and the globalization of corporate power* (pp. 13-22). New York: Earth Island Press.

Mander, J. (1996). The rules of corporate behavior. In J. Mander and E. Goldsmith (Eds.), *The case against the global economy* (pp. 309-322). San Francisco: Sierra Club Books.

Marquardt, M. and Engel, D. (1993). *Global human resource development.* Englewood Cliffs, NJ: Prentice Hall.

Martino, J. P. (1972). *Technological forecasting for decision making.* New York: American Elsevier.

Mathews, J. T. (1997). Power shift. *Foreign Affairs.* 76(1), 50-67.

Maucher, H. (1994). *Leadership in action.* New York: McGraw-Hill, Inc.

Maynes, C. W. (1998). The perils of (and for) an imperial America. *Foreign Policy,* Summer, 36-48.

McDonald, I. S. (1999). Growth projections for 1999 revised downward, but global economic situation is stabilizing. *IMF Survey,* January 11, 1-15.

McGrew, A. (1992). Conceptualizing global politics. In A. McGrew and P. Lewis (Eds.), *Global politics: Globalization and the nation states* (pp. 1-28). New York: Polity Press.

McGrew, A. G. and Lewis, P. G. (1992). *Global politics: Globalization and the nation-states.* Cambridge, UK: Polity Press.

McLuhan, M. (1960). *Understanding media.* London: Routledge.

McNamara, R. (1999). Misreading the enemy. Available FTP: <www.Lexis-nexis.com>, April 29.

Mengisteab, K. (1996). *Globalization and autocentricity in Africa's development in the 21st century.* Trenton, NJ: Africa World Press.

Meredith, R. (1999). In Detroit, a sex change. *The New York Times on the Web,* May 16, <www.nytimes.com>.

Merrill Lynch (1997). *Merrill Lynch 1997 Annual Review.* New York: Merrill Lynch.

Middle East Report (1998). Better living through chemistry. Fall, 7.

Milner, H. V. (1998). International political economy: Beyond hegemonic stability. *Foreign Policy,* Spring, 112-123.

Mintzberg, H. (1983). *Structure in five.* Englewood Cliffs, NJ: Prentice-Hall.

Mitchell, A. (1996). Clinton urges Japanese to exercise leadership. *International Herald Tribune,* April 19, 1.

Mitchell, J. (1992). The nature and government of the global economy. In A. McGrew and P. Lewis (Eds.), *Global politics* (pp. 174-196). Cambridge: Polity Press.

Mitroff, I. (1995). Review of *The Age of Paradox*: *Academy of Management Review,* 20(3), 748-750.

Mobil (1993). Don't fear NAFTA. Web page, <www.mobil.com>.

Mobil (1994). Going to bat for GATT. Web page, <www.mobil.com>.

Mobil (1997a). The sanctions debate. Web page, <www.mobil.com>, May 1.

Mobil (1997b). The sanctions: Our perspectives. Web page <www.mobil.com>, May 1.

Mobil (1997c). Climate change. Web page, <www.mobil.com>, May 1.

Mobil (1998a). Parents: The indispensable teachers. Web page, <www.mobil.com>, April 9.

Mobil (1998b). Trade: It matters more than you imagined. Web page, <www.mobil.com>, May 28.

Mobil (1998c). Technology: Tools for the 21st century. Web page, <www.mobil.com>, August 20.

Mobil (1998d). Nigeria: A lesson for investors. We page, <www.mobil.com>, Nov. 19.

Mobil (1999). A special moment. Web page, <www.mobil.com>, February 11.

Modelski, G. (1987). *World politics.* Seattle: University of Washington Press.

Moller, J. (1991). The competitiveness of U.S. industry: A view from the outside. *Business Horizons,* November/December, 27-34.

Moller, J. (1997). The coming world governance. *International Economy,* May/June, 62-67.

Moran, R. T., Harris, P. R., and Stripp, W. G. (1993). *Developing the global organization.* Houston: Gulf Publishing Co.

Morley, J. (1881). *Life of Richard Cobden.* London: Chapman and Hall.

Morris, D. (1993). Free trade: The great destroyer. In R. Nader (Ed.), *The case against free trade: GATT, NAFTA, and the globalization of corporate power* (pp. 139-157). New York: Earth Island Press.

Morse, R. A. (1997). Japan's new techno-nationalism: Balancing global competitiveness and national security needs. In D. F. Simon (Ed.), *Techno-security in an age of globalization.* Armonk, NY: M. E. Sharp.

Mueller, J. and Mueller, K. (1999). Sanctions of mass destruction. *Foreign Affairs,* 78(3), 43-53.

Mydans, S. (1999). Cambodia town's "luck" leaves illness in its wake. *The New York Times,* January 4, <www.nytimes.com>.

Nader, R. (1993). Introduction: Free trade and the decline of democracy. In R. Nader (Ed.), *The case against free trade: GATT, NAFTA, and the globalization of corporate power.* (pp. 1-11). New York: Earth Island Press.

Nader, R. and Wallach, L. (1996). GATT, NAFTA, and the subversion of the democratic process. In J. Mander and E. Goldsmith (Eds.), *The case against the global economy* (pp. 92-107). San Francisco: Sierra Club Books.

Naim, M. (1997). Editor's note. *Foreign Policy,* Summer, 5-8.

Naisbitt, J. (1994). *Global paradox.* New York: William Morrow.

NationsBank (1996). *1996 Annual Report.* Charlotte, NC: NationsBank Corporation.

NationsBank (1997). NationsBank international banking. *The Net@Work Archives.* Available FTP: <159.5.26.131/html/cvrd.html>.

Navarro, M. (1999). Guatemalan army waged 'genocide,' new report found. *The New York Times,* February 26, <www.nytimes.com>.

Neier, A. (1994). Watching rights. *The Nation,* December 19, 751-753.

Nelan, B. (1992). How the world will look in 50 years. *Time,* Special Issue, Fall, 36-38.

Nestlé (1997). *General organization.* Vevey, Switzerland: Corporate Communications, July.

The New York Times (1998). Coping with economic crisis. Editorial, October 11. *The New York Times on the Web,* <www.nytimes.com>.

The New York Times (1999). Half-measures for poor nations. Editorial, June 9, A20.

Nike (1997). *Nike 1997 revised code of conduct.* <www.Nike.com>.

Nixon, R. (1991). Why U.S. policy is right in the Gulf. In J. Ridgeway (Ed.), *The march to war* (pp. 185-187). New York: Four Walls Eight Windows.

Nixon, R. (1994). *Beyond peace.* New York: Random House.

Norberg-Hodge, H. (1996). The pressure to modernize and globalize. In J. Mander and E. Goldsmith (Eds.), *The case against the global economy* (pp. 33-46). San Francisco: Sierra Club Books.

Northern Telecom (1997). *The anatomy of a transformation 1985-1995.* January.

Novartis (1996a). *Health, safety, and environmental report 1996.* Basel, Switzerland: Novartis.

Novartis (1996b). *Novartis operational review 1996.* Basel, Switzerland: Novartis.

Ogura, K. (1991). Japan and America: Pride and prejudice. *The New York Times,* November 14, 17E.

Ohmae, K. (1989). Planting for a global harvest. *Harvard Business Review,* July-August, 136-145.

Ohmae, K. (1991). *The borderless world.* New York: Harper Perennial.

Ohmae, K. (1995). *The end of the nation state.* New York: The Free Press.

Passell, P. (1993). Regional trade makes global deals go round. *The New York Times,* December 19, E4.

Passell, P. (1998). Economic scene: IMF is no good, critics say, but who's better. *The New York Times,* February 12.

Pearce, J. and Robinson, R. (1988). *Strategic management.* New York: Irwin.

Pearce, J. and Robinson, R. (1997). *Strategic management.* New York: Irwin McGraw Hill.

Pepper, J. (1991). Globalization and its significance to P&G. Speech at Stanford University, Stanford, CA, October 10.

Pepper, J. (1998). P&G pursues greatest growth ever. Press release. September 9. Cincinnati: Public Affairs Division.

Perlez, J. (1999). Head to head, Albright and Russia's Prime Minister do not see eye to eye. *The New York Times on the Web,* January 26, <www.nytimes.com>.

Perlmutter, H. (1992). The tortuous evolution of the multinational corporation. In C. Bartlett and S. Ghoshal (Eds.), *Transnational management* (pp. 92-100). Boston: Irwin.

Perrella, J. E. (1998). Impact of trade sanctions—A global CEO's perspective. *Vital Speeches of the Day,* 64(22, September 1), 681-684.

Peters, T. (1985). Something is out of work in US business management. *US News and World Report,* July 15, 53-54.

Petre, P. (1990). Lifting America. *Fortune Magazine,* April 23, 56-66.

Pfaff, W. (1995). A new colonialism? *Foreign Affairs,* 74(1), 2-6.

Pfaff, W. (1996a). "Benevolent hegemony" in foreign policy. *Los Angeles Times Syndicate, Indiana Gazette,* July 28, 2.

Pfaff, W. (1996b). It's time to challenge the orthodoxy of trade liberalization. *International Herald Tribune*, April 9, 8.

Pfaff, W. (1996c). U.S. presence not needed in Gulf. *Indiana Gazette,* July 6, 2.

Pfaff, W. (1997). Should labor bear globalization costs? *Los Angeles Times Syndicate, Indiana Gazette,* January 11, 2.

Pfaff, W. (1998). Policies unreasonable, unrealistic. *Los Angeles Times Syndicate, Indiana Gazette,* October 16, 2.

Pfaff, W. (1999a). Davos takes critical look at globalism. *Los Angeles Times Syndicate, The Indiana Gazette,* January 29, 2.

Pfaff, W. (1999b). Japan calls for alliance against U.S. *Los Angeles Times Syndicate, The Indiana Gazette,* January 12, 2.

Phatak, A. (1995). *International dimension of management.* Cincinnati: South Western.

Phillips, K. (1994). *Arrogant capital.* New York: Little, Brown and Company.

Pollack, A. (1999). U.S. and allies block treaty on genetically altered goods. *The New York Times on the Web,* February 25, <www.nytimes.com>.

Popoff, F. (1994). Issues management. Interviewed by S. Ainsworth. *C&EN*, March 23, 25-27.

Porter, M. (1985). *Competitive advantage: Creating and sustaining superior performance.* New York: The Free Press.

Porter, M. (1990). *The competitive advantage of nations.* New York: The Free Press.

Porter, M. (1995). The determinants and dynamics of national advantage. In J. Drew (Ed.), *Readings in international enterprise* (pp. 26-47). New York: Routledge.

Prahalad, C. and Doz, Y. (1986). Controlled variety: A challenge for human resource management in the MNC. *Human Resource Management,* 25(1), 55-71.

Prahalad, C. and Doz, Y. (1987). *The multinational mission: Balancing demands and global vision.* New York: Simon and Schuster.

PricewaterhouseCoopers/World Economic Forum (1999). Inside the mind of the CEO: The 1999 global survey report. *The PricewaterhouseCoopers Web page,* January 30, <www.pwcglobal.com>.

Primakov, Y. (1991). The inside story of Moscow's quest for a deal. *Time,* March 4, 40-48.

Rapoport, C. (1994). Nestlé's brand building machine. *Fortune Magazine,* September 19, 147-156.

Rapoport, C. and Martin, J. (1995). Retailers go global. *Fortune Magazine,* February 20, 102-108.

Read, D. (1968). *Cobden and Bright.* New York: St. Martin's Press.

Ready, D. (1995). Don't be an ugly-American manager. Quoted in *Fortune Magazine,* October 16, 225.

Reese, C. (1993). NAFTA sweet deal for transnational. *King Features Syndicate, Indiana Gazette,* July 19, 2.

Reese, C. (1997). Big foundations determine policies. *King Features Syndicate, Indiana Gazette,* May 5, 2.

Reich, R. B. (1990). Who is us? *Harvard Business Review,* January-February, 53-64.

Reich, R. B. (1991). Who is them? *Harvard Business Review,* March-April, 77-89.
Reich, R. B. (1998). The real policy makers. *The New York Times on the Web,* September 29, <www.nytimes.com>.
Reinicke, W. H. (1997). Global public policy. *Foreign Affairs,* 76(6), 127-138.
Rhinesmith, S. H. (1996). *A manager's guide to globalization.* New York: McGraw-Hill, Inc.
Rhodes, M. (1996). Globalization, the state and the restructuring of regional economies. In P. Gummet (Ed.), *Globalization and public policy* (pp. 161-180). Cheltenham, UK: Edward Elgar.
Ricupero, R. (1997). Transnational corporations, market structure and foreign policy. In *World investment report—Overview.* United Nations Conference on Trade and Development. New York and Geneva: UN.
Ricupero, R. (1998). *Concise report on world population monitoring, 1998: Health and mortality.* United Nations Commission on Population and Development, 31st session, February 23-27. New York and Geneva: UN.
Ridgeway, J. (1991). *The march to war.* New York: Four Walls Eight Windows.
Rifkin, J. (1996). New technology and the end of jobs. In J. Mander and E. Goldsmith (Eds.), *The case against the global economy* (pp. 108-121). San Francisco: Sierra Club Books.
Ritchie, M. (1996). *Globlization vs. globalism.* <wwwpanix.com>.
Robertson, R. (1992). *Globalization: Social theory and global culture.* London: Sage Publications.
Robinson, W. I. (1996). *Promoting polyarchy: Globalization, US intervention and hegemony.* Oxford: Cambridge University Press.
Roddick, A. (1995). Reflections on management education and the global change agenda. Paper presented at the Academy of Management Conference on Organizational Dimensions of Global Change. Cleveland, Ohio, May 3-6.
Roddick, A. (1998). Another year. In *The Body Shop 1998 annual report* (p. 3). <www.bodyshop.com>.
Rodgers, J. R. (1998). From Bretton Woods to the World Trade Organization and the formation of regional trading blocs. In A. Levy-Livermore (Ed.), *Handbook on the globalization of the world economy* (pp. 199-225). Northampton: Edward Elgar.
Rodrigues, C. (1994). Think local. *International Management,* January-February, 52.
Rodrik, D. (1997a). Sense and nonsense in the globalization debate. *Foreign Policy,* Summer, 18-36.
Rodrik, D. (1997b). *Has globalization gone too far*? Washington, DC: Institute for International Economics.
Rohter, L. (1994). Close to home: Remembering the past: Repeating it anyway. *The New York Times,* July 24, Section 4, 1.
Rosenthal, A. M. (1999). 100 brave Arabs. *The New York Times on the Web,* May 7, <www.nytimes.com>.
Rosenthal, E. (1998). In North Korea hunger, legacy is stunted children. *The New York Times on the Web,* December 10, <www.nytimes.com>.

Roth, K. (1995). Human wrongs and international relations. *International Affairs,* 71(1), 103-126.

Rothenberg, R. (1996). The age of spin. *Esquire,* December, 70-77, 124-125.

Rothkopf, D. (1997). In praise of cultural imperialism? *Foreign Policy,* Summer, 38-53.

Rubin, R. E. (1998). Strengthening the architecture of the international financial system: The financial crisis in Asia and the IMF. *Vital Speeches of the Day,* 64(14), 421-425.

Rugman, A. (1997). Canada. In J. Dunning (Ed.), *Government, globalization, and international business* (pp. 175-202). Oxford: Oxford University Press.

Sachs, J. (1998). International economics: Unlocking the mysteries of globalization. *Foreign Policy,* Spring, 97-109.

Sanger, D. E. (1997). Look who's carping most about capitalism, *The New York Times*, April 6, E1.

Sanger, D. E. (1997). Playing the trade card. *The New York Times,* February 21, A1.

Sanger, D. E. (1999a). Clinton's foreign policy lacks coherence, but so does the world. *The New York Times on the Web,* March 7, <www.nytimes.com>.

Sanger, D. E. (1999b). U.S. aide due in North Korea with deal to lift sanctions. *The New York Times on the Web,* May 21, <www.nytimes.com>.

Sanger, D. E. (1999c). How a push by China and US business won over Clinton. *The New York Times on the Web,* April 15, <www.nytimes.com>.

Saporito, B. (1996). Parched for growth: Pepsi had a grand plan for global expansion. Alas, Coke was thirstier. *Time Magazine,* September 2, 48-49.

Sassen, S. (1993). *Losing control? Sovereignty in an age of globalization.* New York: Columbia University Press.

Sauer-Thompson, G. and Smith, J. W. (1996). *Beyond economics*. Sidney, Australia: Avebury.

Sauvant, K. P. and Mallampally, P. (1996). Transnational corporations in services. In United Nations. *Transnational corporations and world development* (pp. 359-393). Boston: International Thomson Business Press.

Schlesinger, J. and Forman, C. (1993). Japan seeks to play a bigger role on the global stage. *The Wall Street Journal,* September 21, A18.

Schrempp, J. E. (1997). Thriving on global economic changes. *Vital Speeches of the Day,* 63(10), 306-309.

Schrempp, J. E. (1998). Letter to the shareholders. In Daimler-Benz, *1997 annual report* (pp. 2-5). Stuttgart, Germany: Daimler-Benz AG.

Schwab, K. (1999). Finding the right balance. World Economic Forum Annual Meeting, January 28-February 2, 1999, Davos, Switzerland. *The World Economic Forum Web Page,* January 28, <www.live99.weforum.org>.

Schwab, K. and Smadja, C. (1996). Start taking the backlash against globalization seriously. *International Herald Tribune,* February 1, 4.

Schwab, K. and Smadja, C. (1999). Globalization needs a human face.World Economic Forum Annual Meeting, January 28-February 2, 1999, Davos, Switzerland. *The World Economic Forum Web page,* January 30, <www.live99. weforum.org>.

Sera, K. (1995). Corporate globalization: A new trend. *The Academy of Management Executive,* 6(1), 89-96.

Shell Chemical (1998). Health, safety and environment. *Shell on the Web,* <www.shell.com>.

Shenon, P. (1995). A Pacific island nation is stripped of everything. *The New York Times,* December 10, 3.

Shenon, P. (1999). U.S. to train police leaders for Indonesia in riot control. *The New York Times on the Web,* May 9, <www.nytimes.com>.

Shultz, G. (1997). Ideas and issues on foreign policy. *Vital Speeches of the Day,* 63(15), 454-457.

Siemens (1996). *Annual report 96.* Munich, Germany: Siemens.

Siemens (1997). *Factbook.* Munich, Germany: Siemens.

Siemens (1998). *Annual report.* Munich, Germany: Siemens.

Simon, D. (1997). *Techno-security in an age of globalization.* Armonk, NY: M. E. Sharp.

Smart, T. (1993). GE's brave new world. *Business Week*, November 8. Reprint.

Smith, J. (1997). *Letter to Shareholders—GM annual report.* Detroit: General Motors.

SmithKline Beecham (1996). *SmithKline 1996 annual report.* Middlesex: SmithKline Beecham.

Sobek II, D. K., Liker, J. K., and Ward, A. C. (1998). Another look at how Toyota integrates product development. *Harvard Business Review,* July-August, 36-49.

Soros, G. (1997). The capitalist threat, *The Atlantic Monthly,* February, 45-58.

Soros, G. (1998). Testimony to the U.S. House of Representatives, Committee on Banking and Financial Services. Washington, DC, September 15. Available <www.soros.org>.

Soros, G. (1999). Capitalism's last chance. *Foreign Policy,* Winter, 55-65.

Spero, J. E. (1996). The challenges of globalization. Remarks at the World Economic Development Congress, Washington, DC, September 26.

Stevenson, R. W. (1998). Hedge fund's failure raises disturbing questions. *The New York Times on the Web*, September 26, <www.nytimes.com>.

Stiglitz, J. (1998). The role of the financial system in development. Presented at the Fourth Annual Bank Conference on Development in Latin America and the Caribbean. San Salvador, El Salvador Juneza.

Stonecipher, H. C. (1996). At what price peace. *Vital Speeches of the Day,* 62(8), 250-251.

Stopford, J. (1997). Implications for national competitiveness. In J. Dunning (Ed.), *Government, globalization, and international business* (pp. 457-480). New York: Oxford University Press.

Stopford, J. (1999). Multinational corporations. *Foreign Policy,* No. 113, Winter, 13-24.

Stopford, J. M., and Wells, L. T. (1972). Managing the multinational enterprise. New York: Basic Books.

Strange, S. (1997). An international political economy perspective. In J. Dunning (Ed.), *Governments, globalization, and international business* (pp. 132-145). New York: Oxford University Press.

Sutherland, P. D. (1998a). *Answering globalization challenges.* Washington, DC: Overseas Development Council.

Sutherland, P. D. (1998b). *The 1998 Per Jacobsson Lecture: Managing the international economy in an age of globalization.* Washington, DC: Overseas Development Council.

Suzuki, T. (1997). To our shareholders. In *Ito-Yokado Co. 1997 Annual Report.* Tokyo: Ito-Yokado.

Talbott, S. (1998). Hegemon and proud of it. *Slate Magazine*, June 26, 1-5.

Tang, R. (1981). Career issues in international assignments. *Academy of Management Executive,* 2(3), 241-244.

Tarantino, D. A. (1998). Principled business leadership—global business and the Caux Round Table at a crossroads. *Vital Speeches of the Day,* 64(18), 559-562.

Teeple, G. (1995). *Globalization and the decline of social reform.* Atlantic Highlands, NJ: Humanities Press.

Thatcher, M. (1993). *The Downing Street years.* New York: HarperCollins Publishers, Inc.

Thompson, K. W. (1981). *Cold war theories.* Baton Rouge, LA: Louisiana State University Press.

Thompson, M. (1994). Going up, up in arms. *Time,* December 12, 46-57.

3M (1999). *Organization chart.* St. Paul, MN: 3M Corporate Marketing and Public Affairs, April 1.

Thurow, L. (1992). *Head to head.* New York: William Morrow and Co.

Thurow, L. C. (1996). Taking charge. *World Business,* 2(3), 3.

Thurow, L. C. (1997). The revolution upon us. *The Atlantic Monthly,* March, 97-100.

Time (1996). *Time*'s 25 most influential Americans, June 17, 53-79.

Toffler, A. and Toffler, H. (1993). *War and anti-war: Survival at the dawn of the 21st century.* New York: Little, Brown and Company.

Toffler, A. and Toffler, H. (1998). The discontinuous future: A bold but over optimistic forecast. *Foreign Affairs,* 77(2), 134-139.

Tokyo Business Today (1992). The Japan that can say enough is enough. August, 22-23.

Toyota (1996). *Annual report 1996.* Toyota City, Japan: Toyota Motor Corporation.

Trotman, A. (1996). The climate for change. *Vital speeches of the Day,* December 1, 121-123.

Tyler, P. E. (1999). Seeing China's challenge through a cold war lens. *The New York Times on the Web,* February 14, <www.nytimes.com>.

UNDESA (1998). *World population projection to 2150.* UN Population Division Department of Economic and Social Affairs with support from the UN Population Fund. New York: United Nations.

UNCTAD (1996). *Globalization and liberalization.* New York: United Nations.

UNCTAD (1997a). *Trade and development report.* New York: United Nations.

UNCTAD (1997b). *Transnational corporations, market structure and foreign policy.* World Investment Report—Overview. New York and Geneva: United Nations.

UNCTAD (1997c). *Outlook: UN conference on trade and development—The least developed countries.* New York: United Nations.

UNCTAD (1998a). *Foreign direct investment on the rise.* Press release TAD/INF/2762.

UNCTAD (1998b). *World investment report 1998.* New York: United Nations.

UNCTAD (1998c). *Trade and development report 1998.* New York: United Nations.

UNCTAD (1999a). *Trade and development report 1999.* New York: United Nations.

UNCTAD (1999b). *World investment report 1999.* New York: United Nations.

Unilever (1996a) *Annual report to employees—North America.* New York and Toronto: Unilever.

Unilever (1996b). *Introducing Unilever 1996.* London: Unilever Corporate Relations Department.

Unilever (1996c). *Unilever's Organization.* London: Unilever Corporate Relations Department.

Unilever (1997). *Annual Review 1996.* London: Unilever Corporate Relations Department.

United Nations (1997). *Human Development Report. UN on the Web:* <www.un.org>.

United Nations (1998). *Human Development Report. UN on the Web:* <www.un.org>.

United Nations (1999). *Human Development Report. UN on the Web:* <www.un.org>.

United Nations Commission on Population and Development (1998). Official United Nations Documents, Press Release, 31st session, February 23-27.

United Nations Population Division (1998). *World population projections to 2150.* 31st session, February 1. New York: United Nations.

United Nations Statistics Division. Indicators on income and economic activity. *Year Book of Labour Statistics,* Geneva, various years up to 1997.

VEBA (1996). *VEBA 1996 annual report.* Dusseldorf: VEBA.

VEBA (1997). *Strategy and key figures.* Dusseldorf: VEBA, March.

Vernon, R. (1997). Epilogue: Research on the transnationals: Mapping a course. In United Nations, *Transnational corporations and world development* (pp. 559-572). Boston: International Thomson Business Press.

The Wall Street Journal (1993a). Halloween for NAFTA. Editorial, September 9, A20.

The Wall Street Journal (1993b). The world wins one. Editorial, December 15, A16.

The Wall Street Journal (1995). Restive sheikdom. Editorial, June 12, A1.

The Wall Street Journal (1996). The WTO's successful debut. Editorial, December 17, A18.

The Wall Street Journal (1997a). The virtual empire. Editorial, January 10, A10.

The Wall Street Journal (1997b). Japan's diplomatic offensive. Editorial, January 24, A14.

The Wall Street Journal (1998). The world's 100 largest public companies, September 28, R27.

Warder, M. (1994). The role of think tanks in shaping public policy. *Vital Speeches of the Day,* 60(4), 434-437.

Washington Spectator (1997). The bridge to the 21st century leads to gridlock in and around decaying cities, 23(12), 4.

Waters, M. (1995). *Globalization.* London and New York: Routledge.

Watkins, K. (1997). Globalization and liberalization: Implications for poverty, distribution and inequality. *UN on the Web:* <www.un.org>.

Wayne, L. (1998). Wave of mergers recasts the face of business. *The New York Times on the Web,* January 19, <www.nytimes.com>.

Webber, A. (1994). Surviving in the new economy. *Harvard Business Review,* September-October, 76-92.

Wehling, R. L. (1997). Principles for global branding. Speech at General Motors Global Branding Conference in Orlando, Florida, April 23.

Welch, J. (1993). Turning soft values into hard results. Interviewed by *Leaders Magazine,* 16(4), GE Reprint (n.p.)

White, D. (1996). The frontiers. In *The American Century.* New Haven, CT: Yale University Press. Available <www.yale.edu/yup/books/whitechap1>.

Whitman, D. (1994). The right way to go global: Interviewed by R. F. Maruca. *Harvard Business Review,* March-April, 135-145.

Whitney, C. (1999a). French premier assails U.S. over Iraq air stike. *The New York Times on the Web,* January 7, <www.nytimes.com>.

Whitney, C. (1999b). NATO at 50: With nations at odds, is it a misalliance? *The New York Times on the Web,* February 15, <www.nytimes.com>.

Wilkin, P. (1996). New myths for the south: Globalization and the conflict between private power and freedom. *Third World Quarterly,* 17(2), 227-238.

Williamson, J. G. (1998). Globalization, convergence, and history. In J. Foreman-Peck (Ed.), *Historical foundations of globalization* (pp. 103-132). Northampton: Edward Elgar.

Wills, S. and Barham, K. (1994). Being an international manager. *European Management Journal,* 12(1), 49-58.

Wolf Jr., C. (1997). Asia in 2015. *The Wall Street Journal,* March 20, A16.

Wolf, J. (1997). The ancient art of globalization—We truly will be a global industry only when we produce globally. *Vital Speeches of the Day,* 60(14), 437-440.

Wolfensohn, J. D. (1997). Towards global sustainability—Remarks to the United Nations General Assembly Special Session on the environment. *World Bank on the Web,* June 25, <www.worldbank.org>.

Wolfensohn, J. D. (1998a). Whither globalism. Remarks at the Economic Strategy Institute's Seventh International Trade Conference. Washington, DC, May 6. *World Bank on the Web,* <www.worldbank.org>.

Wolfensohn, J. D. (1998b). The other crisis. Address to the Board of Governors—World Bank Group. Washington, DC, October 6. *World Bank on the Web,* <www.worldbank.org>.

World Bank (1992). *World Bank Policy Research Bulletin,* 3(3, May-July). Washington, DC.

World Bank (1999). *World development report 1998/99.* Washington, DC.

World Business Council for Sustainable Development (WBCSD). (1998). A platform for Sustainable Business . . . Sustainable Development Challenges. *WBCSD on the Web,* <www.wbcsd.ch>.

World Business Council for Sustainable Development. (n.d.) What is the WBCSD? *WBCSD on the Web,* <www.wbcsd.ch>.

World Economic Forum (1998). *1998 global competitiveness report.* Davos, Switzerland: World Economic Forum.

World Food Programme (1998). Emergency operation DPR Korea No. 5959.01. <www.Wfp.org/op/>

Wright, R. and McManus, D. (1991). *Flashpoints.* New York: Alfred Knopf.

WTO (1998). World trade growth accelerated in 1997, despite turmoil in some Asian financial markets. Press release, March 19.

Yergin, D. (1991). *The prize.* New York: Simon and Schuster.

Yip, G. S. (1995). *Total global strategy: Managing for worldwide competitive advantage.* Englewood Cliffs, NJ: Prentice-Hall, Inc.

Yoshida, S. (1996). Japanese corporations react to new global economic pressures. *Vital Speeches of the Day,* 63(3), 92-96.

Zachary, P. G. (1999). An era for mice to roar. *The Wall Street Journal,* February 25, B1.

Zahra, S. A. (1998). Competitiveness and global leadership in the 21st century. *Academy of Management Executive,* 12(4), 10-12.

Zahra, S. A. and O'Neil, H. M. (1998). Charting the landscape of global competition: reflections on emerging organizational challenges and their implications for senior executives. *Academy of Management Executive,* 12(4), 13-21.

Zehnder, E. (1993). Conversation. Interviewed by R. Litchfield. *Canadian Business,* December, 40-46.

Zeieh, A. (1996). An iconoclast in a cutthroat world. Interviewed by J. P. Donlon. *Chief Executive,* March. Reprint, n. p.

Zeira, Y. and Banai, M. (1985). Selection of expatriate managers in MNCs. *International Studies of Management and Organization,* 15(1), 33-51.

Index

Page numbers followed by the letter "f" indicate figures; those followed by the letter "t" indicate tables.